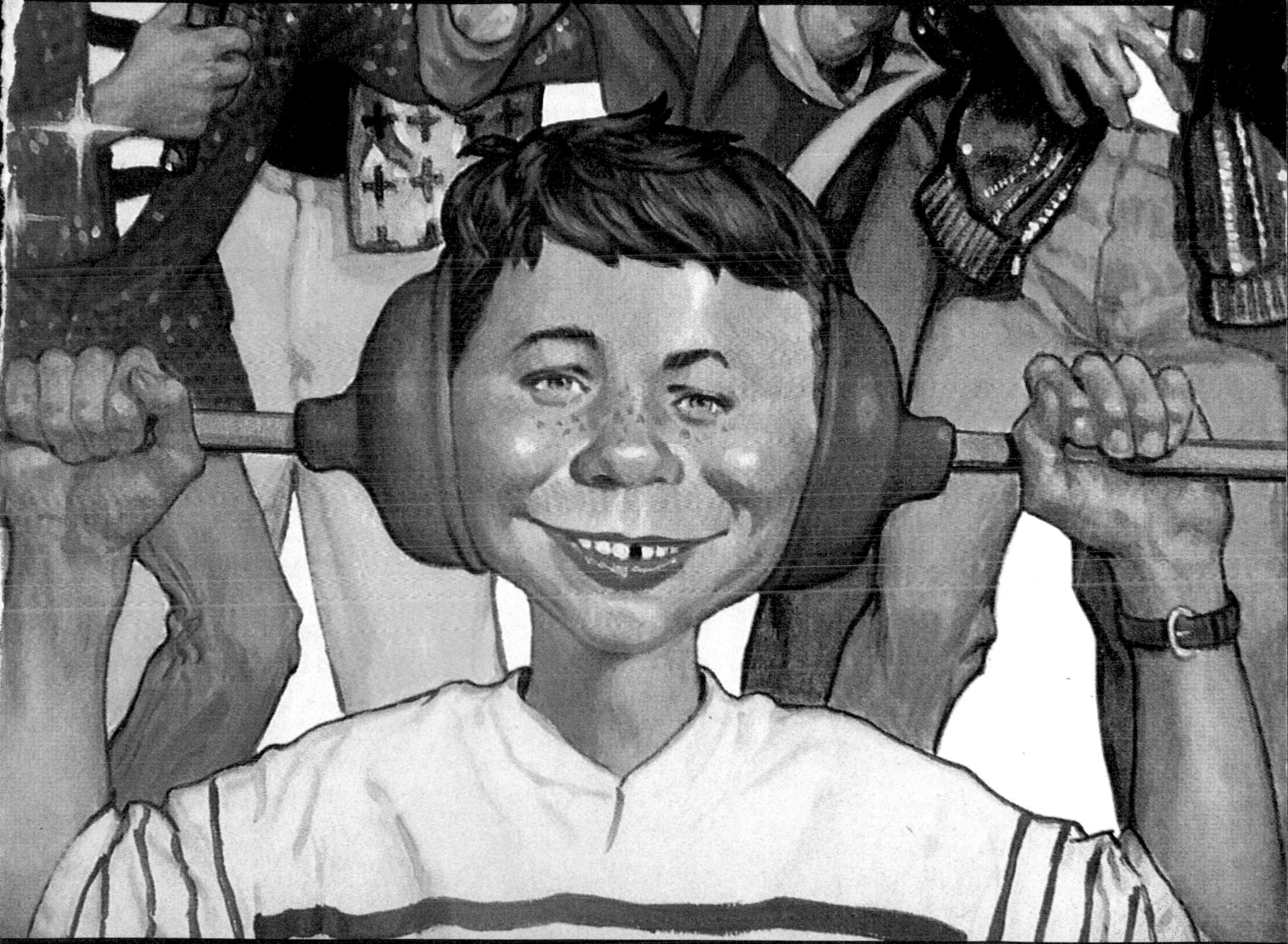

"I never get tired of listening to DeBartolo talk about MAD Magazine"

Alfred E. Neuman

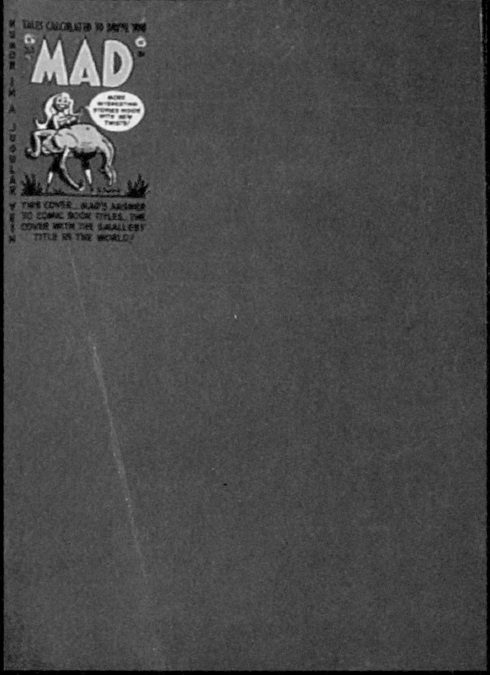
MAD

"An actual cover of the 10 cent MAD comic"

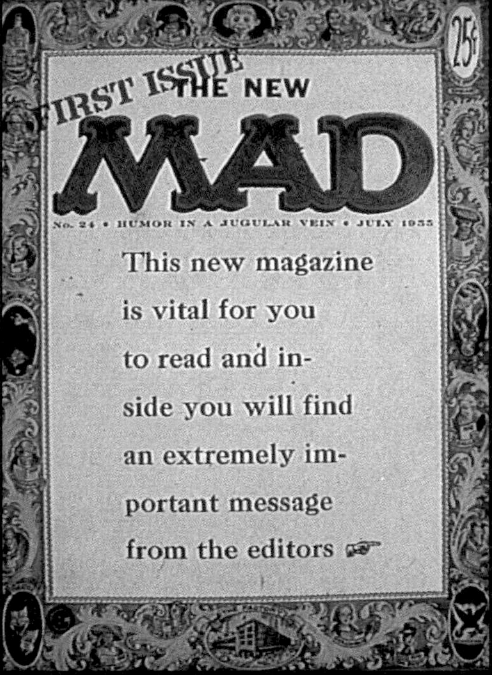
FIRST ISSUE
THE NEW
MAD
No. 24 • HUMOR IN A JUGULAR VEIN • JULY 1955
This new magazine is vital for you to read and inside you will find an extremely important message from the editors

"The first MAD Magazine"

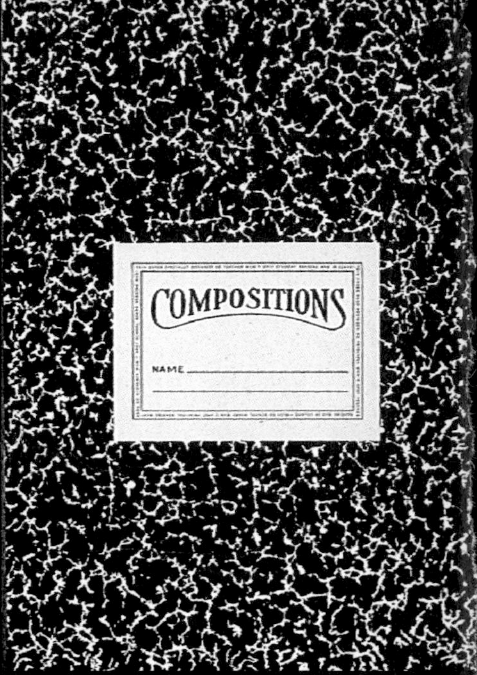
COMPOSITIONS
NAME

"The most popular back cover ever --- it could be read openly in school!!!"

MAD
40¢
CHEAP
No. 151 June '72
UDLY SALUTES AMERICAN INDUSTRY IN ITS ENDLESS QUEST FOR QUALITY, RFECTION, AND GH STANDARDS OF PRODUCTION

"Newsstands starting sending this issue back as defective - we had to send them a note saying: "that's the joke!"

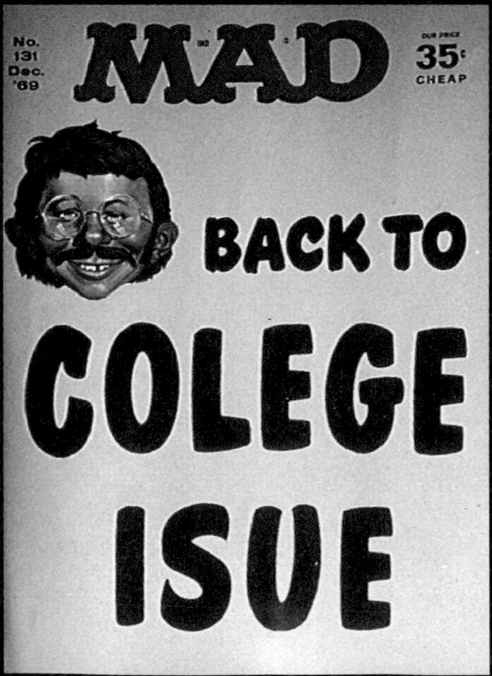
No. 131 Dec. '69
MAD
35¢
CHEAP
BACK TO
COLEGE
ISUE

"we got over 1,000 letters from readers telling us we spelled "issue wrong"

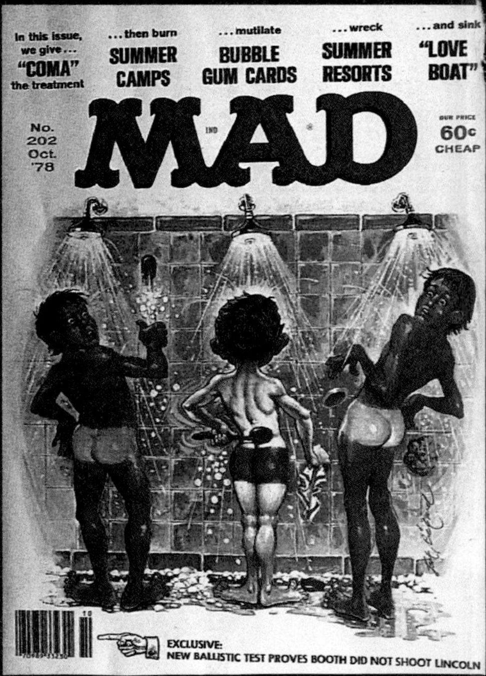
In this issue, we give... "COMA" the treatment
...then burn SUMMER CAMPS
...mutilate BUBBLE GUM CARDS
...wreck SUMMER RESORTS
...and sink "LOVE BOAT"
No. 202 Oct. '78
MAD
60¢
CHEAP
EXCLUSIVE:
NEW BALLISTIC TEST PROVES BOOTH DID NOT SHOOT LINCOLN

"Nothing we can tell you here"

MAD
OUR PRICE
25¢
CHEAP
CONGRATULATES
John KENNEDY
I LIKE JACK
upon his election as
PRESIDENT
We were with you all the way, Jack!

"In the 1960 Presidential election MAD took no chances!

No. 60
MAD
Jan. '61
OUR PRICE
25¢
CHEAP
CONGRATULATES
Richard NIXON
I LIKE DICK
upon his election as
PRESIDENT
We were with you all the way, Dick!

Instead of a front cover and a back cover, we had TWO front covers!!"

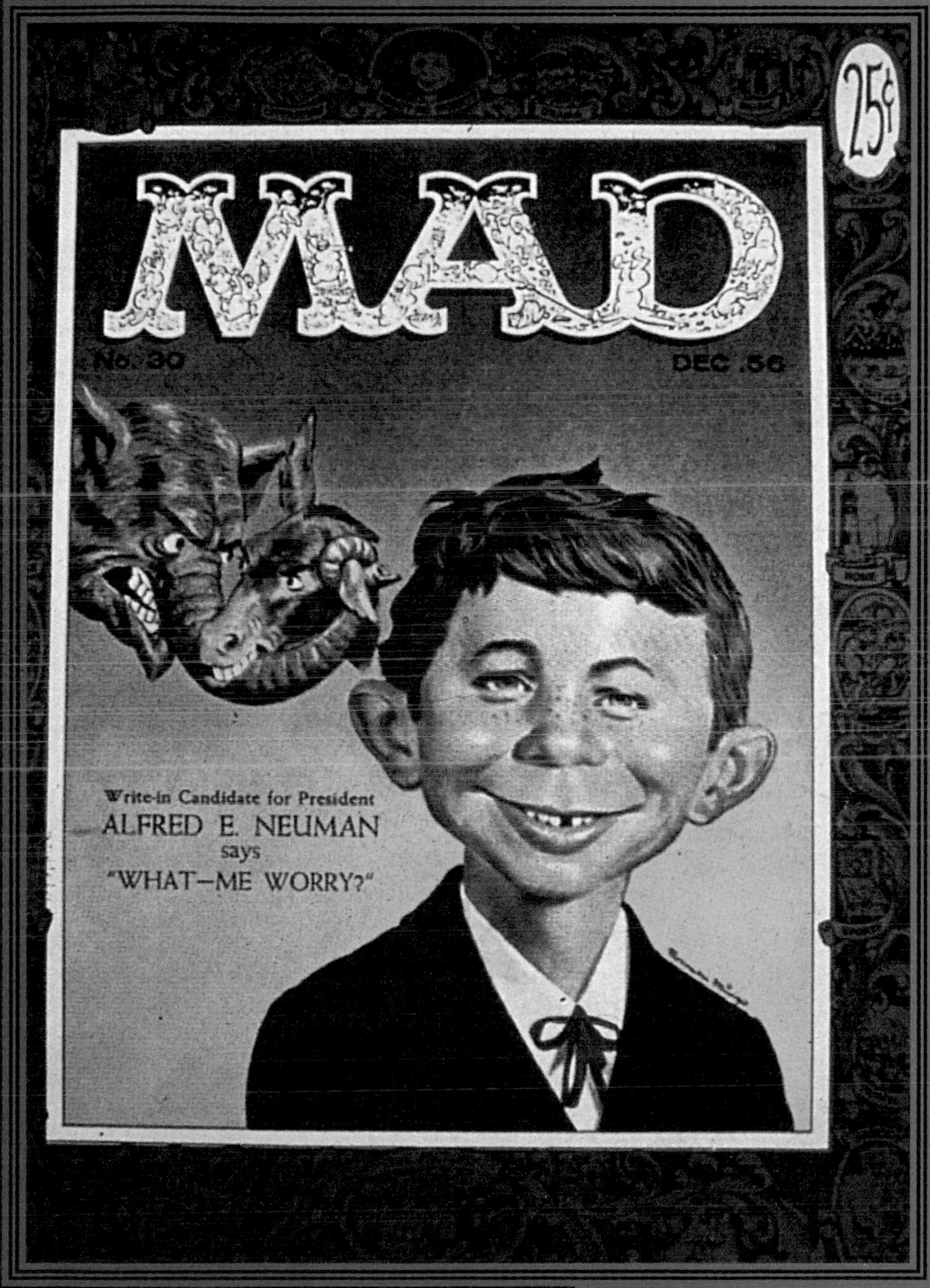
25¢
MAD
No. 30
DEC. 56
Write-in Candidate for President
ALFRED E. NEUMAN
says
"WHAT—ME WORRY?"

"First MAD Magazine with a color cover"

25¢
MAD

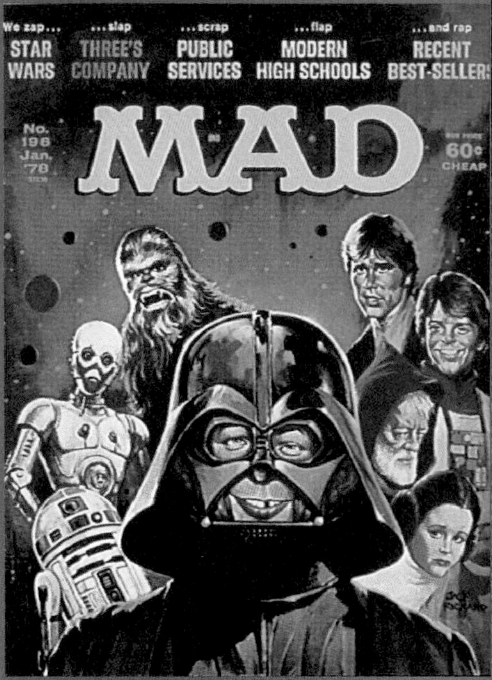
We zap... STAR WARS
...slap THREE'S COMPANY
...scrap PUBLIC SERVICES
...flap MODERN HIGH SCHOOLS
...and rap RECENT BEST-SELLERS
No. 196 Jan. '78
MAD
60¢ CHEAP

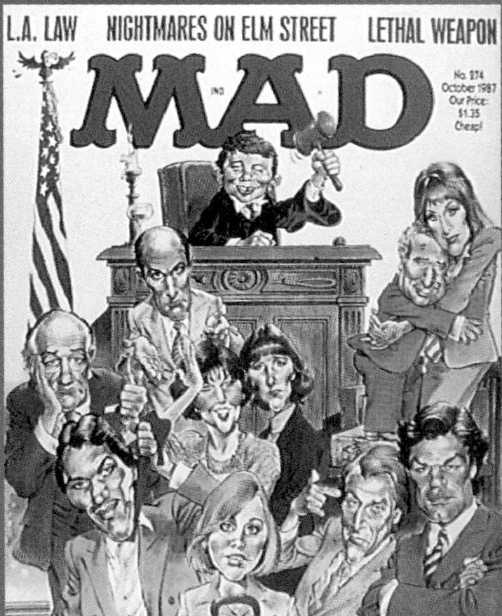
L.A. LAW
NIGHTMARES ON ELM STREET
LETHAL WEAPON
MAD
No. 274 October 1987 Our Price: $1.35 Cheap!

"Actual back cover of first color issue"

MAD
No. 198
April '78
60¢
CHEAP
HOPES THIS ISSUE JAMS EVERY COMPUTER IN THE COUNTRY...
70989 33230
...FOR FORCING US TO DEFACE OUR COVERS WITH THIS YECCHY UPC SYMBOL FROM NOW ON

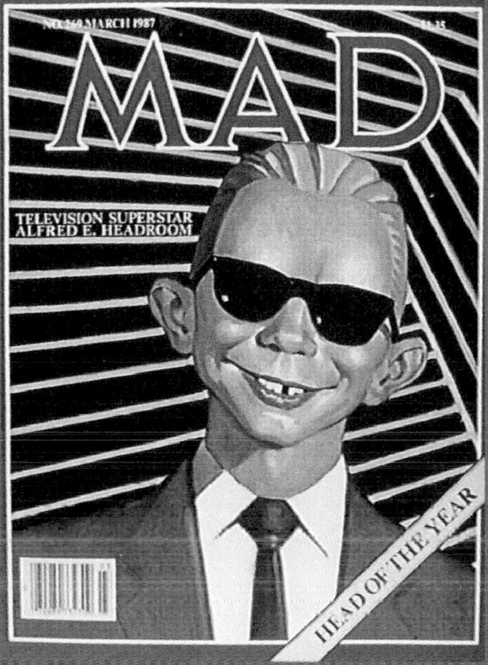
NO. 269 MARCH 1987
$1.35
MAD
TELEVISION SUPERSTAR
ALFRED E. HEADROOM
HEAD OF THE YEAR

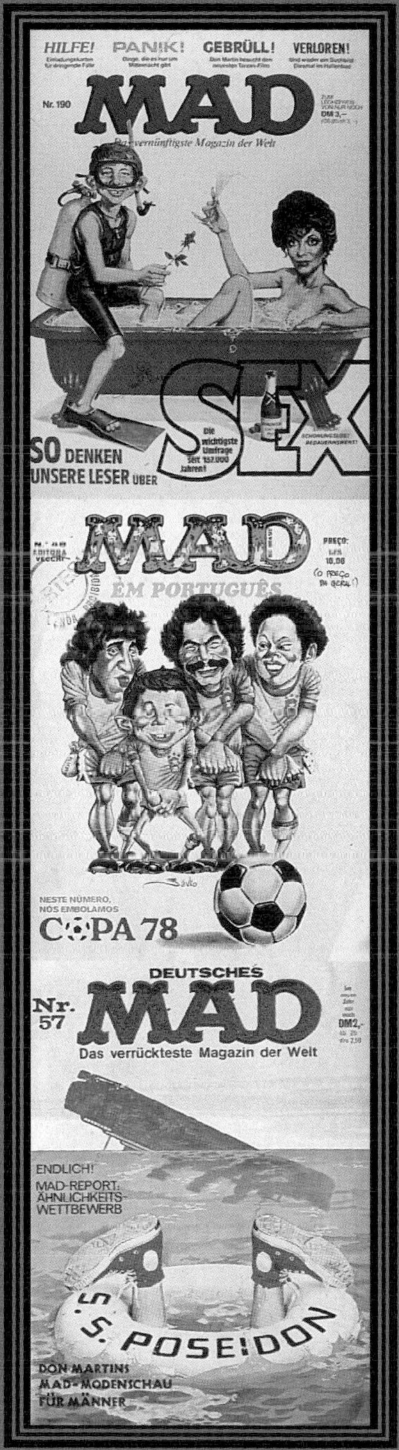
HILFE!
PANIK!
GEBRÜLL!
VERLOREN!
Nr. 190
MAD
SO DENKEN UNSERE LESER ÜBER
SEX
MAD
EM PORTUGUÊS
PREÇO:
NESTE NÚMERO, NOS EMBOLAMOS
COPA 78
DEUTSCHES
Nr. 57
MAD
Das verrückteste Magazin der Welt
ENDLICH!
MAD-REPORT: ÄHNLICHKEITS-WETTBEWERB
S.S. POSEIDON
DON MARTINS
MAD-MODENSCHAU
FÜR MÄNNER

"Foreign MADs (why should only Americas suffer?)"

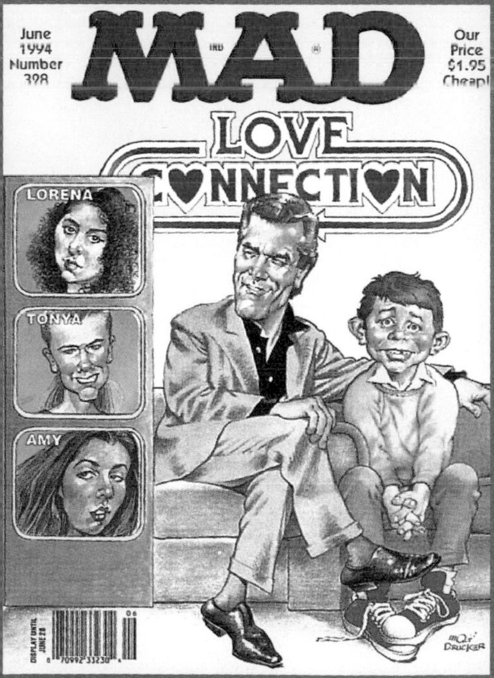
June 1994 Number
MAD
Our Price $1.95 Cheap!
LOVE CONNECTION
LORENA
TONYA
AMY

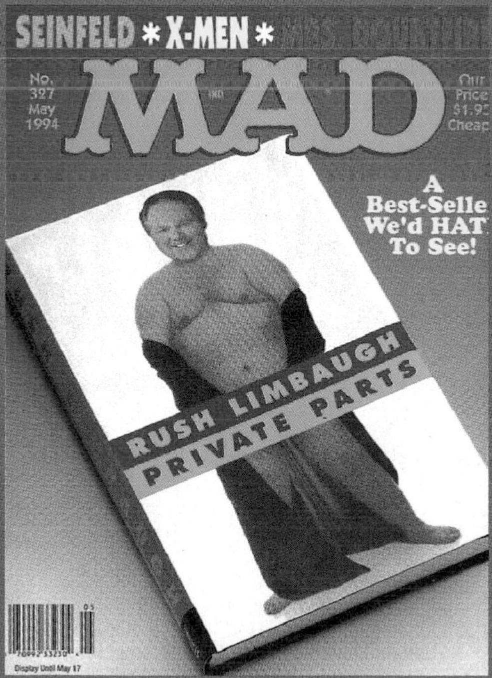
SEINFELD * X-MEN *
No. 327 May 1994
MAD
A Best-Selle We'd HAT To See!
RUSH LIMBAUGH
PRIVATE PARTS
Display Until May 17

MAD
353
The Black
MAD
MAD

MAD

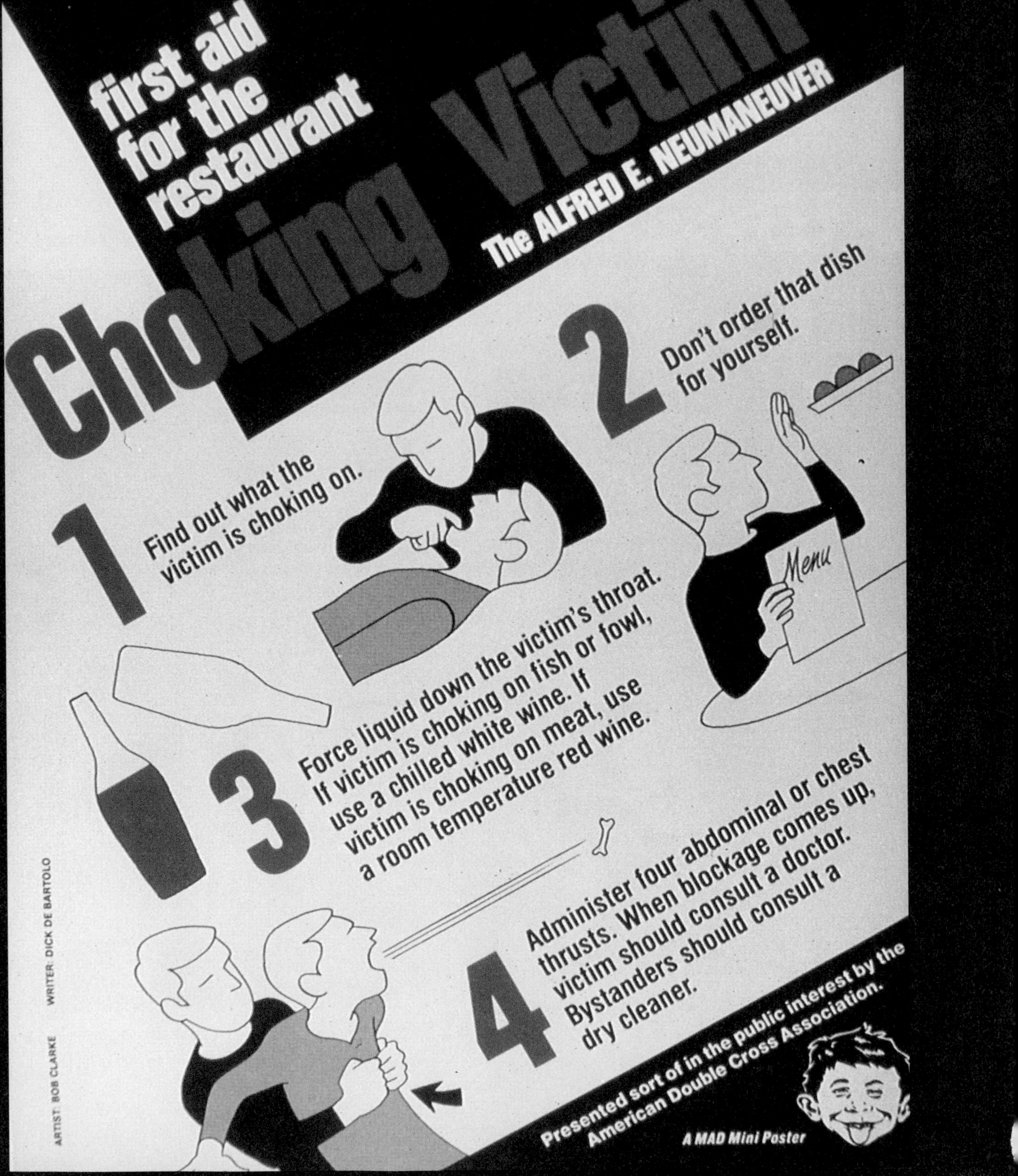
first aid
for the
restaurant
Choking Victim
The ALFRED E. NEUMANEUVER
1
Find out what the
victim is choking on.
2
Don't order that dish
for yourself.
Menu
3
Force liquid down the victim's throat.
If victim is choking on fish or fowl,
use a chilled white wine. If
victim is choking on meat, use
a room temperature red wine.
4
Administer four abdominal or chest
thrusts. When blockage comes up,
victim should consult a doctor.
Bystanders should consult a
dry cleaner.
Presented sort of in the public interest by the
American Double Cross Association.
A MAD Mini Poster
ARTIST: BOB CLARKE
WRITER: DICK DE BARTOLO

Dedicated to the memory of William M. Gaines, and all who appreciate his genius.

First edition, First printing, 1994

Published by Thunder's Mouth Press
632 Broadway, 7th Floor, New York, NY 10012

29.95

Library of Congress Cataloging in Publication Data

DeBartolo, Dick.
Good days and Mad; a hysterical tour behind the scenes at Mad magazine / Dick DeBartolo. -- 1st ed.

ISBN 1-56025-077-1 : $29.95
1. Mad (New York, N.Y. : 1958) I. Title PN6728.M33D43 1994 051--dc20
94-2685 CIP

Printed in the United States of America

Distributed by Publishers Group West
4065 Hollis Street, Emeryville, CA 94608
(800)788-3123

Good Days and MAD ®

11-15-94 BxT 16.92

GOOD DAYS AND

A ~~Historical~~ *Hysterical* Tour Behind the Scenes at MAD Magazine

Dick DeBartolo

THUNDER'S MOUTH PRESS

DEAR READER:

As you might imagine, negotiating to write a hardcover book is a long, drawn-out affair. (as a matter of fact, it's probably the only long, drawn-out affair I've had in my life, but that's material for a totally different book!)

If the truth be told, and I guess that's what one does in a nonfiction hardcover book, I never planned on writing this memoir. As a matter of fact, when literary agent Jim Hornfischer telephoned me to discuss the possibilities, I told him I wasn't interested. I did, however, agree to have lunch with him, since he was kind enough to seek me out and suggest the project. During that lunch, Jim said something that changed my mind.

While chatting about William M. Gaines, MAD's founder and one of my favorite subjects, Jim said, "Dick, you knew Bill for more than thirty-two years. If you think of writing a book as a way to keep Bill's memory alive, you might reconsider. Your book would be a tribute to his bizarre ways of running a business! Just from the little you told me today, there'll never be another boss, or friend, like Bill. And I think readers will find your escapades together outside of the MAD offices fascinating. Not many employees get their boss stuck in the arm of the Statue of Liberty!"

This agent was pushing all the right buttons, but I'm no pushover, so I said, "If I agree to write the book, will you pay for lunch?" Jim agreed, I agreed, and the wheels for this volume were set in motion.

In searching my memory and my archives, and in talking to MAD's "usual gang of idiots" about Bill and MAD, I realized more than ever that there really will never be another William M. Gaines, and certainly no business will ever again be run the way he ran MAD.

MAD's getting more corporate now, and we have to do many "professional" things like write memos, have job reviews, and fill out forms (lots of forms), but this book doesn't go into any of that. It's MAD, the way Bill ran it and I lived it—and even loved it!

SOME TECHNICAL NOTES

GOOD DAYS AND MAD is organized chronologically but not necessarily in any particular order. Within this rigid framework, I have told many stories about what has made MAD an institution, and William M. Gaines a person who belonged in that institution!

I have grouped themes into special sections of the book for which I have coined the word "CHAPTERS," and I know that you, dear reader, will be able to follow this daring experiment in publishing. You will also notice that this book does not have an index. Why? It was hard enough writing enough words to fill 300 pages! After all that work, I wasn't about to read all 300 pages AND make up a list of what was on what page! Besides, I'm sure you

ON THIS BOOK

already own a book with an index, so why would you want another one? (And besides that, your name isn't in here—so what do you care? However, I have provided a place for you to actually write in this book, so you **CAN BE** a real part of it!)

With all the technical stuff out of way, I hope you enjoy reading **GOOD DAYS AND MAD!**

MADly,

A NOTE ABOUT THE FOREWORD(S) FROM THE AUTHOR

Not wanting to offend any of my fellow writers and artists at MAD, when any one of them asked who was writing the foreword to my book, I always replied, "Who else??? You!"

Well, it got a little out of hand, and I somehow ended up promising fourteen people, even a couple of non-MAD types, that they would write the foreword. That's why you'll find forewords throughout the book! (If you're going to write a book, think twice before you make promises to your friends about who is going to write the foreword.)

In addition to the forewords, I asked MAD writers and artists to tell their thoughts or their favorite story about Gaines. These wonderful remembrances, including much original art created for this memoir, can be found throughout the book.

AND THEN THERE ARE... THE BONUSES

Just before this book went to press, I had a soul-searching conversation with Neil Ortenberg, the publisher of Thunder's Mouth Press.

I told Neil that I wanted to include something EXTRA in my book, something other books didn't have. After many sleepless nights, I came up with the idea of BONUS PAGES!

Some of the bonus pages would be brand new, original material, created just for GOOD DAYS AND MAD by members of "the usual gang of idiots." Luckily, Annie Gaines, Nick Meglin, John Ficarra, Lenny Brenner, Mort Drucker, Al Jaffee, Duck Edwing, Arnie Kogen, Sam Viviano, George Woodbridge, Joe Raiola, Charlie Kadau, Paul Coker,

Sergio Aragonés, Jack Davis, Frank Jacobs, Dave Berg, Angelo Torres, Paul Peter Porges, John Caldwell, and relative MAD newcomer Andrew Schwartzberg all owed me, so they all created something just for this volume. Other bonus pages would be things from the past, both published and unpublished, that were special or important to me.

Well, Neil listened intently as I outlined what would be on each and every bonus page, and why the reader, who would spend his or her hard-earned money for this book, deserved these extra pages.

When I finished, Neil said, "Oh, so you got my memo saying your book was thirty-seven pages short! I'm glad you found some garbage to fill it!"

Publishers, I love the way they respect a writer's work!

HOW MUCH MORE FILLER STUFF
IS THERE BEFORE THIS BOOK BEGINS?

NONE

See! The book starts now!!!

Oops, sorry! I forgot we need the contents pages !!!

TABLE OF CONTENTS

FOREWORD

Number 1?!...

BY ANNIE GAINES

When Dick DeBartolo (one of my favorite MAD people) told me he was writing a memoir about MAD (one of my favorite subjects), which would include many recollections about my late husband Bill Gaines (MAD's founder and publisher for its first forty years and my ABSOLUTE FAVORITE MAD person), I was delighted! And when he told me he wanted ME to write the foreword, I felt thrilled and very honored. Then I found out he asked about twenty other people to write forewords! I was crestfallen until Dick told me that one of the other forewords would appear before each chapter, and that mine would appear at the beginning of the book, so mine would be the REAL foreword. So, dear reader, if you find this foreword anywhere else than at the beginning of this book, take it back to your bookstore and demand your money back!!

Anyway, you have to hand it to DeBartolo, that clever guy—he's managed to get a lot of other people to write part of HIS book—for FREE! Every page of "foreword" written by someone else is a page of this book that Dick DeBartolo did not have to write!

But I digress, and must get back to the task at hand—writing this foreword. Mr. DeBartolo's outrageously hilarious articles have been making MAD readers laugh for 33 years, and his humor is sometimes so off-the-wall that for many years now he's been billed as "MAD's Maddest Writer," a title he relishes (I'll skip the mustard and ketchup jokes)! Dick is a funny, warm, sweet, endearing guy, and I'm sure you will find this memoir to be the same.

As you read through the book, I want you to pay close attention to the parts about Bill Gaines, another funny, warm, sweet, endearing guy—also clever, wise, generous, caring, hardworking, honest, thrifty, brave, clean, and reverent—and he wasn't even a Boy Scout! Bill was the best! He loved fiercely and was fiercely loved. He was loyal to people he loved and he inspired and admired loyalty in others. He was a wonderful person and I want the world to know it! So I'm glad Dick decided to write this book—it will add more "Gaines Lore" to the already existing mass that's out there! You have a treat in store for you, so start reading!

MAKING THE FIRST CONTACT

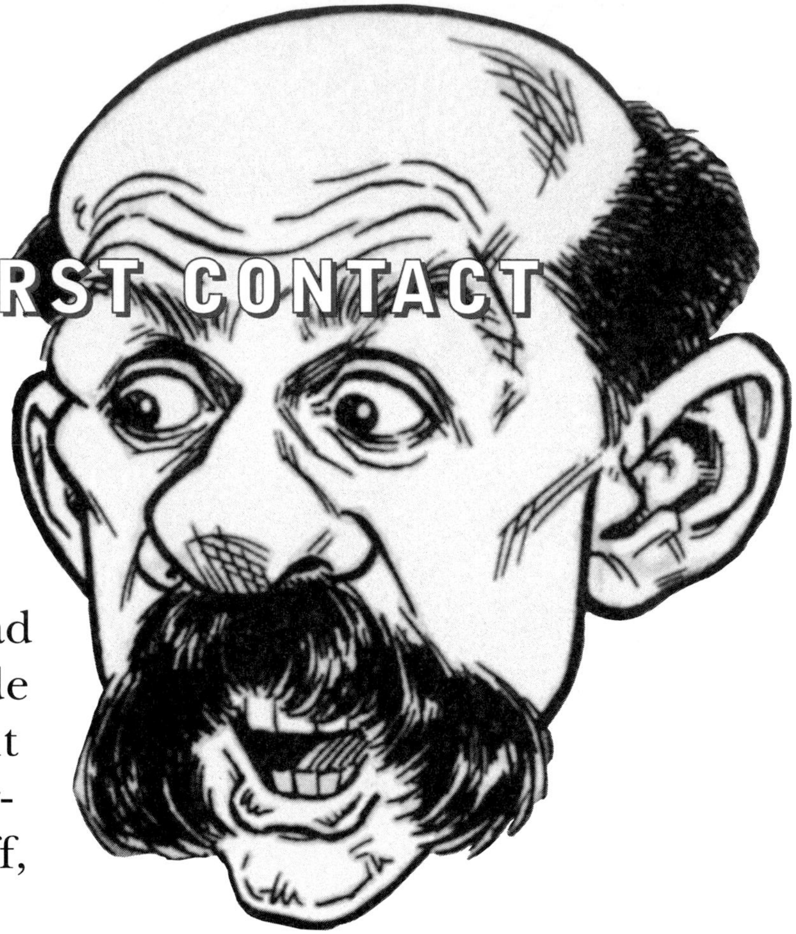

The beginning of my career at MAD Magazine was...well, MAD! I had just started high school when I started reading MAD Magazine. But instead of making me laugh, it made me feel ill! Sure, I thought it was funny, but I wanted desperately to *write* that kind of stuff, not just read it.

I felt I *belonged* at MAD—and the next thirty-plus years proved my feelings were right! (I also felt I should be rich and famous. Well, one out of three isn't bad!) Now I'm MAD Magazine's Maddest Writer; I've had work in every single issue of MAD for the past 26 years. *And* I've written eleven original MAD paperbacks, plus this hardcover book you're holding in your hands. (If it's not hardcover complain loudly to the bookstore! Call the publisher! I was promised it would be hardcover!)

Anyhow, my flair for writing MAD satire was discovered by Nick Meglin. Back then, Nick was an associate editor at MAD. I was still in high school, living at home with my parents, when I sent my first submission to MAD. The piece was a take-off on those "live" Imperial Margarine Tests being conducted in supermarkets at the time, and it raised an honest question: How come everybody they film is so normal? What would those tests be like if they were *really* done live? So I depicted a bimbo-type starlet doing anything to stay on camera and a dowdy old lady freaking out because she thought she was answering questions on a game show. Not wildly hysterical, but it did get me a job that's lasted over thirty years (and there's still no end in sight)!

But I almost didn't find out that I had the stuff to be a MAD writer. When I sent that first piece in, I knew from an article in *Writer's Guide* that a self-addressed, stamped envelope had to be sent along with any submission to a magazine. I complied. Weeks later when that thick envelope arrived back at my house, I was disappointed and I threw it in a drawer, thinking, "Well, maybe MAD's not that funny after all!" Later that day I had another thought—perhaps it was a handwritten rejection, which would at least indicate that my piece had been read by a human. So, I opened the envelope—it was stuffed with cardboard. And scribbled on the cardboard were the words that changed my life:

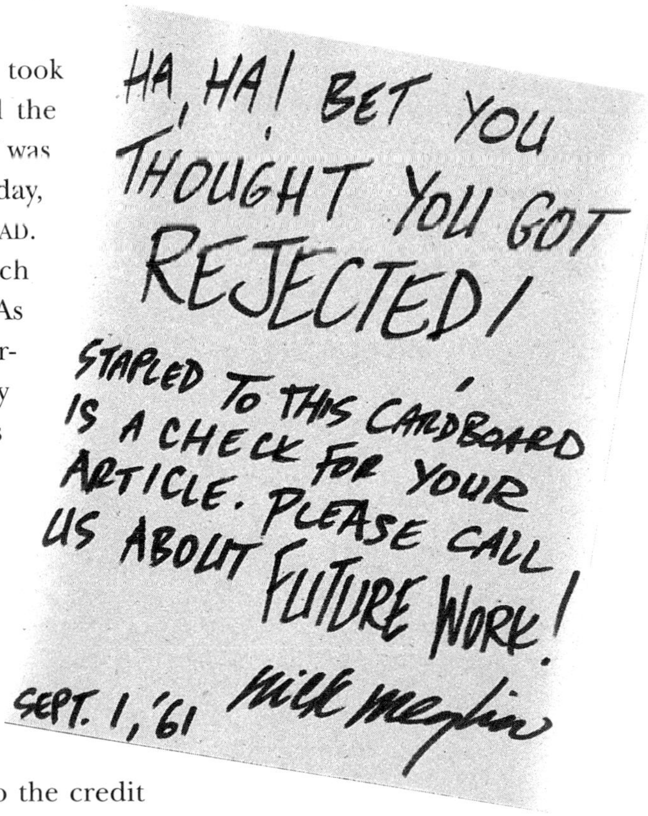
HA, HA! BET YOU THOUGHT YOU GOT REJECTED!
STAPLED TO THIS CARDBOARD IS A CHECK FOR YOUR ARTICLE. PLEASE CALL US ABOUT FUTURE WORK!
SEPT. 1, '61

I was so excited, I could hardly believe my luck! I'd sold something to MAD Magazine!

Unfortunately, I had no idea how long it took from the time a magazine bought an article until the time it was actually in print and on the newsstands; I was expecting to see it in the next issue. Every day, I checked the newsstand for the new issue of MAD. When it finally came out, I s-l-o-w-l-y turned each page, hoping that the next article would be mine. As I approached the last pages of the magazine, my spirits dropped. I knew that MAD didn't publish every month and there would be six-and-a-half weeks until the next issue. The waiting was excruciating. But after four painful months, I s-l-o-w-l-y turned a page—and there was my article!! I jumped up and down right there in front of the newsstand, and then I bought a dozen copies. What made me even more excited was that MAD had added a fourth example to the three I'd sent in. The fourth Imperial Margarine Test was written by Al Jaffee, whose work I knew well and admired. So the credit read, "Written by Dick DeBartolo with Al Jaffee." I was some happy camper!!

Hi! Welcome to another unrehearsed Imperial Margarine Test! We've spread two crackers—one with the "expensive spread," and one with new Imperial—and we're going to stop someone now and see if she can tell the difference!

BONUS #1

The Imperial Margarine Tests!

Of course, selling MAD an article the first time out didn't necessarily mean that my every submission to them would result in a sale. And as a matter of fact, my next three or four submissions were rejected. But each one was returned with a personal note, or better yet, a phone call from Nick Meglin, who encouraged me to keep sending stuff in. Nick was also kind enough to explain that several of my pieces were rejected not because the material wasn't funny, but because my premises were too close to things they already had in the works. He told me that was further proof that I was on the right road to being a more-than-one-time MAD contributor. Which was great news.

Pardon me, Ma'am. I wonder if you would mind making the Imperial Margarine Test!
You mean like they do on Television?
Yes. . . .
OH, YOU DON'T KNOW HOW LONG I'VE WAITED FOR THIS!! Ever since six months ago, when you first started showing the test on TV, I've wanted to do it!
As a matter of fact, I've shopped ten hours a day in different supermarkets, looking for you!
Oh, really? That's a compliment, but. . . .
You know my grocery bill is over $4000 a week!
$4000. . . .!!
Well, you just can't spend ten hours a day in a supermarket and not B U Y something. . . .
RICKARD
36

I guess that's true . . .
I'm wanted in five states for not paying my grocery bill!
Well, to. . . .
The "A&P" has my picture on a wanted poster!
That's terribl—
I owe "Piggly Wiggly Markets" $6000. . . .
I wish I could help, but. . . .
Fortunately, I have $2000 worth of empty deposit bottles to return!
Yes, well, if we could proceed with. . . .
Have you ever made this test in Murray's Kosher Delicatessen on Delancy Street?
I don't think so, but. . . .
I figure I'd spent ten lost hours in that place!
Look, lady — you've waited six months to make this test! Can we do it N O W ?
I'd love to . . . only I'm on a "fat-free" diet!

But MAD came out only eight times a year, and since I was in business high school I could figure out that I was going to need another occupation besides selling material to MAD.

My high school was in Manhattan, and classes were held on split sessions. For my last two years there, I went to school on the 7:30 a.m. to 1 p.m. shift. I HATED that schedule because I hate to get up early, but it did make getting a part-time job easier. I got lucky and my very first job was in TV with Barry-Enright Productions. They produced game shows like "Tic Tac Dough," "Twenty-One," and "Dough Re Mi," and although my job was office boy, I got to deliver scripts and props to the different television studios, so I felt like I was in the thick of show biz. Here I was, writing for MAD Magazine *and* working in TV!

Through this job I made a few contacts and started writing monologues for some up-and-coming comedians. For one wanna-be funny guy, I wrote a piece based on those old submarine movies. Now these movies had really formula plots and dialogue. For example, every one of them had a scene where the submarine crew would shoot their clothes

Pardon me, Ma'am. I wonder if you would mind making the Imperial Margarine Test!
Oh, yes! God, yes. . . .
Er . . . we're on television, Ma'am. . . .
Pictures that fly through the air and come out of little boxes in living rooms across the nation! The inventive genius of man!!
Y-yes. Now, one of these crackers has been spread with the "expensive spread.". . .
The "expensive spread.". . . .?
You know. Like Mother used to churn?
I'm glad you said that! There aren't many of us left today who remember Mama! You and I think alike!
..If GIGI PERREAU married photog WEEGEE . . .
Look — would you taste this cracker?
For you, my love, I would go to the end of the Earth!
And now, eat this cracker, please!
Do not say "please!" EXPECT it of me! We know each other well enough!
Now, would you please tell us which is better?
Anything but that, my precious! Who am I to condemn one man's product, and praise another's! Free enterprise must survive! The very future of Mankind depends upon it! Four score and seven years ago. . . .

out of the torpedo bay, so the enemy ship above would think they had hit the sub and blown it apart underwater. In my spoof, the captain has a special plan IF the submarine is actually hit. He'd have the crew hang on to every piece of debris from the explosion, so the enemy floating above would never have the satisfaction of knowing if they were successful! Another cliche in those films was that anytime the captain gave a command the first officer would have to repeat it. I wondered why the first officer didn't get angry about that, so in my piece, the poor guy finally blurts out, "Captain! Why do I always have to repeat what YOU say! Tomorrow, I want a turn at making up the commands, and YOU'LL have to repeat them!" Anyway, the monologue had all sorts of off-the-wall observations like that.

Well, the comedian liked it, but his wife didn't, so he gave it back to me. *I* thought it was funny, but I also thought, Hey, maybe this guy's wife knows better. So I decided to ask Nick Meglin at MAD to read it. MAD doesn't use monologue material, but I valued Nick's opinion. Now, the funny thing about Nick, which I didn't know at the time, is that he's only a

Sir, this may sound like a scatter-brained idea, but why not stuff our clothes and some junk and a little oil into one of the torpedo tubes and shoot it to the surface? When they see the oil slick and stuff, they'll think they got us!
Not bad, Lieutenant, but I've got one even better. Why not wait till they hit us, then hold on to everything so that nothing floats to the surface and drive them crazy wondering!

few years older than me. Here I was, a teen-aged kid in awe of Nick and his power to pass judgment on MAD material, when he was barely out of high school himself. But Nick sat behind a desk, and he had an office, so I assumed that meant he was MORE professional than I was! (Today, I have an office and a desk too, but Nick can approve pay vouchers and I can't, which still makes him MORE professional than I am!)

After he read the monologue, Nick said, "Not only is this funny, but if you rewrite it as movie dialogue, and we get Jack Davis or Mort Drucker to illustrate it, it would be a wonderful feature for MAD!" Well, I did, and they got Jack Davis to illustrate it, and that started a long career of writing movie satires for MAD. At first I did take offs on generic movies: war movies, airliners-in-trouble movies, giant-animals-gone-nuts movies, et cetera. Later on I did two paperback books on the subject: *A MAD Look at Old Movies* and *The Return of a MAD Look at Old Movies.* Although MAD publishes anthologies and collections which contain material from the magazine, my books for MAD were all original material, as are many of the other paperbacks from MAD writers and artists.

Captain, Sir, we're entering **mined water.**
Yours, mine, what's the **difference.** Out here, Lieutenant, the water belongs to **everyone!**

1

I said **"mined,"** Sir. You know, "hit and make big **boom?"**
Captain, Sir, I'm picking up a signal on the Sonar. It may be an **enemy ship.**
Let me look at the **horoscope!**
5¢

2

After a few of these generic-movie assignments, Nick asked me to take a shot at satirizing current movies, and writing those turned out to be my favorite kind of work for MAD. Over the years, I've written dozens of them, along with take-offs on hit TV shows.

When Nick asked me to do these pieces, I felt honored because I was going to join the ranks of Stan Hart and Larry Siegel, who had written so many great MAD movie satires that really broke me up. As a matter of fact, in addition to writing for MAD, for years Larry and Stan were head writers for Carol Burnett. They're the guys who wrote many of those fantastic movie take-offs that Carol, Vicki Lawrence, Tim Conway, Harvey Korman, and Lyle Waggoner did on "The Carol Burnett Show."

Stan still writes for MAD. I'm still at MAD. Mort Drucker and Jack Davis are still at MAD. In fact, Nick Meglin, my discoverer, is still at MAD, and today, he's co-editor, along with John Ficarra. (What if I hadn't opened that envelope?? Today I might be working in a bookstore, selling this book instead of writing it, and someone else would have gotten to be me! And *I* wanted to be me! Wait, I AM me! I got my wish! It was the power of positive thinking!)

You mean **periscope,** don't you Captain?
I mean **horoscope!** I never do anything unless my **stars** are right! Let me see . . . I'm a **Leo . . .**

3

And I'm a **Stanley,** Sir, but all that isn't going to matter if that ship gets any **closer!**
A **Cancer** is what you are, Stanley! Stop bothering me with your **meaningless** interruptions so I can think! Now, the best way to avoid detection is to kill the **engines . . .**
Shut all engines!

4

FOREWORD
Number 2?!...

BY NICK MEGLIN
CO-EDITOR, MAD MAGAZINE

It's both an honor and a privilege to be selected by the author of this book to write a few words about him for this classic (not to mention classy) edition. To be chosen for this, in view of my humble background, just goes to show that where else but in a country like ours can an orphan like myself, wretched and poor, pick himself up by his bootstraps and rise above his environment to the point where he can be even considered to write a foreword about a man like the author of this book. It wasn't easy, believe me! I mean, how would you like to be the only kid out of an orphanage class of 45 that wasn't chosen by foster parents? No, I'm sure you wouldn't like it either. "Too sensitive," I would hear them whisper about me as they took their Johnnies and Jimmies back to their warm homes and chocolate cake. "Too shy," they would say as that fink Harvey Stonebreaker climbed on a new black and white Schwinn bike his new foster parents bought him. Well, I don't need anyone to buy me a bike, Harvey Stonebreaker, wherever you are! I hope you're reading this so you'll know that I made it! I can buy all the bikes I want! With money I earned writing, Harvey! Writing things like forewords for important people like the author of this book, Harvey. People who wouldn't have anything to do with the likes of you!

But I've gotten off the subject a bit, haven't I? I guess you want to know what happened to me after I left the orphanage. Well, I was eighteen, and one of my poems ("There once was a girl from Dodge City") caught the attention of MAD's publisher, William M. Gaines. The rest is history.

I've certainly enjoyed this opportunity to write about the author of this book who, I'm sure, must be a great guy. Not like that spoiled brat Harvey Stonebreaker.

FEELING AT HOME IN TV LAND

Things were looking good. Like Nick had predicted, I was selling MAD more articles *and* I was writing for budding comedians, when my TV career took a whole new turn. I had been an office boy at Barry-Enright for three whole months, when I thought it was time to move on to bigger things. So I decided to take an old cliché from the movies and put it to work for myself. But how?

What I did was this: I wrote a take-off on one of the game shows Jack Barry and Dan Enright were producing. I recorded it on my tape recorder at home and then one day, when Jack and Dan were having lunch in the office, I played it real loud outside their door. When Dan stuck his head out the door, I acted innocent and said, "Oh, is this too loud?" But Dan told me to let it play, that he thought it sounded funny, and then he came out with Jack to be able to hear it better. After they listened, Dan said, "That's funny stuff! Why don't you take a shot at writing scripts for our kids' show 'Winky-Dink and You'."

"...by the next week, I was a TV writer, at triple the office-boy salary! Gee, just like in the movies!!"

I wrote a sample sketch, and by the next week, I was a TV writer, at triple the office-boy salary! Gee, just like in the movies!! But unlike the movies, while writing "Winky-Dink" scripts, I still had to do most of the office boy chores! And I had to lie about my age. Dan said no one at the studio would respect a fifteen-year-old script writer. So along with my raise, Dan gave me an eight-year increase in my age! (Although I normally don't tell my age, I will in this book, and I'll get the age thing out of the way right now. My age equals the difference between the height of the Empire State Building and the length of the Queen Elizabeth 2, plus or minus an unknown percentage. But please, DON'T tell anyone else!)

Things were going incredibly well, so I wanted to make even more sweeping changes in my life. I wanted to move out of my parents' house in Brooklyn and live in Manhattan. I wanted to be able to stay up as late as I wanted; to eat dessert for three meals a day; to have a dog, or two or three; to have a speed boat, or two or three. And I wanted it all by the time I graduated. And I didn't want to have to be left back for a term or too, I wanted to graduate on time. So to keep on schedule, I had to work fast. And I did.

Actually, a lot of my success was due to my talks with a therapist, Dr. Isabel Wright. She totally changed my conception of time. She said that when one's work was important, hours were not important, and that you could and would work as long as necessary to achieve what you wanted. Consequently, I worked at least a part of each day, all seven days of the week, and it worked! I did it back then and I follow that schedule today. And I never go anywhere without a pen and paper to jot down ideas.

SORRY
LIFT
NOT.
WORKING
SERVICE

MEETING THE GREAT WHITE HULK

During my first year as a contributor to MAD, I didn't meet, or even talk to, my idol, William M. Gaines. MAD had been around for ten years by then, and Gaines had already developed a cult following, but it was Nick who handled all the writing assignments.

Then one day I had a question about money. Nick said the only person who handled financial arrangements was Bill Gaines, and so he would switch me over to Bill. I started to shake, and I said to Nick, "You mean Bill himself, or his secretary?"

"Bill himself. He doesn't have a secretary," said Nick.

I tried again. "Shouldn't you switch me over to the accountant instead?"

At that point, Nick just wanted me off the phone. "Bill does all the financial stuff himself. Just hang on!"

It was happening...I was being switched over to William M. Gaines! Do I call him Bill? Do I call him William? Do I call him Mr. Gaines? Your lordship? Should I be funny? *Could* I be funny while I was this nervous? My heart was pounding. I couldn't believe I was going to actually talk to my hero.

I heard a click, and then a booming voice in the background. It had to be Bill's voice. He wasn't talking directly into the mouthpiece, but I could hear everything he was saying, and that was unfortunate.

"DeBartolo's on the phone??? Who the hell wants to speak to him? Did you tell him I'm in?? Oh, Christ, what the hell does he want??? He's a pain in the ass!" Then he picked up the phone. "Hellllooo....," he said soothingly.

I stammered and fell over my words. "Bill, er, I don't know if you know who I am, but Nick INSISTED I talk to you an...an..." As I was attempting to speak, I was trying to think of a reason why he hated me. We'd never even met! I was a nice guy, at least I THOUGHT I was a nice guy. I was in a panic. For a few seconds Bill listened to me stutter and then he broke up laughing. "Dick, I'm pulling your leg, relax....I do that to all the new guys! I love to scare them! Welcome to MAD!"

Well, that was exciting. In fact, every new phase of working for MAD was exciting. Getting that first check. Seeing that first article in print. Talking to Bill for the first time. Then it was time for the next adventure—going to see the MAD offices in Manhattan.

As all diehard MAD fans know, MAD started out on the Bowery in lower Manhattan, but they had moved up to Third Avenue by the time I sold them my first piece. It was a fancier address, but when I entered the offices, I was surprised. *These are the MAD offices?? They're so small! They're a mess! And where is everybody??* (This is much the same way visitors to the current MAD offices feel, but you'll see for yourself when you take the MAD tour later on in this book. You'll sit in on meetings and learn a lot about life behind the scenes at MAD. Excited? Then let's get back to the chapter in progress!)

"...DeBartolo's on the phone??? Who the hell wants to speak to him? Did you tell him I'm in?? Oh, Christ, what the hell does he want??? He's a pain in the ass!"

Then I was introduced to William M. Gaines.

When Nick went into the office to see if Bill was free, he closed the door behind him and from behind that closed door, I could hear Gaines bellow. "DeBartolo's here?? What the hell does he want? Who let him in?!" But this time I knew he was kidding....Well, I was HOPING he was kidding. But Bill was laughing as I entered the room, which gave me a pretty good reassurance that he didn't hate me.

As I later found out, Bill always kept his office door closed. He once confided to me that he did it so he wouldn't know who came in late, who left early, who took a two-hour lunch, who was sleeping on the hall floor, et cetera. He said, "As long as the magazine gets out on time, and it's funny, let the staff do whatever they want!"

One of my favorite quotes from Bill is, "I get the best writers and artists and merely provide the atmosphere in which they can thrive." And thrive we did—and still do.

FOREWORD

Number 3?!...

BY JOHN FICARRA
CO-EDITOR, MAD MAGAZINE

Dick DeBartolo is a very talented, prolific writer who has played an enormously important role in MAD Magazine for the past 33 years. I know this because Dick emphatically told me so the first time we met and he continues to remind me of it on an almost daily basis. I never really gave it all that much thought until recently, when Dick got down on his hands and knees and begged me to write this foreword. That's when I went back and did some checking.

Dick first wrote for MAD in 1962. In June 1966, he began (and continues to this day) an impressive streak of contributing at least one article to every issue of MAD. Many of his contributions have been TV and movie satires such as "The Odd Squad," "The Moronic Woman," and "201 Minutes of a Space Idiocy." Others include such infamous MAD classics as "The MAD Choking Victim's Poster" and "A Psychedelic Diary." My point is, like it or not, there's no denying that our boy Dick has pounded out hundreds of pages of MAD material. True, many people would say this is not something to be very proud of, but it is an achievement of sorts, in the loosest sense of the word, however dubious.

And Dick deserves all the corresponding credit/blame. Now, in my opinion, there is no one whose life is more deserving of a book than Bill Gaines. Never have I met a more extraordinary 300 pounds of human being. Outrageous, eccentric, hilarious, some might say dangerous, I firmly believe Bill Gaines was a true American hero. His birthday should be a national holiday (or, at the very least, me, Dick, and the rest of the MAD staff should get the day off every year, with pay. But that's another story).

So why am I not more thrilled to be writing this foreword? One word: fraud. There is a real question in my mind as to just how well Dick DeBartolo knew Bill Gaines. I know from firsthand experience that Bill was not a fan of Dick's and ducked him whenever possible. Sometimes Bill would spend hours hiding out in a bathroom booth when Dick came into the MAD offices. Bill absolutely refused to be photographed with "that little bastard" as Bill liked to refer to Dick and, on the rare occasions that they were photographed together, Bill spent thousands of dollars buying up all the prints and negatives before gleefully burning them in his office spittoon. To date, I've seen no evidence to convince me that Dick DeBartolo met Bill Gaines face-to-face more than two or three times in the 31 years they knew each other. In fact, I have an ugly suspicion that this entire book is nothing more than a cheap, elaborate hoax filled with sickening lies, twisted quotes, fabricated tales, absurd half-truths, and worse.

Happy reading!

IT TAKES A THICK SKIN TO WORK AT MAD

It wasn't just Bill's privilege to treat everyone badly—it's a way of life at MAD. Of course it's all done in jest, but everyone is so good at it, it takes a long time to get used to it.

Nick Meglin, for example, can really dish it out. One time I watched while he was reading a script I wrote. I felt pretty good because he'd smiled through much of it, and he'd really laughed out loud several times. When I asked which of the jokes he'd laughed at most, he said, "None of the jokes. I was laughing at the typos. God, are you an awful speller!"

And I'll never forget my first paperback book meeting. Present were Nick, longtime MAD artist Jack Davis, and myself. Nick had called the meeting so we could discuss the artwork and layouts for *A MAD Look at Old Movies,* my first book for MAD. Jack had already done the "pencils," which are the rough sketches of how the panels in each story would look, and Nick was going over them because he wanted to make sure the book was close to the way I visualized it. Nick is also an artist, so he had a much better grasp of the layout than I did, and all during the meeting, he made suggestions as we flipped through the pages. "Jack, can you make this one page into a two-page spread to get better detail?...Can you flip-flop story two and story four? I think it gives the book a better flow." Over the hour-long meeting, Jack eagerly agreed to everything and took careful notes, often adding a nice twist of his own to Nick's suggestions. But when Jack left the room to make a phone call, Nick turned to me and said, "What a temperamental bastard! MAD artists are the most temperamental shits in the world, but Davis is the worst. But don't be depressed. He's arrogant, but he'll do a good job on your book!"

I was truly speechless! Hard to work with??? A bastard?? The guy was a saint!! My God, what did they say about me when I wasn't there?

I was still pretty green and must have looked it, because Nick broke into a smile and said, "Jack's a sweetheart, isn't he? He's great to work with!" I thought, "Oh, I get the routine now!! No matter how good anything or anybody is...you dump on them and their work."

So that's how it goes here at MAD, and over the years, I became real good at it, too. One of my proudest moments came when a camera crew came to MAD to film Gaines and me for an interview. The host of the segment asked, "Are there any sacred cows at MAD?" I pointed to Bill and said, "Just him!" Of course Bill broke up completely.

There were rarely any hurt feelings because, as I said, continuous verbal abuse was a way of life with all of us at MAD, and especially with Bill. When guests would go through the MAD offices, I would often throw open Bill's door and say things like:

"That blithering idiot is William M. Gaines!"

"There he is, the fat millionaire who sucks the blood from the MAD artists and writers, so he can live like a king, while we live in squalor!"

"It's cold in here because Mr. Gaines died two years ago, but we like to leave him propped up at his desk for this tour!"

And often Bill would respond by saying, "He's right, you know" or "He's not kidding, I am a rotten millionaire!"

During that same interview, the host asked me what kind of boss Bill was. I replied, "We joke and kid about Bill being a slave driver and a cheap man, but deep down, he's a despicable creep!"

When the interview was over, Bill took my hand, shook it, and said,

"...There he is, the fat millionaire who sucks the blood from the MAD artists and writers, so he can live like a king, while we live in squalor!"

"I've got a great idea! We'll become a team! I hate doing interviews, so we'll do them together! I'll give the facts, and all the while you sit there and say terrible things about me!" I said, "I can handle that!"

This tactic worked for a lot of interviews, but it kept us off "Late Night with David Letterman." Bill didn't want to do it alone, and Dave's people didn't want to book two guests at one time.

Bill liked abuse so much that one day he buzzed my office and said, "Are you mad at me? You haven't been mean to me in three days."

I screamed back, "I was mean to you just this morning, but you're so old and senile, you don't remember!"

I could picture the smile on Bill's face as I heard him say, "I feel better now! Thanks, cookie!"

FOREWORD
Number 4?!...

BY LENNY BRENNER
ART DIRECTOR,
MAD MAGAZINE

When Dick DeBartolo asked me to write the foreword for his book, my first thought was — Dick DeBartolo — that name sounds familiar!
My second thought was — it can't be a very good book if he wants ME to write the foreword!
Therefore, I want nothing to do with it!

BONDING WITH BILL

As you can imagine, most MAD get-togethers are chaotic. And when twenty or thirty of us MAD writers and artists meet at a restaurant, it's a pretty boisterous affair. The chaos starts the minute we enter the room. We'll ask if we can move some tables together, and usually the waiters, overwhelmed by the mob, reluctantly nod "yes." Tables are quickly moved about, and in short order there is a circle of tables—with the waiters trapped in the middle!!

After we get the table-moving shtick out of our system, we start phase two. The writers try to top each other with one-liners, and the artists try to outdraw each other, using the napkins and tablecloths as their canvas. The waiters reap the benefits, because they take free artwork home to their families and kids. Here's a drawing I rescued before the waiters could get to it. A piece of paper was passed around and the various MAD artists drew impressions of me (see how many of them depict sweets). But Paul Peter Porges summed up the whole story in one little drawing. Notice how in that tiny sketch, my boat has sunk, I'm underwater, but I'm holding my dog safely above the water!

These MAD parties were organized by Bill because he loved good food and good wine and he loved to play host on a lavish scale. But just as important to Bill was the fact that the parties would bring together the MAD staffers. The MAD offices were small, MAD had few full-time employees, and the magazine was mainly a freelance effort, so those who worked for MAD, even those who lived in Manhattan, only rarely saw each other. So periodically Bill would preside over these parties.

WOW!
J.D.
D.M.
DICK
P.P.F.
D.B.

"...The waiters reap the benefits, because they take free art-work home to their families and kids. Here's a drawing I rescued before the waiters could get to it."

Lucy the Elephant

I was very shy the first few times I attended these food orgies. I was afraid to enter into the one-liner competition, and since I was still anxious about authority figures, I was a little disquieted by Gaines. But at one particular MAD party, I decided to speak up. The conversation had turned to hotels, and as an attempt at humor, I mentioned that my favorite place to stay was the Elephant Hotel. Bill froze! Then in disbelief, he inquired, "How did you ever hear about the Elephant Hotel?" I told him it was mentioned in an old book about Coney Island that I'd found at a used bookstore. I added that, in addition to the one at Coney Island, the same architect had built a smaller Elephant, nicknamed Lucy, in Margate City, New Jersey. If I recall the facts in the book correctly, the Elephant at Coney Island was actually an eight-story hotel—guests entered by walking up a flight of stairs in the trunk. The one in Margate City was built as an office and was considerably smaller, about the size of a two-story house.

Bill knew about the one in Margate City, too, and he looked at me as if I had depths he hadn't anticipated. Suddenly, it seemed, we were buddies. "I've been dying to go to Margate City to visit Lucy," Bill said, "but it's a long trip to make alone. Would you like to go with me? We can make a day out of it." And right then and there Bill took out his little diary, and he set up a trip so we could visit Lucy in person.

"...and he looked at me as if I had depths he hadn't anticipated. Suddenly, it seemed, we were buddies."

Even though at first I was nervous about spending so much time with Bill (it was a three-hour drive each way), we had a wonderful time, and we learned a lot more about each other. The trip had a great side benefit too, because Bill introduced me to one of his favorite things to eat: grilled Taylor Pork Roll on a hamburger bun. On the way to Margate City, we stopped in Atlantic City and ate. With Bill, you didn't go to Atlantic City to gamble, you only went for Taylor Pork Roll!

We got to Margate City and we found Lucy the Elephant, but she was in horrible disrepair. Bill said we had to do something about it—with Bill, that meant then and now. I told him we should find the Chamber of Commerce to see if they had any plans to help Lucy.

I'm not sure of the exact series of events that took place, but in short order Bill and I were at the home of the mayor of Margate City and Bill was sitting there, telling the mayor how important it was to restore the Elephant. Then Bill stood and said he wanted fund-raising to start immediately, and here was his contribution—he handed the mayor a fifty (or was it a hundred?) dollar bill. I added ten dollars of my own. (It might have been five, but ten dollars looks better in print!)

Bill and I visited the Elephant many years later. Lucy had been restored—she now had a small museum—and she had been moved to a few blocks from the ocean. And yes, on the way to Margate City, we did stop in Atlantic City for grilled Taylor Pork Roll!

After that day with Bill, I could open his office door without fear of rejection. (Real rejection, that is. Of course I expected him to continue to abuse me.) At long last, I was one of those people who could sit behind Bill's closed door and just talk. In the past, I would see Bill's closed door and wonder if he was in there alone, or talking to the one of the MAD staffers he liked better than me.

Now that we had bonded, Bill and I found other areas in which we thought alike—like the way we thought about money. Bill took a kind of paternalistic interest in his staff; he genuinely worried about us. One way he showed this to me was that he would often ask what I was getting paid for writing jobs that had nothing to do with MAD. He wasn't being nosy, he just wanted to make sure I wasn't being ripped off.

One day when Bill asked, I told him that for one writing job I had just done, I had charged $188. Bill wanted to know how I had come up with such a weird figure. I told him there was a portable electric typewriter I wanted and it cost $188, so that's the amount I charged. God, did that please Bill! "I used to do the same thing when I first started to work," he said. He literally beamed. "Except I thought of money in terms of frankfurters! If I did a chore for a quarter, I really thought of it as two and a half frankfurters." (Obviously we're talking ten-cent frankfurters here.)

Bill's approach to all things financial was just as skewed, and just as precise. For example, all the freelancers received Christmas bonuses, but the amount of the bonus was never a straightforward, per page deal. Of course that was the basis, but other things would factor into the final figures, like how long they had been there, how often they had sold MAD work, perhaps the ever-rising cost of frankfuters would show up. There was even a special little extra something for the contributors Bill called "the big guns." I was one of the "big guns" but I don't know what that meant in dollars and cents compared to...er, the small guns, I guess. I sometimes thought that Bill had developed this system just so he could play with his calculator. He thought the calculator was a great gadget. Bill just LOVED gadgets—another bond between us.

Bill's cheapness was legend, but the truth is that he would be cheap in one transaction and extravagant in another. I'll explain the biggest extremes I can recall.

In the early eighties, Bill asked if I'd like to be on staff at MAD. Being on staff meant showing up and putting in actual hours for a certain number of days per week. (Freelancers just wandered in at will and left after dropping off their jobs.) My schedule was already pretty hectic, but I said I would be able to devote one full day a week to MAD. We kicked around titles, but coming up with one that really fit was difficult because there were going to be so many different things for me to do. We finally zeroed in on "creative consultant." That would appear on the masthead, but I would continue doing articles freelance and those would bear my name as "writer." After we'd ironed out the details of the job, I told Bill I would need an electronic typewriter. I'm a pretty fast typist, and although I had started using a computer at home, I didn't want to ask Bill to get one, because a computer at MAD ten or twelve years ago would have been totally out of place. (Just about everyone at MAD got a computer about three years ago, but we didn't plug them in till two years later!) Bill asked how much an electronic typewriter cost, and I told him about $450. He said fine, go buy one.

TOM KEENE

At that time, the newest feature on electronic typewriters were special backspace keys that let you correct mistakes. The machine would remember the last complete line you had typed; to erase the line you would hold down this special key and the machine would back up and remove each letter from the paper automatically. You would then have a blank line and could start over and put in the correct words. This was not as advanced as the spell-check features which came out a year or two later, but it did eliminate the need to use those little pieces of correction tape, which was time-consuming and messy. So I purchased the typewriter I wanted, Bill paid for it, and I didn't think anymore about it.

Then one day, I got a call at home from Bill. He was livid! At first I thought it was another one of his jokes, but he was serious, and he was screaming into the phone: "The ribbons for that %$#ing machine aren't reusable??? You have to keep putting in new ribbons??" What was going on was that while I wasn't doing all that much typing, this was the newest typewriter the office had seen in many years. Everyone was using it, and we were going through yards and yards of typewriter ribbon.

I tried to explain to Bill that the whole idea of the one-use carbon ribbons was that you could correct scripts so easily, saving time and...he didn't want to hear it! Bill got someone on the staff to start calling around the country, until he found a supplier of fabric ribbons that fit the machine I had. Of course it defeated the lift-off feature, but Bill was happy! He'd spent $450 on an electronic typewriter and saved $6 a month on ribbons!

That was the frugal side of Bill. Then there was the generous side of Gaines. (You know, as I write this, I'm having a thought that never occurred to me before. Maybe the difference was that the ribbons came out of MAD's budget, but the trip you're going to read about next came out of Bill's personal budget. Hmmmm....Anyway, on with the story.)

Bill told about a dozen of his friends to set aside a certain Saturday in March. He wouldn't tell us the reason, only that we should plan on being with him for the entire day. When it got closer to that special Saturday, we were told to meet at Penn Station at 8 a.m. under the big clock. But we were given no further details. We all met at eight, but Bill was still silent as to why. When the station master announced the 8:45 Metroliner to Boston, Bill told us to go to the track for the Boston train, BUT NOT TO GET ON IT! Hey, this was pretty

The Black
L.V.
Diamond

exciting! What was Bill up to??

The train pulled in, and we stood there, waiting for further instructions from Gaines. A few minutes later, we heard the sound of another train, and out of the tunnel came a small switch engine pushing a totally restored passenger car from the late 1800s!! And hanging off the open-air observation deck on top of this gorgeous piece of railroad equipment was a group of smiling Pullman waiters!!

The vintage railroad car was hooked to the end of the Metroliner, and then Bill made the announcement we were all waiting for: "Hop aboard, we're going to Boston for the day!"

That trip was one of the best times I ever had. I love trains, especially the older ones, and this car, which once belonged to a railroad tycoon, couldn't have been more beautiful. It had a dining room, three private compartments for those who wanted to nap, and that grand observation deck.

A champagne brunch was served on the way up to Boston; we had a three-hour layover to shop; and then our Pullman was attached to the 8 p.m. Metroliner for the ride back to New York. While we waited for the train to pull out, a group of us stood on the observation deck. Everyone going to board the regular Metroliner had to pass by our luxurious car and several people stopped to ask what was going on. We told them Amtrak was trying out a new service, but that it cost $3 extra, and that we were sorry, but this particular trip was sold out!

On the ride back to New York, the waiters served us a seven-course gourmet dinner by candlelight. (God, if only Amtrak would go back to that kind of service! Heck, if they did, I'd take a job in Boston, just so I could do the daily commute from New York.)

That trip was a truly grand gesture. And then there were the "little" things that Bill would do, like the time my houseboat sank. Bill was very upset for me, and asked if I was insured. I was, but the company had never bothered to tell me I didn't have "contents insurance." In other words, anything that was on the boat when it came from the factory was covered, but nothing else inside the boat was insured. Bill asked me to tell him some of the things I had lost and I told him I was particularly upset about losing my good 35mm camera. Bill told me to buy a new one and send him the bill. And he even apologized that he didn't do more. I was so overwhelmed, I couldn't be mean to him for several days!

OFTEN ANNIE

Many of the adventures in this book **often** involve **Annie** Gaines, Bill's widow. Annie started with MAD and Bill the exact same way I started with MAD—through the mail! Actually, it was a bit different because Bill, not Nick, discovered her. In 1970 when Annie was a sophomore at Penn State, the students there all had to submit "grade projects." They could write about any subject they wanted, and Annie chose pollution. She remembered that MAD writer Frank Jacobs had done an article on the subject, called "America the Beautiful Revisited," but looking through her pile of MADs (Annie was a big MAD fan, and had quite a collection), she couldn't find the issue with that particular pollution article (or more correctly, that anti-pollution article).

...Bill said to himself, "Hmmm, if she was dating one fat guy, she might take up with me!"

So Annie wrote William M. Gaines, figuring that the publisher of MAD would know what issue it was in. To cover the cost of photocopying and postage, she enclosed a one dollar bill.

Now it was Bill's habit to read all the mail that came to MAD—from subscription mail to requests for reprints—and a short time later Annie got a note from Bill. The note said, "Never send cash through the mail." Bill had returned Annie's dollar, but of course, since **he** didn't send cash through the mail, he sent her a **check** for $1! And he said he'd send her the Frank Jacobs article for free if she would send him a picture of herself. Annie sent Bill a centerfold picture from a *Playboy* magazine with a note of her own. She said she looked exactly like the photo, except—and then she listed a dozen ways she was different from the centerfold.

When Bill sent her the article, he told her he was going to visit relatives near Penn State, and that he and Annie should meet in person. They did. Then Bill invited Annie to New York for a visit. They had a wonderful time. Over a period of a couple of years, Bill and Annie kept writing and visiting each other. Then one day, Annie visited MAD with a former boyfriend. Bill was heartbroken that she was with another man. But then for a couple of reasons, his spirits picked up. Reason one was, as Annie explained, the guy was a **former** boyfriend. But, even more important, this former boyfriend was a very heavy man. Bill said to himself, "Hmmm, if she was dating one fat guy, she might take up with me!"

Well, Annie and Bill dated, moved in together, and fell madly in love. Make that MADly in love. At their wedding, Gaines invited, introduced, and publicly thanked her former beau for coming to the office with Annie that day. When he saw the man's enormous size, it was the first time he realized (to use Bill's own words) that "Annie was a chubby chaser! I knew I stood a good chance to win her, and I did!" Early in their courtship, Annie started working full-time at MAD, helping Bill with his various chores. My guess is that unknown to Bill, she made a point of pre-screening the mail, to make sure Gaines didn't get any more letters from young ladies asking for reprints!

WHEN SAVING A BUNDLE COSTS A FORTUNE

When it came to bargains, Bill Gaines and I fell into the same trap. While I can't speak for Bill, I inherited some of my bargain-hunting traits from my parents, although sometimes for them it was the idea of saving money that was important —much more important than what they bought.

I'll never forget the day they came back from a shopping trip with a case of plastic Santa Clauses. My father was beaming because he'd paid only ten cents apiece, and they had originally been a dollar each. He told anyone that would listen, how he had saved ninety percent! Of course this was two weeks *after* Christmas... and even if it was two weeks BEFORE Christmas, what does one do with 144, six-inch high, plastic Santa Clauses?

But my father didn't care, because it was a great buy. After showing them to the neighbors, that gross of Santa Clauses went right to the attic, and I never saw them again. Some bargain!

One day I was talking to Annie about Bill's love of bargains and saving money, and she related the story of their first date. When they were ordering dinner, Bill asked Annie if she would like blue cheese dressing on her salad. Annie said, "But Bill, it's fifty cents extra!" Right then and there Bill felt he had found the girl for him—a girl who would save him money! Shortly after that, they made a plan to eat in every three- and four-star restaurant in the world. And for years after, Bill complained to Annie, "That fifty cents you saved me on our first date was the most expensive fifty cents I ever saved!!"

Anyway, here's the story of how a real bargain I found cost Bill a fortune. Even before I became TV's "Gadget & Gizmo Guy" (yes, my love of gadgets turned into yet another exciting career), I was collecting every kind of gadget I could afford. But I also kept an eye out for any gadget I thought might interest Bill. You see, if I found a gadget and I could get Bill to buy it, I would at least get to play with it for a while before I delivered it to him. This was something he didn't mind; as a matter of fact, he encouraged it. If I got it first, I'd figure out how to operate it and then I could show him how to use it, which would save him the trouble of having to read the instruction book.

I found a real winner in Seiko's Language Translator Watch, which was quite ingenious for its time (pun intended). It had a dictionary of about 350 words in English that you could scroll through on the face of the watch. You would stop at a word and then, using a series of buttons on the side of the watch, you could translate it into one of five foreign languages. It was an engineering masterpiece, but it cost $189, which was pretty expensive twelve years ago. Bill said he'd like one, but not for that amount of money. So, as usual, he said, "Keep your eyes open for one at a bargain price."

Not too long afterwards, I was at an importers' trade show and I saw the Translator Watch on display...and the guy wanted only $35 for it! I snapped it up, of course I bought a second one for myself, and I excitedly called Bill to tell him the great news. Bill couldn't believe it either, and told me to buy forty of them! Right then and there he'd decided to give a watch to each MAD writer and artist going on the next MAD trip. (Ah yes, the MAD trips. They came out of what is possibly the world's most famous and most expensive practical joke, and they lasted over thirty years, with "Father" Gaines taking his family all over the globe! But you'll get all those fascinating facts later, after you've finished *this* fascinating chapter!) But, as I pointed out to Gaines, our next trip was to Italy, and for some reason, Italian was not one of the five languages on the watch. "Well they can get an idea of the translation from one of the other languages," Bill said. "And besides, who can resist paying only thirty-five dollars for a hundred and eighty-nine dollar watch??" Of course even at $35, forty watches cost Bill over $1,400!! But all the MAD staffers were very impressed with the watch.

But that's not all—there's a nice little twist to this story. It occurred when Bill was scrolling through the watch's English vocabulary section. Under

"M" was the word "MAD," and believe it or not, the next word to come up was "MAGAZINE." So if you held your finger just right on the forward button the watch face read "MAD Magazine." For years Bill was convinced that since I had ordered forty watches, I had been able to persuade someone at Seiko to program the watch to do that. But that just happened to be the way the watch came from the factory. (Of course, I could have told Bill that I had paid a little extra to have them program the watches to read "MAD Magazine." And, if I had added that Seiko normally charged $25 extra to program special words into the watch, but that I had gotten it done for $10, he would have bit immediately!! But, Bill was always fair, so I just couldn't do it to him.)

I'll tell you another story about getting Bill a bargain on a bizarre gadget. I was among the very first to buy a VCR. At the time it cost $1,500, could record only in black and white, and then only for an hour. It didn't even have a timer. When the Sony Betamax came out, it did have a timer and it could record in color; still, it recorded only for one hour. But, of course, I bought one of those, too! I got Bill to jump on the Beta bandwagon when a second, two-speed model that could record up to two hours came out.

"...And that one million dollars in cash is still there today."

Bill was immediately hooked on his video recorder and naturally he wanted more recording time. Others wanted more recording time too, and to solve this problem, Sony came out with this strange add-on device: You stacked three blank tapes into this Rube Goldberg-type thing that sat on top of the VCR. As each tape finished recording, a mechanical finger would hit the stop button, and another one would hit the eject key. (Back then VCRs didn't have electronic keys; you had to push each key rather firmly to engage it, hence the mechanical fingers.) Then a tractor feed would remove the recorded tape and drop it down into a waiting receptacle, while another tractor feed lowered the new, blank tape into position. This thing had a million belts and gears, but it worked! Yet as clever as it was, it was a bit too expensive—$230 to be exact. Bill wanted one desperately, but not at the retail price, so every time I went to our favorite electronics store to buy blank videotapes, I'd ask if the price of the Betamax tape changer had come down any. Finally one day, I hit pay dirt! "Yeah, it's thirty dollars," the salesman told me. "It came down two hundred dollars??" I inquired in a soft voice, hoping no one else would hear. Yes, it had been reduced by $200.

I called Bill right from the store and he told me to buy all they had, up to a half dozen units. They only had four, so I bought them all. Of course the fire sale on this weird device signaled the oncoming of VHS and four- and six-hour Betamax machines. But Bill and I loved our original Betamaxes! As a matter of fact, it wasn't until all three of Bill's tractor feeders broke (he had given one to his friend Lyle Stuart, a book publisher) that he gave in and switched to the much more popular VHS format.

Then for years there were no real new wrinkles to video recorders until the introduction of the "dubbing deck." I really wanted to play with one of those Go Video dual dubbing decks, so I told Bill about it, and sold him on the idea of how convenient it would be. Previously you'd had to wire two VCRs together, one to play the tape, and one to record the copy. The Go Video deck had two wells, one for the recorded tape and one for the blank tape. All you had to do was put the original in one slot and the blank in the other and push a button to start the dubbing process. After I pointed all this good stuff out to Bill, he had me buy him one, which of course, I could use to dub my own tapes!

MAD tattoos appeared as a special bonus. Lots of luck trying to use these.

FOREWORD *Number 5?!...*

The one question everyone at MAD faced for forty years was, "Is Bill Gaines for real?" We always answered, "Yes." But the truth is more like "Yes" and "No." Now the truth can be told. *There was no Bill Gaines.*

The big, fat, hairy guy in droopy drawers was actually an actor named Felix Ginsberg. He was hired as Santa Claus at the first MAD Christmas party to hand out gag bonuses. To make the gag funnier, wives, friends, and freelancers were told he was the famous publisher, "Bill Gaines."

AL JAFFEE

Later, this "Bill Gaines" thing took on a life of its own as mail and phone calls started coming in for him. Felix was called and offered the job on a permanent basis. He eagerly accepted and at a pitiful salary to boot.

The years passed, the myth grew, and so did "Bill"—to a spectacular 300 pounds. But his public and private personas could not have been more different.

The "Bill Gaines" the public saw was that of a slothlike creature to whom yawning was an act of strenuous physical exertion. But in private this same "Bill Gaines" was a closet exercise freak who thought nothing of doing hundreds of push-ups nightly before retiring.

Another popular myth perpetuated by "Bill Gaines" was his voracious appetite. It was all pretense. Actually he had a large plastic bag strapped around his waist with a tube hidden in his beard. Mountains of food disappeared surreptitiously into the bag, while other diners either gaped or were too embarrassed to look. Later at home he'd have his usual cottage cheese and yogurt.

"Bill Gaines" also developed and promoted his legendary prowess as a fierce negotiator whose entire business vocabulary consisted of the word *NO!* This, too, was pretense and illusion. After every vicious contractual bout he'd call his bloodied adversary and apologize profusely. Then he'd draw up a new secret deal that practically "gave away the store." But on one condition. No one must ever know.

Then there's the matter of attire. It has been rumored that he would not wear anything that hadn't been run over by Amtrak at least twice. This may or may not be true. But one thing is true: In private, he was the picture of sartorial splendor, immaculately dressed in the latest designer fashions.

Oh, I could go on and on but I think I've made the point. Now that he's gone the legend of "Bill Gaines" is all that remains.

Farewell "Bill Gaines," and farewell Felix Ginsberg, wherever you are.

XRAY VIEW OF "BILL GAINES" DINING.

TRUTH DECAY

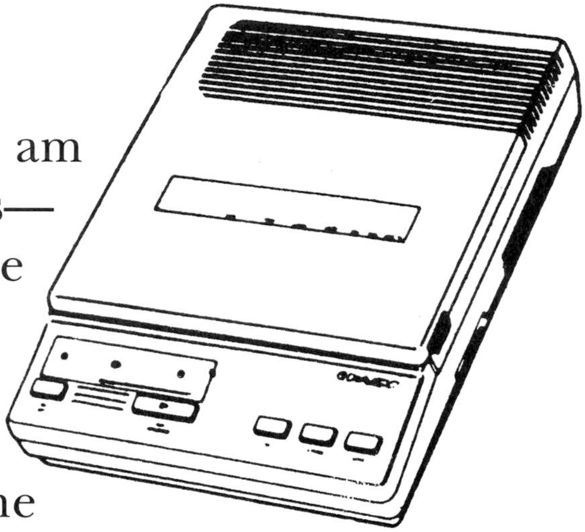

Sometime during this century (I am REALLY bad at remembering dates—but probably in 1962), Bob Noah, one of the producers at Barry-Enright, left to join Goodson-Todman Productions, where he was involved in developing a new show called "The Match Game." Bob had liked my writing on "Winky-Dink," which by then was history, so he asked me to submit sample questions for "The Match Game." I did, and he liked those, too, so I got the job writing the questions for the show. Hard-hitting questions like:

Name a red flower.
Name a kind of sandwich.
Name a president whose picture is on currency.

Well, the show was canceled after a year and a half and when that happened, I got an idea. I went to Mark Goodson and said, "Mark, I write silly stuff for MAD, how about doing silly questions on 'The Match Game'?" I had written a couple of samples:

John liked to put gravy on his (blank).
Mary had a flower growing out of her (blank).

Goodson said, "Dick, we have six more weeks of shows to tape. Do what you want. Since 'The Match Game' is already canceled, they can't cancel it again!"

The silly questions brought lots of laughs, as Gene Rayburn, the original host of the show, read the word "blank" for the missing part of the question. Of course (at least in their minds), people couldn't help but fill in the blanks with all sorts of weird things, and a whole new life was given to the show. "The Match Game" got renewed, and it ran for about a total of twelve years, with a break somewhere in between. When the show moved out to California, Mark asked if I wanted to relocate to the West Coast. I told him I really loved New York, and that MAD was in New York, and I'd rather stay. He told me he'd never forget what I'd done for "The Match Game," and I'd always have a job at Goodson-Todman, no matter where I lived. Thirty-two years later, I'm still there, too! After Bill Todman died, the company became Mark Goodson Productions, and these days I'm one of the writers developing questions for Mark's show, "Family Feud." (Actually, by the time this book is published, it may be "The New Family Feud." I do know for sure, the show will have a new host. Well, not a new host, but Richard Dawson, the show's original host, will be back.)

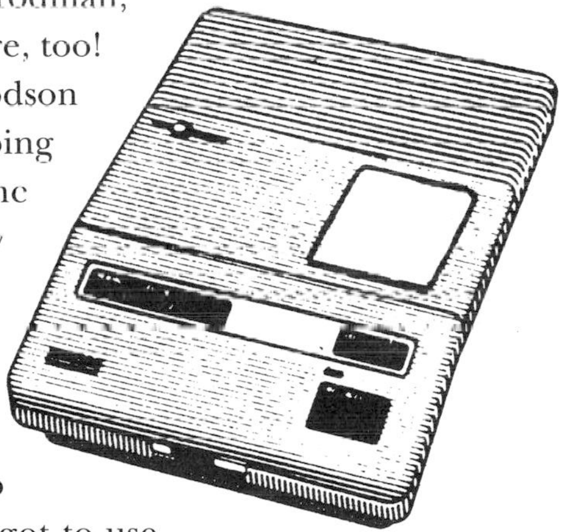

Somewhere in between "The Match Game" and "Family Feud," I worked on Goodson-Todman's "To Tell the Truth." It was while working on that show that I got to use Bill's love of gadgetry to play a great practical joke. I may have bought one of the first video recorders, but Bill was the first person I knew to get an answering machine. So after Bill got his machine, for a period of about two months, I asked every guest on "Truth" to call Bill's home and leave him a message saying they were returning his call or asking if he'd like to have lunch—anything that came to mind. "To Tell the Truth" taped during the day, so it was safe to call Bill's home—they'd get the machine because he was at the MAD offices.

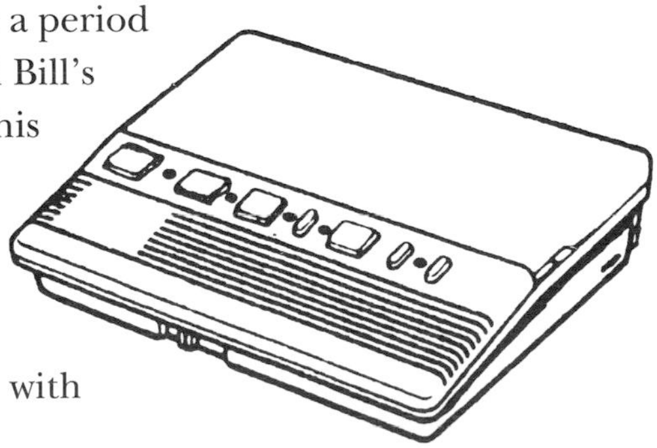

Well, Bill's answering machine was bombarded with

messages—from Bill Cullen, Orson Bean, Soupy Sales, Garry Moore, Nipsey Russell, Joe Garagiola, Kitty Carlisle, Peggy Cass, Tom Poston, and every other guest on the "Truth" panel I could muster. At MAD one of the things that makes a joke work is NEVER giving the joke away. So I never mentioned to anyone what I was doing to Bill, and he never mentioned it to me... until months later.

We were in Rome, on one of those famous MAD trips. I was telling Bill that I had bought a telephone speakerphone, which was a hot innovation back then. I'd gotten it just before the trip to Italy, so I could talk to my dogs when I called home. Bill rolled his eyes heavenward and said, "So, does it work?"

"According to the friend staying at my house, it does," I said. "When he clicks it on, the dogs listen to my voice, stare at the phone, and then run in circles!"

"Speaking of telephones," Gaines said, "Do you know Rich Little?" I didn't, and I inquired why he'd asked. "Because last fall someone left message after message on my answering machine, and all the messages were in the voices of famous people. And the guy who did the voices was very good, because they all sounded like the real people. I was thinking that since you work in television, you might know Rich Little, and you might have put him up to doing that."

"Bill, you jerk! That wasn't Rich Little! That WAS Peggy Cass, and Kitty Carlisle and Garry Moore—and all the others!!"

"Now you tell me! After I erased them all! If I had known they were the real people, I would have saved the tapes! Especially Kitty Carlisle. You know how much I love *A Night at the Opera*, and she's in it!"

After that incident, I got to thinking that Bill would make a great contestant on "To Tell the Truth." The staff liked the idea, and Gaines was invited to be a central character on the show. If you're not familiar with the game, it went like this: There were three people on stage, in this case, Bill and two people posing as Bill Gaines. The panel of four celebrities would ask questions and from the answers they would try to guess which one of the three gentlemen "was the real William M. Gaines." The most important rule of the game was that the real person HAD TO tell the truth, while the imposters could lie. Bill told the truth, but the truth of how Bill ran a multi-million dollar enterprise was so bizarre that no one believed him, and no one voted for him as the real William M. Gaines! Bill was proud of that. But what made him especially proud was that when Garry Moore asked Kitty Carlisle who she thought was the real William M. Gaines, she pointed to Gaines himself and said, "It's obviously not him. The publisher of MAD is a successful businessman—and well, just look at him!" Bill was dressed in his usual slovenly way, the way he always went to work.

Wait a minute! How did I get into that story about "To Tell the Truth"? Oh, I remember. It started when I was talking about Bill's answering machine. Which is a good way to get back to what we were talking about just a few pages ago—gadgets.

Knowing a lot about the latest in electronic wizardry had a downside for me, because sometimes Bill would ask me to pick out something real expensive for him, and I would have to do tons of research to make sure I got him the optimum unit at the best price. One of my toughest assignments was getting Bill a giant-screen TV.

BILL: I want one of those giant TVs. You know the ones I mean, a thirty- or thirty-two inch set.

DICK: Do you know you're talking about spending anywhere from eighteen hundred to twenty-five hundred dollars?

BILL: That's okay. Just make sure it's a good one.

DICK: That's the whole assignment? Run out and buy you a thirty-two inch TV? And when do you want it by? Lunchtime? Those things weigh a couple of hundred pounds.

BILL: So, take until tomorrow. (getting serious) No, shop around, take a couple of weeks, and—oh, yeah, make sure the top of the set is big enough so my stereo and VCR can sit on it.

DICK: Am I supposed to guess how big those components are, or are you going to tell me?

BILL: (Takes out his notepad and writes memo to remind himself to measure components. Bill was forgetful) I'll call you tonight.

...This is the only place in the book, the name Dave Durian appears.

I shopped around for a while and got an excellent buy on a 32-inch set with a Carver sound system built into the base. It even had a remote-control swivel feature so you could turn the set to face you if you changed chairs. I arranged delivery and told the store manager that the set was going to the publisher of MAD Magazine, so *p-l-e-a-s-e*, no screw-ups! The set arrived on time, but it didn't work the way Billy wanted it to. So I got the kind of call I hated: "Dick, this set doesn't work. Come over and fix it!" That meant dropping everything at home, grabbing my box of assorted connecting cables, and jumping into a cab. This was one of the downsides of being a gadget freak. You were expected to know how to get the most complicated TV or VCR up and running in short order. Often over the phone, no less! And I felt an extra obligation to Bill: He was my boss; I did order the TV; and even though it was at his request, I wanted to make sure he was happy with my choice.

While Bill and I devoted lots of time and energy to finding the best possible gadgets at the cheapest prices, we weren't only interested in saving money on big-ticket items, we were just as delighted by saving twenty cents on a roll of paper towels! Since shopping in New Jersey was far cheaper than shopping in Manhattan where we all lived, Bill, Annie, and I made monthly trips across the border, armed with coupons collected from the Sunday papers. Bill and Annie were fairly organized, and even had a shopping list. They knew exactly what they wanted and shopped intensely with a mini-train of carts—two or three wagons long. For me, these trips were more like "supermarket sweeps"—you know, that game show where shoppers are given seventeen seconds to pick up whatever they can. I'm a spur-of-the-moment shopper. If it's on sale, I need it. Hey, there's a two-for-one sale on frozen squash! I don't like squash, fresh or frozen, but two-for-one is hard to resist.

One thing that made the expedition fun (read "fun" as "scary") was that Bill and Annie were the perfect driving couple. Bill could drive, but couldn't see very well. Annie didn't know how to drive, but she had great eyesight and a great sense of direction. Between the two of them, they made one good driver! Going **to** the supermarket was always worse than going home because I could clearly see just how close Bill came to road dividers, lampposts, and other cars. The trip home was much easier to take because I was in the backseat, which was loaded to the roof with groceries, so I couldn't see. (As a matter of fact, after I got in the car, Annie would often load my lap with the groceries that wouldn't fit anywhere else!) Once we took freelance artist Dennis Wunderlin along for the experience, but a fourth for shopping was almost over the limit. Our car was so loaded, you could hear the rear end scraping along the ground for the entire trip home—so the ride was scary in both directions! Once, MAD's art director, Lenny Brenner, heard we were going shopping and asked if we could pick up some stuff for him. I explained that with the way we stacked the car with OUR stuff, we could probably pick him up a pack of matches, or a roll of toilet paper—single ply toilet paper, that is. There would be no room for a roll of *double* ply!

Because Bill, Annie, and I were such fans of clipping coupons—to this day, Annie and I still swap coupons—I developed a MAD back cover that I wish

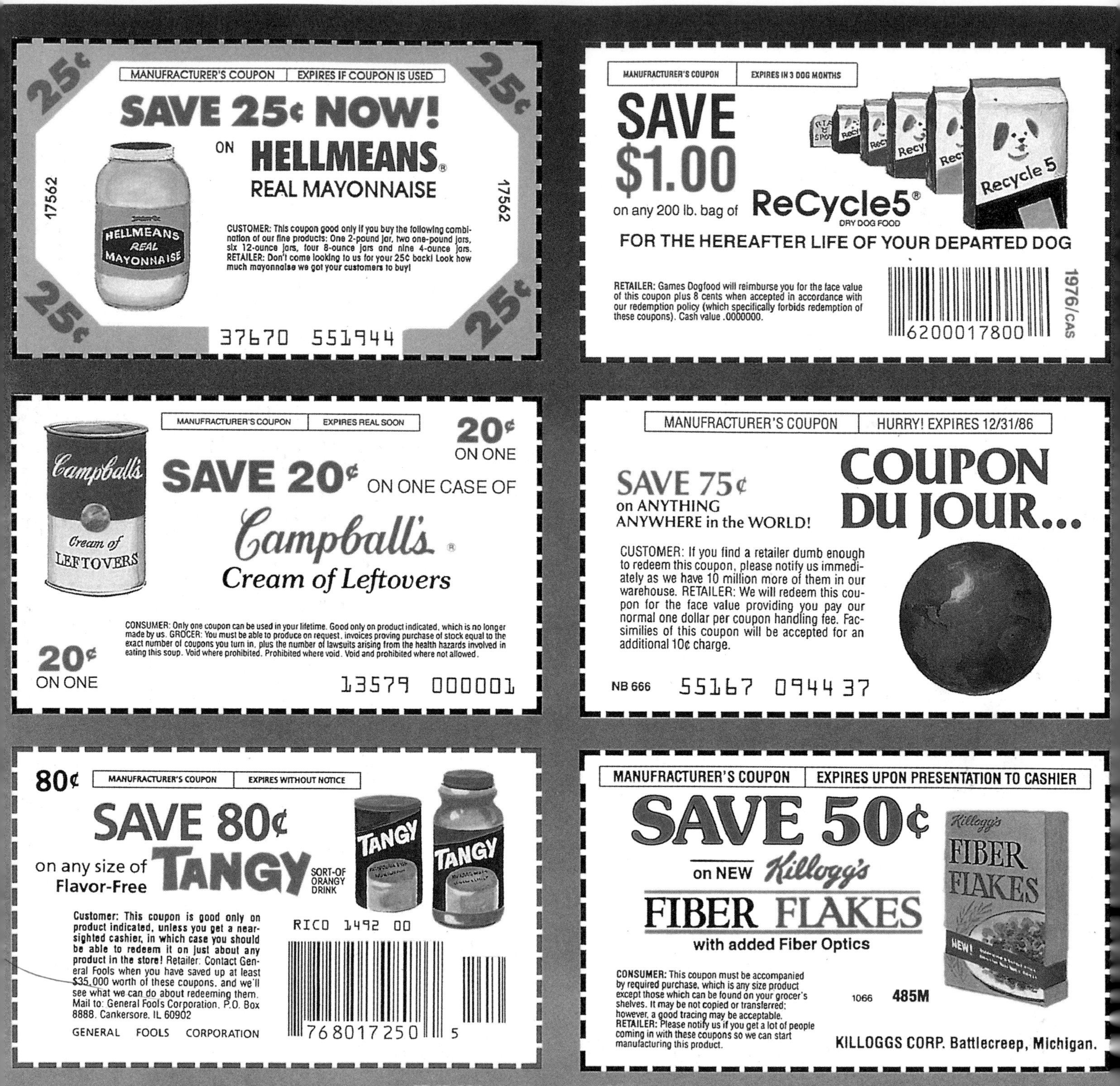
25¢
MANUFRACTURER'S COUPON
EXPIRES IF COUPON IS USED
SAVE 25¢ NOW!
ON HELLMEANS®
REAL MAYONNAISE
17562
HELLMEANS REAL MAYONNAISE
CUSTOMER: This coupon good only if you buy the following combination of our fine products: One 2-pound jar, two one-pound jars, six 12-ounce jars, four 8-ounce jars and nine 4-ounce jars. RETAILER: Don't come looking to us for your 25¢ back! Look how much mayonnaise we got your customers to buy!
37670 551944
MANUFRACTURER'S COUPON
EXPIRES IN 3 DOG MONTHS
SAVE $1.00
on any 200 lb. bag of ReCycle5®
DRY DOG FOOD
Recycle 5
FOR THE HEREAFTER LIFE OF YOUR DEPARTED DOG
RETAILER: Games Dogfood will reimburse you for the face value of this coupon plus 8 cents when accepted in accordance with our redemption policy (which specifically forbids redemption of these coupons). Cash value .0000000.
6200017800
1976/CAS
MANUFRACTURER'S COUPON
EXPIRES REAL SOON
20¢ ON ONE
Campball's
Cream of LEFTOVERS
SAVE 20¢ ON ONE CASE OF
Campball's®
Cream of Leftovers
CONSUMER: Only one coupon can be used in your lifetime. Good only on product indicated, which is no longer made by us. GROCER: You must be able to produce on request, invoices proving purchase of stock equal to the exact number of coupons you turn in, plus the number of lawsuits arising from the health hazards involved in eating this soup. Void where prohibited. Prohibited where void. Void and prohibited where not allowed.
20¢ ON ONE
13579 000001
MANUFRACTURER'S COUPON
HURRY! EXPIRES 12/31/86
SAVE 75¢
on ANYTHING
ANYWHERE in the WORLD!
COUPON DU JOUR...
CUSTOMER: If you find a retailer dumb enough to redeem this coupon, please notify us immediately as we have 10 million more of them in our warehouse. RETAILER: We will redeem this coupon for the face value providing you pay our normal one dollar per coupon handling fee. Facsimilies of this coupon will be accepted for an additional 10¢ charge.
NB 666
55167 094437
80¢
MANUFRACTURER'S COUPON
EXPIRES WITHOUT NOTICE
SAVE 80¢
on any size of Flavor-Free TANGY
SORT-OF ORANGY DRINK
TANGY
Customer: This coupon is good only on product indicated, unless you get a near-sighted cashier, in which case you should be able to redeem it on just about any product in the store! Retailer: Contact General Fools when you have saved up at least $35,000 worth of these coupons, and we'll see what we can do about redeeming them. Mail to: General Fools Corporation, P.O. Box 8888, Cankersore, IL 60902
GENERAL FOOLS CORPORATION
RICO 1492 00
768017250 5
MANUFRACTURER'S COUPON
EXPIRES UPON PRESENTATION TO CASHIER
SAVE 50¢
on NEW Killogg's
FIBER FLAKES
with added Fiber Optics
Killogg's FIBER FLAKES
NEW!
CONSUMER: This coupon must be accompanied by required purchase, which is any size product except those which can be found on your grocer's shelves. It may be not copied or transferred; however, a good tracing may be acceptable. RETAILER: Please notify us if you get a lot of people coming in with these coupons so we can start manufacturing this product.
1066 485M
KILLOGGS CORP. Battlecreep, Michigan.

ARTIST: BOB CLARKE WRITER: DICK DeBARTOLO

we could have published without Gaines' knowledge. This was, of course, MAD's money-saving coupons back cover. The coupons weren't real, but they looked very real, and I would have loved to cut them out and slip them into Billy's coupon envelope. Then, from a safe distance in the grocery store, I could have watched as he tried to figure out how in God's name to comply with the bizarre coupon rules so he could save money.

BONUS #2

The money-saving coupons. Why not cut them out and slip them into a friend's coupon collection?! And for even more fun buy several copies of this book, so you'll have extra coupons for future practical jokes!

MAD'S CLIP'N SAVE
MONEY SAVING COUPONS
BONUS • BONUS • BONUS • BONUS • BONUS • BONUS

FOREWORD

Number 6?!...

BY CHARLIE KADAU AND JOE RAIOLA
ASSOCIATE EDITORS, MAD MAGAZINE

(Phone rings, Joe answers.)

JOE: Hello?

CHARLIE: Joe, it's Charlie. Dick DeBartolo just asked us to write the foreword to his new book about Bill Gaines.

JOE My God, he's so lazy—why doesn't DeBartolo write his own foreword?

CHARLIE: Because he's the author and the author traditionally doesn't write the foreword to his own book.

JOE: And he wants us to do it? He must be desperate.

CHARLIE: I think it's quite an honor. Imagine all the other people he could have asked—and he chose us!

JOE: Maybe you're right—that was awfully nice of him. So what do you want to do? You and I probably saw Bill and related to Bill very differently.

CHARLIE: I'm not so sure. We both had great affection and admiration for him.

JOE: Yes, but we had different perspectives on the man.

CHARLIE: I agree.

JOE: And what I'd like to do is get clear on the things we agree on. What is our common ground regarding Bill?

CHARLIE: I don't know.

JOE: Let's see if we can find out, okay?

CHARLIE: Okay.

JOE: Bill was fat.

CHARLIE: Yes.

JOE: Bill was unhealthy.

CHARLIE: Yes.

JOE: Bill was a profoundly disturbed person.

CHARLIE: Well...I think we all are.

JOE: But Bill was especially disturbed. He had a replica of King Kong coming through his office window and zeppelins hanging from his ceiling and he always had his air conditioner going—even on the coldest winter day.

CHARLIE: Would you point to these things as the keys to his success?

JOE: Those things in particular, no. He was successful because he was ruthless, inventive, inscrutable, determined—and he did things on his own terms. He had a vision.

CHARLIE: I saw Bill in his underwear.

JOE: Really?

CHARLIE: Yes. I'd never seen any of my other bosses in their underwear.

JOE: Come to think of it, I saw him with his shirt off once. Between the both of us we've pretty much seen him naked.

CHARLIE: But not completely naked, I'm happy to say. I'm really grateful for that.

JOE: Where did you see Bill in his underwear?

CHARLIE: It was generally on the MAD trips—in Switzerland and on the cruise to Bermuda. Bill tended to not get dressed when he was on vacation, except when he went to dinner. Where did you see him with no shirt?

JOE: I walked into his office one day and he had some kind of machine attached to his chest. The phone was hooked up to it. I said to him, "What are you doing?" He said, "I've called to have my pacemaker monitored."

CHARLIE: It was probably a toll-free number.

JOE: "You're wasting your time," I told him. "You're putting your faith in science—that's a big mistake. It's absurd."

CHARLIE: What was his response?

JOE: He said, "Get the fuck out of my office!"

CHARLIE: Yes, I'll always remember him as a man of action...

JOE: But wait a minute...to be honest, I don't want to write anything for Dick's book. It would be much easier to just record a conversation and give him a transcript.

CHARLIE: That would really be the cheap way out.

JOE: What better way to honor Bill?

CHARLIE: You may have a point...

A BRIEF, BUT SHORT, HISTORY OF MAD MAGAZINE

And now, come with me as we delve into the dark, secret beginnings of MAD! (Don't read this part aloud or let your lips move if you're in a public place!) What you are going to read right now has NEVER been published before!

MAD began when a small group of artists and writers, working under fake names, set up shop in a tiny room behind an illegal gambling parlor. They yearned for artistic freedom, journalistic integrity, and a place that delivered pizza in under 45 minutes! At the helm of this effort was William M. Gaines, working under the name J. Edgar Hoover, so as not to arouse suspicion.

MAD
1

J. Edgar Hoover, it was rumored at that time, was working under the name Claire Hansen, so his real name was available for Bill to use! What luck! (Now the reason this information has never been published before is that it's 4 a.m., and I have an editor's note here that says, "Dick, this chapter needs something to grab the reader's attention!" Hopefully, I have your attention and you will read on and I can go to bed.)

To be a little bit serious, before this book is over you should have a good inside view of what has made MAD an unequaled phenomenom in the publishing world. Here are some *real* facts: MAD is 42 years old and has survived without accepting advertising (you'll learn the minor exception) *and* without advertising itself! (You'll learn how we managed to stay visible.) *And* without losing money during those 42 years. That's a real record! And, in what must be another record, some of the most famous names in MAD belong to people who have been there from the very beginning, and who are still contributing today. They include Al Jaffee, Mort Drucker, and Jack Davis. There are others, but hey, this isn't the *definitive* history of MAD.

Anyway, as MAD Magazine's Maddest Writer, *and* its creative consultant, I am frequently asked to lecture on the workings of MAD. And now you don't have to pay my lecture fees or come to New York City to take the office tour. For the paltry price of this book you will be privy to the inner sanctum of MAD.

To begin, here is how I open my "Backstage Peek at MAD Magazine" slide show! Enjoy!

MAD
2

MAD
The End!
3

1- MAD started out as a ten-cent comic book...

2- ...and ended up as an overpriced magazine.

3- The End! (Here, the audience usually laughs but you don't have to, especially if you're still in a public place.)

Okay, so perhaps you would like a little more! Well, I really don't have the inside scoop on the very beginnings of MAD because my first article was published in 1962, and MAD was first published in 1952. (I used to tell Gaines that I let the magazine struggle for a decade without me before jumping in to save it.) Since I wasn't there for the first ten years, my history of MAD for that time period is based mainly on stories told to me by Bill.

As I understand it, Gaines was publisher of a vast empire of comic books, the most famous of which was *Tales from the Crypt.* (It's still famous today because of the TV series of the same name, which is on HBO and in syndication.) Other titles were *Two-Fisted Tales, The Vault of Horror,* and *Weird Science.* Al Feldstein was writing and editing most of them, while Harvey Kurtzman was editing the war comic books. Harvey wanted to make more money, and since Gaines paid his editors by the title, the only way to make more money was to get another title. Bill told Harvey he was a funny guy, so why not add a funny comic to the EC line? They talked about a comic that would satirize other comics...and MAD was born!

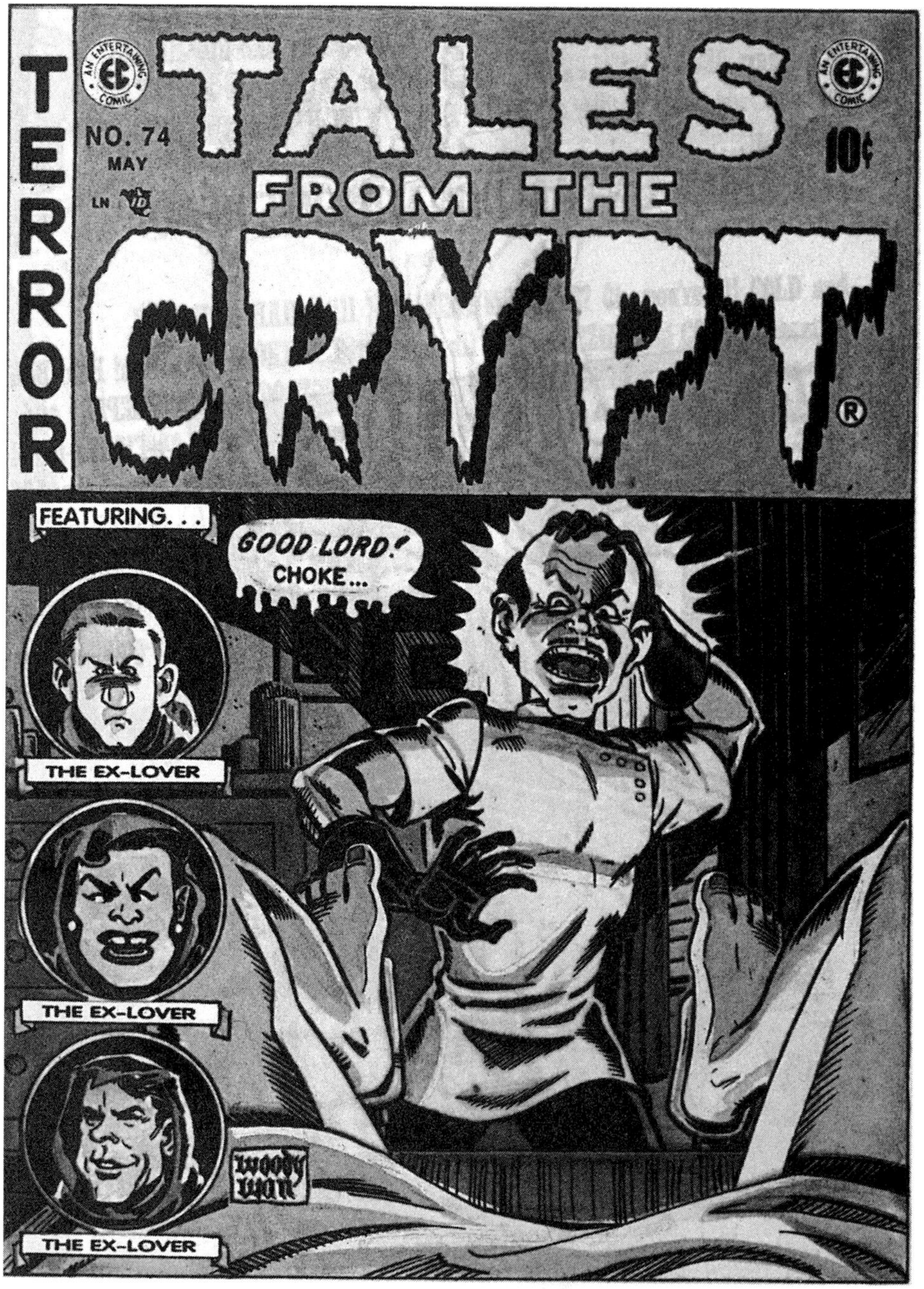
TERROR
TALES FROM THE CRYPT
NO. 74
MAY
10¢
FEATURING...
GOOD LORD!
CHOKE...
THE EX-LOVER
THE EX-LOVER
THE EX-LOVER

During that same period, the early 1950s, someone got the bright idea that comic books were tools of the devil—maybe even run by Communists as a way to ruin the minds of American children. So that put the heat on the comics, especially the bloody ones like Gaines was publishing. In Senate subcommittee hearings about this sinister plot, Bill testified that he thought the whole Communist hypothesis was nuts—or maybe MAD. Rather than have government interference, the comic publishers decided to censor themselves by establishing a board to approve the contents of their comics. So a Comics Code was drafted. Except it wasn't very comic, especially to Gaines, and that's when he decided to chuck the whole deal. He hated censorship in any form. Sales were starting to slump for the scary titles anyway, and besides, the Comics Code dictated that certain words couldn't be used, and most of those words were in the titles of the EC comics! So Gaines had most of his writers and artists put their effort into a new line of "nonthreatening comics," which included one called MAD. The other new titles fell by the wayside, but the ten-cent comic MAD ran for 23 issues. Then in July 1955, MAD turned into a 25-cent magazine. Although Alfred E. Neuman's face was in the ornate MAD Magazine logo, it was almost another year before he took over the entire cover. He's been on most MAD covers ever since. And at first, he didn't have a name. Different names were tried, but Alfred E. Neuman was the one that stuck!

The only way I can authenticate all this is to say that Gaines sat through my slide show dozens of times and never changed anything I said. In fact, before I performed it anywhere I gave Bill a private showing. After hearing my version of the history of MAD, Bill said, "It's close enough!"

(Perhaps others have more accurate descriptions of MAD's beginnings, so I promise to buy THEIR book when they write it! In the meantime—hey, it was over forty years ago! Does it matter all that much?)

...Mathieu Arnaud was in charge of checking to see that all these marginal notes were properly placed.

HISTORY DOESN'T REPEAT ITSELF

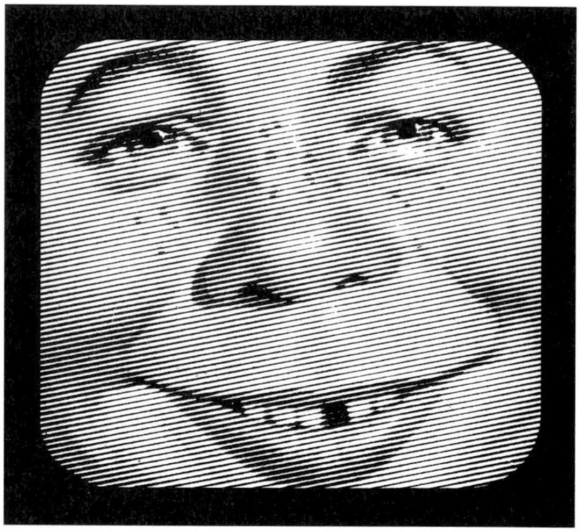

Actually, one historical analysis of MAD was written—Maria Reidelbach's 1991 book, *Completely MAD*. In the book are the complete details of how MAD Magazine ended up being a part of Time Warner. (Time Warner, you didn't know?) It's all fuzzy to me, but I *think* it went something like this: Bill sold EC Publications, MAD's parent company, to Premiere Industries. They sold it Kinney Corporation, which was originally in the rent-a-car and the rent-a-hearse business.

Then Kinney merged with Warner, and became part of Amalgamated By-Products. They merged with World Wide Rust, a division of International House of Flannel. MAD was spun off into the cooking division until three years later, when it was discovered that MAD was not edible. MAD's stock split several times during that period, which led Gaines to believe we had to buy a better kind of stock—one that wouldn't split so often! Then one morning we all woke up to find we were owned by Time Warner.

On that morning I asked Bill what sort of impact being owned by Time Warner would have on MAD. Bill said, "Don't give it a thought. It will take Time one to two years before they realize they own us." And Bill was right on target —they were oblivious to us! Although I never saw the contract for myself, Bill told me that when he sold MAD he was given a contract to continue as publisher for a three-year period. He inserted a clause in that contract that read, "I, William M. Gaines, retain the right to be unreasonable!" Apparently, Time Warner never gave it a thought.

But I found out for myself just how right Bill was about a year later when Time Warner started NY-1, a cable station for Manhattanites. I had begun doing some very well received consumer reporter spots on various cable stations in the area, so I thought I would see if NY-1 was interested. When I called, I told the woman that I was MAD's Maddest Writer and I did light-hearted TV consumer spots. The woman said that sounded "very interesting," but they were staffing NY-1 from various Time Warner divisions. I told her MAD Magazine was a division of Time Warner. She said she doubted that. After a few minutes, I convinced her to check further. She called back later that day to say I was right, MAD *was* owned by Time Warner and "they'd get back to me." I'm still waiting!

"...I was MAD's Maddest Writer and I did light-hearted TV consumer spots."

IN THE SHRED OF NIGHT

At one time MAD had a very successful line of paperback books. There were two kinds of MAD books being published: anthologies, which were reprints from MAD Magazine; and original titles. I wrote eleven of the original titles, which were illustrated by the likes of Jack Davis, Mort Drucker, Don Martin, Al Jaffee, and Angelo Torres—all MAD artists who started at the magazine even before I did.

For a long time the paperbacks sold well, and the royalties were good. And it seemed that every time I signed a contract for a new book, my advance got larger. I asked Bill if the higher advances were a sign that my name was getting to be a bigger draw and he said, "Not really. It's just something I discovered about the book contracts."

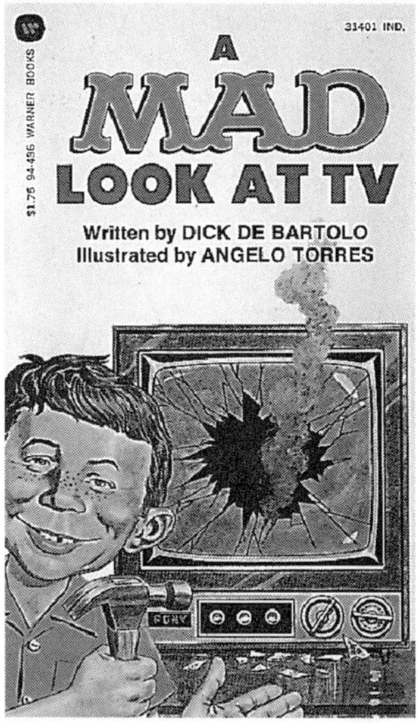
A
MAD
LOOK AT TV
Written by DICK DE BARTOLO
Illustrated by ANGELO TORRES

What Bill had discovered was that the publisher of the paperbacks never really read the endless pages of the contract. Bill told me he had found this out when on one contract, just as a joke, he'd put in an unreasonably large print order. The contract came back signed. So each time he sent out a new contract, he boosted the advance and the print order. Sure enough, it was automatically signed. Finally, it got to the point where the advances were so large, the sales of the books never even covered them. (Another of Bill's clauses, which I think is unique, was that the book had to be published and on sale for six years! At the time I didn't think it was unique, but that was before I ever dealt with another publisher. Thunder's Mouth Press has a much different contract. They are required to publish this volume and keep it on sale for six

MAD
VERTISING
OR,
UP MADISON AVE.
31311 IND.
BUY NOW AND SAVE!
NEW and IMPROVED
An Accumulation of Asinine and Atrocious Advertising Approaches
Attributed to Dick De Bartolo and Bob Clarke

days, and one of those can be a Sunday. And my advance MUST BE PAID to me "prior to my death." Boy, they're tough!)

Then the book contracts Bill drew up started being read more carefully....As matter of fact, they were read *too* carefully, and advances plummeted from a high of $22,000 to about $2,000. I should explain something about the advances. They weren't author's advances; they were divided between MAD, the writer, and the artist. MAD got something like 25 percent, and the writer and artist each got 37 1/2 percent. (With Bill, you learned to expect odd percentages. *Nothing* was ever fifty-fifty. He liked it much better when it was more like 50.5 percent and 49.5 percent, and I don't think it mattered who got the larger percentage. Odd percentages enabled Bill to use his calculator more, and he LOVED using his calculator.)

At that point I was too spoiled to even consider writing a book for a $750 advance, and I'm sure the other writers felt the same. But pretty soon we didn't have the choice. Over the years MAD had kept adding new titles to the paperback line, but none of the old ones were dropped. Over time, the line grew to over a hundred titles, an unwieldy number for any publisher to handle. I guess it was too much

THE RETURN OF A
MAD
LOOK AT
OLD MOVIES
WRITTEN BY DICK DE BARTOLO
ILLUSTRATED BY JACK DAVIS

trouble to figure out how to shrink the line; so the entire line was dropped, and the MAD paperbacks were phased out. But, unlike their material for MAD Magazine, the writers and artists retained the rights to the paperbacks after the contract expired. So, perhaps one day MAD paperbacks will rise again.

But before the paperback books bit the dust, I was able to write one of my favorite pieces ever, which unfortunately, met with tragedy. (It wasn't even around long enough to be dropped by the publisher.) The book was *MAD Murders the Movies* and I'd loved doing it because I got to write satires of the most famous classic movies of all time. The book had been illustrated by Duck Edwing, and the fact that I still found the book humorous after it was murdered by Duck's art proved that the material was really solid when I wrote it! Duck, of course, claimed that his art improved the humor (as if that was possible). But you can see for yourself because I'll show you a few samples from *MAD Murders the Movies.* It's possible you've never seen them before—very few people did.

I found out that *MAD Murders the Movies* was one of those casualties

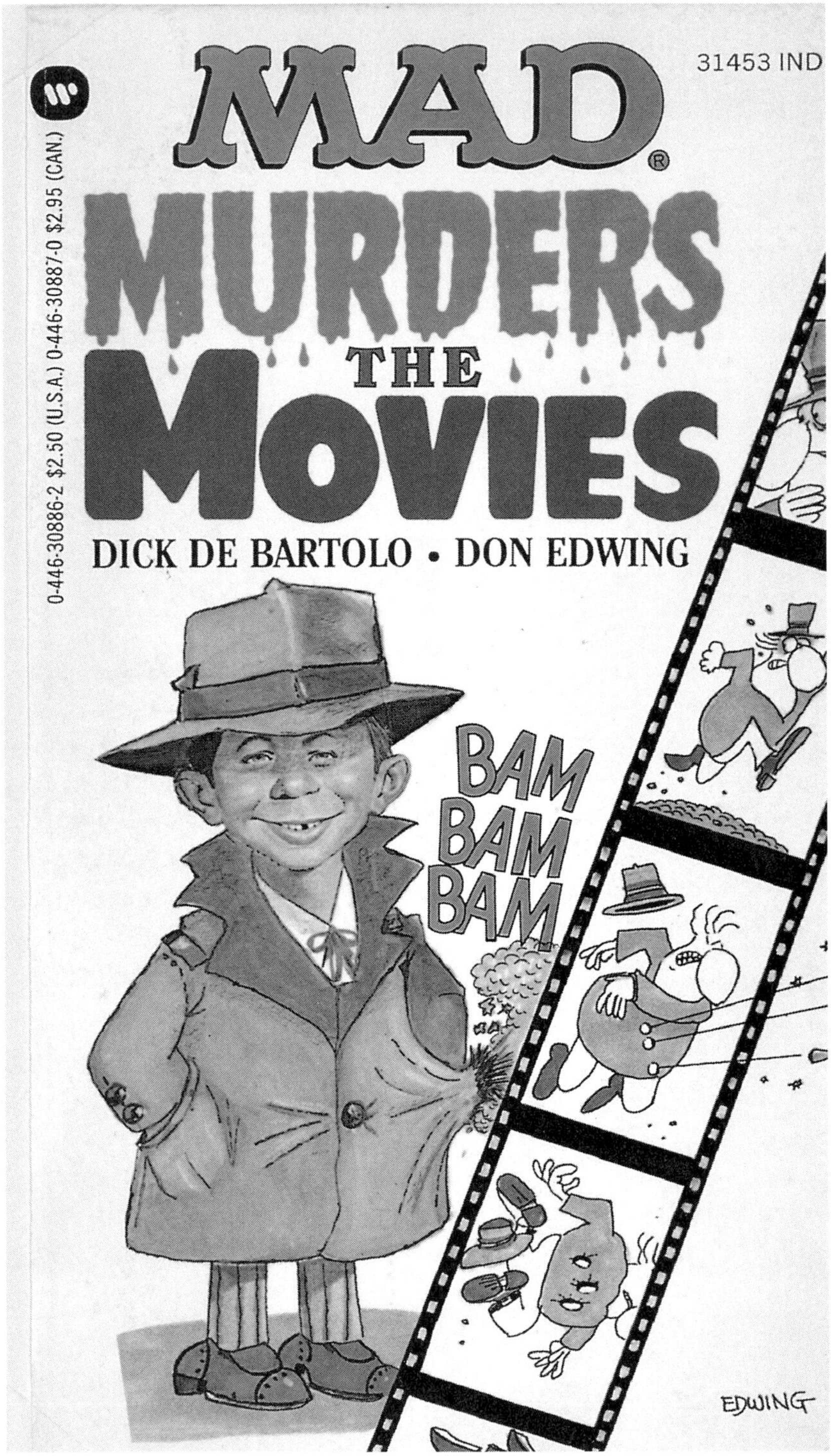
31453 IND
MAD
MURDERS THE MOVIES
DICK DE BARTOLO • DON EDWING
0-446-30886-2 $2.50 (U.S.A.) 0-446-30887-0 $2.95 (CAN.)
BAM
BAM
BAM
EDWING

I'll climb the tallest building, it's my duty
I'll play the **beast** for you, my raving **beauty**
I'll fight off planes, although it's clear to see
You've made an awful **monkey** outta me . . .

The Case Of
THE MAN WHO DIED A LOT

The PHANTOM OF THE UPROAR
I LIKE IT, JAKE. CAN I GET IT WHOLESALE?
SURE... LEAVE A DEPOSIT... TAILORING IS EXTRA!
239.99

GROAN WITH THE WIND
CONFEDERATE ARMY
ENLIST NOW!
AH WANT YOU ALL!
UNION ARMY
I WANT YOUSE!
ENLIST NOW!

of the corporate world soon after it was published, when I asked Bill to order me two cases of the books. (Yes, we pay for our own books at MAD, but we do get them at a nice discount.) A day later Bill called me with some interesting news: My order had been sent back because the book was out of print. "Didn't this book just came out?" he asked.

"Yeah, maybe two or three months ago," I replied. So the phone calls started, and slowly the picture became clear. Somehow, this newly released book had ended up on the out-of-print list and had been shipped off to the shredders. Thank God, we had gotten a pretty good advance, because the book was probably on sale for seven minutes in one obscure bookstore in Saratoga Lake.

I've always done the MAD Slide Show at the Warner publishers' convention, and for the one held later that year, I had a special slide made. It showed a printing press that delivered freshly printed books directly into a paper shredder. The slide was titled "The Latest Labor Saving Device," and it got a big laugh, so I guess things being accidently shredded was not totally unheard of.

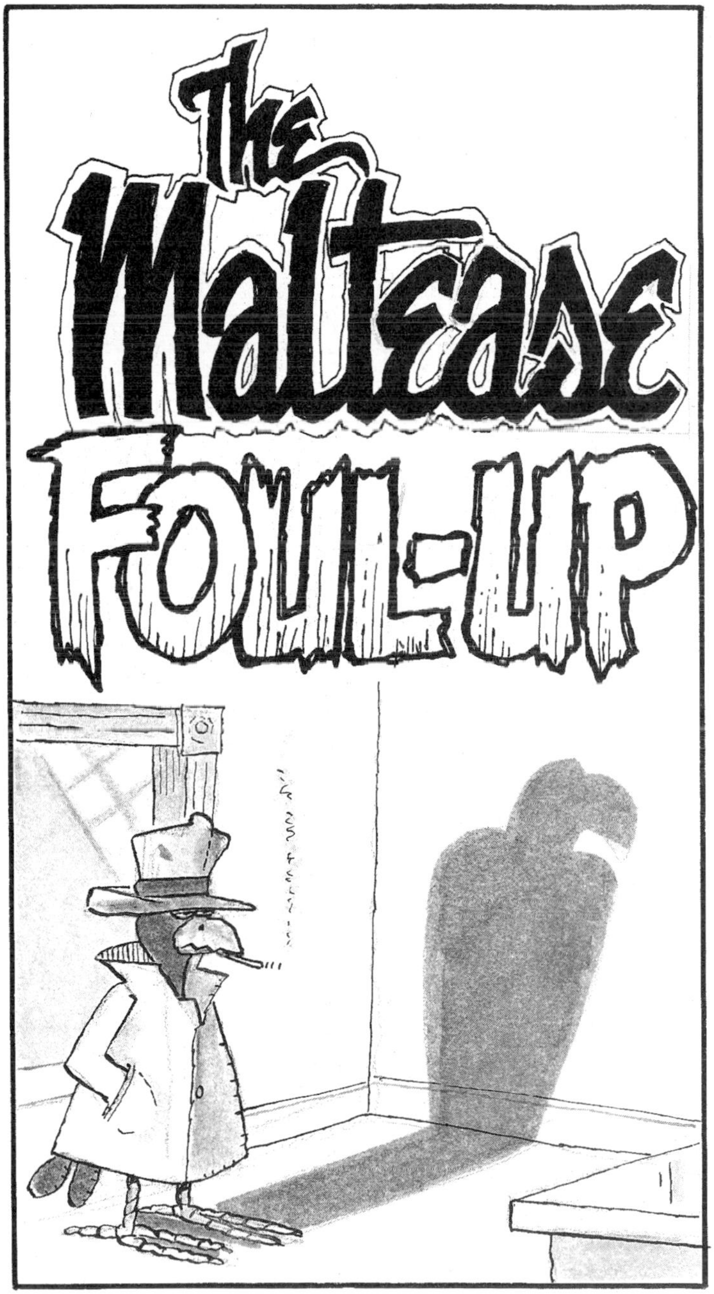
The Maltease
FOUL-UP

MAD AT THE OFFICE

But anyway, we were discussing the history of MAD, weren't we? And I promised you an inside peek. Okay, here goes.... At Bill's memorial service, William Sarnoff, chairman of Warner Books, said, "Bill ran his empire with all the tools of the nineties...the 1890s!" Although that's a funny way to state it, it was quite true. As I mentioned earlier, MAD only got computers a few years ago—even then it took us two years to hook them up! And for years we only had three phone lines (now we have a big FIVE phone lines for nine people).

But Bill's empire-running style wasn't really old-fashioned, just highly individual. Bill didn't have a secretary; but what he did have was a series of rubber stamps:

VIA
ZEPPELIN
AIR MAIL

To Bill, it was the IDEAL system. He did not need a secretary, because there was nothing to file. Getting an answer from Bill meant you got your own letter back with his comments in the margin. So he didn't have your letter to file, or his reply to file. (Obviously, contracts and other legal documents had to be filed, but Bill liked to have as little as possible cluttering his office. I should say that he liked to have as little paperwork as possible cluttering his office to save room for the important stuff, like the dozens of model zeppelins hanging from the ceiling or the King Kong or the display of MAD gifts the staff gave him each Christmas.)

As far as office procedure goes, there were very few rules at MAD, but Bill wanted those followed to the letter! The one he seemed to feel most strongly about was the rule about phone calls.

Bill monitored the phone bills as if he were paying for the calls out of his own pocket. He required you to fill out a slip of paper for every long distance call you made. On that paper you had to list the number you called, the city you called, and the reason for the call—business or personal. If it was business, you had to put down that reason, too. You also had to say which of MAD's three phone lines you'd used and, naturally, you'd have to give the date and the time. It was such a tedious process that I put all my personal calls on my phone credit card. Of course, that's exactly what Bill intended.

When the phone bill came each month, Gaines carefully matched every slip with every long distance call. If, God forbid, a phone number showed up on the bill without Gaines finding a corresponding white slip, he would storm into whatever meeting was going on and demand to know who had called 623-555-1212! The meeting would come to a dead stop while everyone tried to think if indeed they'd made a long distance phone call without the proper paperwork. I'm sure that stopping a cover conference with seven MAD staffers to find out who'd called across the river without writing it down cost far more than the call, but that didn't matter. Like I said, there were only a few rules at MAD, and keeping accurate phone records was number one!

People ask what a typical day at MAD is like. For openers, there are no "typical" days. Staffers start to arrive at 9 a.m. and must be coherent (open to interpretation) by 10 a.m. Art director Lenny Brenner has a schedule all his own. He arrives at 6 a.m., does his work, and is sound asleep by ten. He does wake up for meetings. Lenny also tends to go to the office on many Saturdays and Sundays. We think he uses this bizarre schedule to assert his independence, but it could be that he hates the staff, and doesn't really want to be there when we are. In fact, we do tend to keep our distance, because Lenny is the ultimate garlic user. He eats cloves of garlic whole, with a bit of bread for a chaser. When someone asks, "Is Lenny in?" you don't buzz his office, you take a deep breath. If you smell garlic, Lenny is in!

SPEED REPLY
IN ORDER TO GIVE YOU THE FASTEST POSSIBLE RESPONSE, WE HAVE MADE THESE MARGINAL NOTES. IN THIS INSTANCE WE BELIEVE YOU PREFER SPEED TO FORMALITY.

Co-editor Nick Meglin always arrives at work carrying bags of stuff. It could be something to eat, but more likely it's something from his bookcase or closet. Nick cannot throw anything out, and the only way he can part with something is to give it away. Sometimes the stuff he lays out has great historical value—that's the food he brings! There are often other neat finds, too: stereo headphones from Pan American; slippers from National Airlines; a necktie so wide, you could wear it on a bare chest and no one would notice you didn't have a shirt on. And then there are the books. Nick gave me a first-aid book to keep on my boat. I don't know what year it was published, but the book offers this advice to prevent seasickness: "Just two tablespoons of ordinary Buffalo Lithia Water before a sea voyage will calm the stomach." But hey, this is the same Nick Meglin who discovered me and started my career at MAD, so I wear that tie, and I carry that first-aid book on my boat!

All our meetings are held in John Ficarra's office. The main reason John's office was chosen is because he has a few chairs that are not filled to overflowing with art, but another reason is that his office has the most sound effects. John, himself, prefers a cymbal and drum, which he uses to punctuate punchlines, especially BAD punchlines. Joe Raiola uses the "applause box," which he activates whenever he says something he feels is truly great. Charlie Kadau, who along with Joe is an associate editor, likes the little cylinder that makes the sound of a cow mooing when you turn it over. I have a key chain with several sound effects, including a bomb dropping and machine-gun fire. We have these to keep the meetings moving—sometimes they are the only activity coming out of a meeting.

...If you can read this, you don't need glasses.

Like any good executive, John has devised various techniques to keep the staff focused, which is not easy for any of us. Sometimes John will post "THE LIST OF THINGS **WE MUST** DO TODAY" on the front of the TV set to make sure we see it. As each item is accomplished, say, writing the ad copy for a new MAD Special, John does a drum roll, as one of us s-l-o-w-l-y crosses the item off the list.

The most difficult thing we do is coming up with cover ideas—those meetings are the worst. In John's office about the only thing that resembles what one finds in a regular executive office are the pencils, but these pencils are stuck in the ceiling. (When no one at the meeting has come up with a good cover idea, even after we've been sitting there for three hours, we see who can throw a pencil and get it to stick into the ceiling tile.)

MAD covers have a four- to five-month lead time, which makes it really hard to come up with good ideas. It means that we have to decide today what is going to go on the cover of an issue that won't be on the newsstands for five months, which also means that very topical things are out, because people will have forgotten about them five months down the line. Celebrities who are hot now may be cold by then—like Roseanne Arnold could have gotten back with Tom and split with Tom three more times in that amount of time. So MAD covers have to be something solid. Hit movies are often a safe bet, provided we know it's going to be a hit movie. Movies from George Lucas and Steven Spielberg are usually big box office; *Jurassic Park* is a good example. When the MAD with the "Jurass Has Had It Park" cover hit the stands some four months after the movie opened, it was still hot. I wrote that satire, but I've also written some satires on movies that turned out to be total losers. Back in 1974, I wrote the take-off on a movie that, fortunately, we didn't feature on the cover of MAD. The movie was called *The Tamarind Seed.* (I bet you never saw it. I bet you probably never even heard of it!) It starred Julie Andrews and Omar Sharif, and was directed by Blake Edwards. They were all hot box office and that, coupled with the fact that the movie opened at Radio City Music Hall, made us all think it would be big. But it wasn't. Julie Andrews, Omar Sharif, and Blake Edwards probably saw it. And I saw it. But that was about it.

Other meetings are called to vote on material for the "filler pieces." (Filler piece is the name given to an article that will appear just once.) These are mixed in with the regular features, like "The Lighter Side," "Spy vs. Spy," "Tales from the Duck Side," the movie and TV take-offs, and stuff like that. Since I also sell MAD filler material, I do not vote on submissions from other writers. That way I can't be accused of voting thumbs down on anyone's work in order to make room for one of my own pieces.

The contributors come up with their own titles for the articles they create. I've had pretty good luck coming up with titles for my movie and TV satires, although sometimes Nick and John have to jump in and help me out. Actually, one of the easiest titles was also one of my favorites. My spoof on the

Clint Eastwood movie *In the Line of Fire,* the one where he plays a secret service agent who's about to be let go, was titled "In Line to Be Fired." It sounded exactly like the real title, but it told the readers something about the movie. Then there was *Raiders of the Lost Ark,* which was supposed to remind moviegoers of old-time movies; so I called my spoof, "Raiders of the Lost Art." Other favorites included "Deadwood Scissorham," "Hack Draft," "Prince of Tirades," and "A Few Goofy Men." (You figure it out.) Of the TV satires I've done, among the most appropriate titles were "Highway to Heaving," "Murder She Hoped," and "Smellgross Place."

Although the contributors write the titles for their articles, the staff comes up with the "department heads," and these meetings take up a fair amount of time. Department heads are the additional titles (comments, really), that appear at the very top of most articles. For example in MAD #326, the department head for Desmond Devlin's article "When the Smithsonian Opens an Advertising Wing" was *They're the Disease and We're the Curator Dept.* The department head for my take-off on "Rescue 911," the TV show with William Shatner, was *A High Price Toupee Dept.*

The whole editorial staff sits in on those meetings. The whole editorial staff is John Ficarra, Nick Meglin, Joe Raiola, Charlie Kadau, Andrew Schwartzberg, Amy Vozeolas, and myself. (Okay, I'll mention EVERYONE else in the office, so no one feels left out.) The entire in-house art staff is Lenny Brenner. The entire production staff is Tom Nozkowski and Marla Weisenborn. Subscriptions and stuff are handled by Lillian Alfonso, Freddie Maloney, and Greta Wood-Webster. We're very lucky to have Greta because no else on the staff has a hyphenated name. Our general manager is, of course, Annie Gaines.

Unlike the real corporate world, where I'm sure meetings go on without interruption, MAD meetings are constantly interrupted. And we all thank God for that! While we no longer have Gaines to break in ranting and raving over the phone bill, fortunately, we have Fedex coming with packages of artwork from Mort Drucker, Jack Davis, Sergio Aragonés, Duck Edwing, and all the other artists who live far from the tiny MAD offices. And we have local artists like Al Jaffee, Sam Viviano, Angelo Torres, Paul Peter Porges, and George Woodbridge stopping in to pick up or drop off jobs. So there are lots of neat interruptions. In fact, sometimes there are so many interruptions, we don't have to use our sound effects to keep things alive! Somehow through it all, the magazine gets out. And quite frankly, if we were all dressed in suits and had much more of a structured life at MAD, I don't think the results would be as good.

So you might ask, what do I *really* do all day, other than go to meetings. As you know, my job title is "creative consultant"; my business card, however, says, "IN CHARGE OF A LOTTA STUFF." Which is about the best description—because I do take care of a wide variety of things. Like I do radio interviews with d.j.s who phone in, write press releases for new foreign editions, appear at comic conventions, and stuff like that. Sometimes I write the copy that appears on the MAD products. For example, for the new 500-piece Alfred E. Neuman puzzle that just came out, the manufacturer wanted something "MADlike" to print on the box, so I came up with "Alfred E. Neuman's 500 piece puzzle—500 times more difficult than our old ONE piece puzzle!" (While we're at it—yes, there will be more MAD merchandise in the future.)

I've had many MAD business cards over the years. They include:

Dick DeBartolo
WRITER—LECTURER—EXTERMINATOR

Dick DeBartolo
LONDON—PARIS—FLATBUSH

I have new cards on the way. They say:
Dick DeBartolo
FRIGHTFULLY IMPORTANT

The other chores I do at MAD vary from week to week. I often work on the ad copy for up-coming MAD Specials. I wrote the rules for the "Spy vs. Spy Combat Game" that appeared in a recent special. In case you missed that handsomely produced issue, which contained a whole set of plastic coated playing cards, here are a few of the rules for playing "Combat":

...ld be divided into...
...n each team.

2. THE CARDS

...led Spy Vs. Spy Combat Cards should also be dealt equally. For those of...
...n, that's 19 cards each! No, wait, 18! The color of the Spies on the cards is not a factor...

3. WHO GOES FIRST?

...y, in most parlor games the player with the cleanest underwear goes first. However, since
...ame all the players begin simultaneously, clean underwear is not necessary.

4. THE NUMBER CARDS

...player turns over a single card from their stack. The player whose card has the higher
...per value wins that round, takes both cards and places them at the bottom of his card stack.
...ering at your vanquished opponent is encouraged!

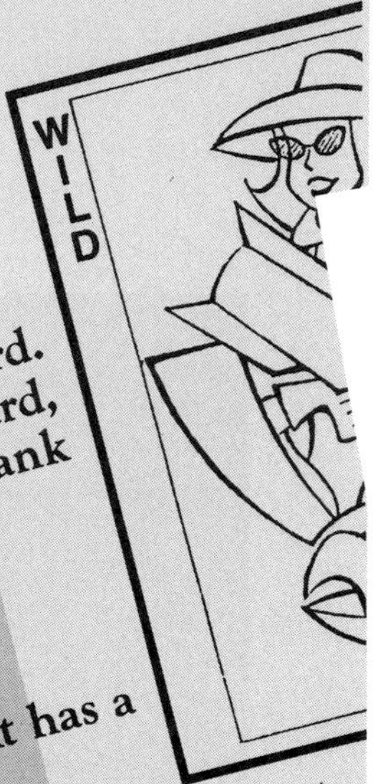
WILD

5. WEAPON CARDS

...here are three types of Weapon Cards: The Dagger Card, the Bomb Card and the Tank Card.
...ocate them now and look at them. The one with the picture of the Dagger is the Dagger Card,
...he one with the picture of the Bomb is the Bomb Card, and the one with the picture of the Tank
...is—yep, you guessed it!! The Tank Card! Are you sure you haven't played this game before??

6. WEAPON CARDS VS. NUMBER CARDS

A Weapon Card ALWAYS wins over a Number Card—unless, of course your opponent has a REAL weapon and not just a picture of one on a card!

2

7. WEAPON CARDS VS. OTHER WEAPON CARDS

You already know a Weapon Card wins over a Number Card. But who wins when two Weapon Cards are played? It all depends on the weapon:

Bomb Vs. Tank: The Bomb blows up the Tank, so the Bomb wins!
Dagger Vs. Bomb: The Dagger cuts the Bomb's fuse, so the Dagger wins!
Tank Vs. Dagger: The Tank runs over the Dagger, so the Tank wins!
Pen Vs. Sword: The Pen is mightier than the Sword, but if you have Pen and Sword Cards, you're playing with the wrong deck!!!

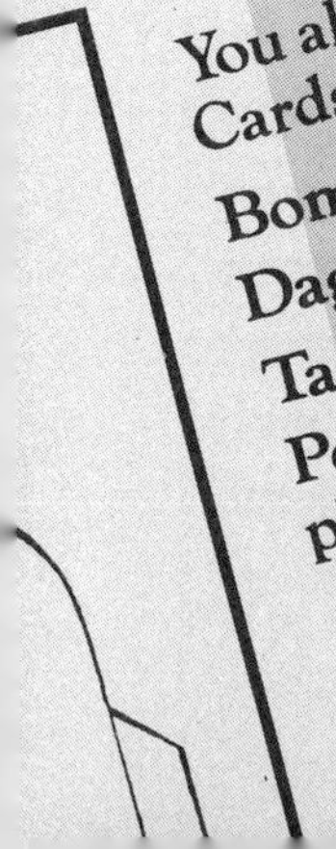

8. WHEN CARDS MATCH—IT'S WAR!!!!

When each player puts down a card that matches (i.e. each player puts down a "4," or each player...

3

Sometimes I write the gags that appear on the plain brown wrappers MAD uses to protect the issues mailed to subscribers. We used to send subscribers their magazines wrapped in plastic but many years ago we switched to paper. (We are environmentally aware at MAD.) Unless you subscribe to MAD, you'll never see the copy on the brown wrapper, so here's a sample of some I've written:

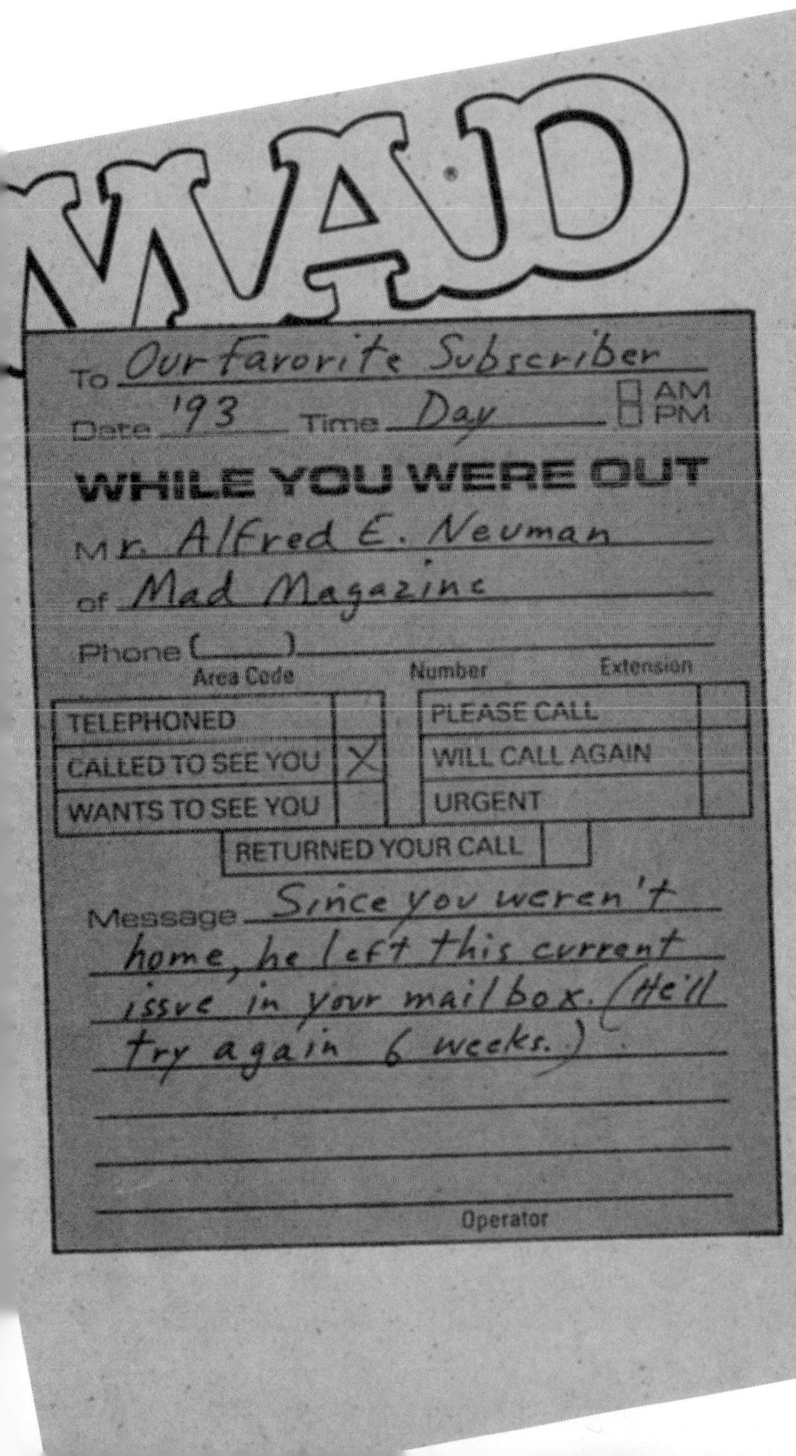
MAD
To Our Favorite Subscriber
Date '93 Time Day AM PM
WHILE YOU WERE OUT
Mr. Alfred E. Neuman
of Mad Magazine
Phone ( ) Area Code Number Extension
TELEPHONED
CALLED TO SEE YOU X
WANTS TO SEE YOU
PLEASE CALL
WILL CALL AGAIN
URGENT
RETURNED YOUR CALL
Message Since you weren't home, he left this current issue in your mailbox. (He'll try again 6 weeks.)
Operator
2ND CLASS

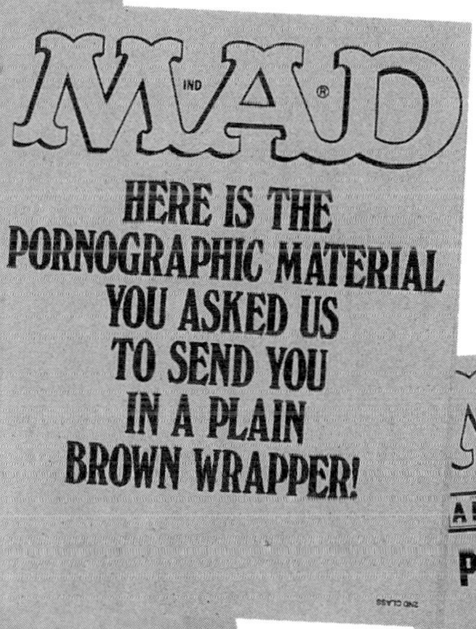
MAD
HERE IS THE PORNOGRAPHIC MATERIAL YOU ASKED US TO SEND YOU IN A PLAIN BROWN WRAPPER!

MAD
A PROFESSIONAL HUMOR MAGAZINE
PUBLISHER ASSUMES NO RESPONSIBILITY SHOULD YOU ATTEMPT THESE JOKES AT HOME!

I also write various "inserts," which is what we call the notes that are mailed out with the MAD premiums. For example, if you order a three-year subscription to MAD, you get a free MAD Pin. Nick and John wanted some sort of note to mail out with the pins, so I wrote the following:

MAD

Dear New Subscriber:

Thank you for subscribing to MAD Magazine. As promised, we are pleased to send you your exclusive bonus MAD pin.

This welcomes you to the MAD family, a very select group whose check or money order cleared the bank. You would be surprised how small this group is! Then again, maybe you wouldn't be!

To ensure that your MAD Pin lasts as long as your subscription, we suggest the following:

CARE OF THE MAD PIN

1. Examine your MAD pin carefully after unpacking. If you find any flaws or imperfections, tough! It looked good when we mailed it, so complain to the post office!

2 Insert three "AAA" batteries in the secret battery compartment. (Be sure to remove the batteries if you are not going to wear the MAD pin for extended periods of time.)

3. If you have received a MAD pin in the past and the serial number begins with "XX3", please return it because it is susceptible to electric short circuits.

4. In an emergency, the MAD pin can be used as a mini door knocker.

5. The MAD pin is backed by an unconditional guarantee. It will be replaced - without charge - for just $33.75 postage and handling. Your replacement pin includes another 24 issue subscription free! Yes, we here at MAD are very generous people!

Once again, thanks for joining the MAD family. As with any family, expect us to drop in for dinner, unannounced, at your house real soon!

MADly,

The Usual Gang of Idiots

The latest insert I've done is for the premium that was sent to all those who responded to MAD's first REAL Reader's Survey—they got a special Alfred E. Neuman pin. The response was unbelievable— more than 60,000 people sent their REAL MAD Survey cards in. That's a lot of pins! (It was also a lot of mail!) Anyhow, Nick and John asked me to write a short note to include with the pin. I don't know which one they've picked (there's a long lead time in books, too), so here are the four choices I gave them:

Choice #1

Dear survey card fillet outer:

Mere words would not be enough to thank you for filling in the MAD survey card. Our accountants would like us to send you **mere words,** but screw 'em — we are enclosing a special "not cheap" Alfred E. Neuman pin! We were also going to enclose wearing suggestions for your pin, but we felt readers (like you) would know were to stick it.

MADly

Choice #2

Dear survey card fillet outer:

We were touched and moved by your heart-felt answers to our survey card. There were succinct, yet telling!!

As a token of appreciation for spilling your guts, we are enclosing a special Alfred E. Neuman pin! Wear it proudly for a job well done!

Choice #3

Dear MAD Reader!!

Out of the **thousands** of survey cards mailed in — yours was one of them! What an honor! Because of that distinction, we are enclosing a very special "not cheap" Alfred E. Neuman pin!

Wear it proudly! We wish we were in your shoes!! On second thought, just wear it proudly!

Choise #4

Dear MAD Reader!!

We were suprised that your survey card was the only one returned.

of course, the cases of unopened mail in our office may contain others, but in the meantime, we want you to have the enclosed gift. You comments were heart felt, moving and gave us the will to carry on.

God bless you!

(Actually, this is the *second* MAD reader's survey. I wrote one years ago, and this classic, MAD FAKE Reader's Survey is coming up as another bonus!)

It's on page 103 ➔

The fact that it took over forty years to do a real reader's survey proves the point: MAD isn't run like a "normal" magazine. MAD has never taken advertising either, and one day I talked to Gaines about his resistance to having ads. Not that I wanted to see ads in MAD, I just wanted to know why Bill didn't want advertising. He told me that he had tried taking ads at the very beginning of MAD as a magazine. But when he ran the ads he felt he had to let people know it was a real ad, so he did just that: The ads said "REAL AD." Then readers wrote in saying, "Oh, now your advertisers will be sacred, and you won't make fun of them."

So in the next issue with ads, Bill had the MAD writers do satires on the real ads. But readers wrote in saying, "Oh, now you're giving your advertisers twice the space by adding the satires!" Bill told me he saw no happy solution, so he decided "No ads, period." And it's been that way for almost 35 years.

To tell the truth, I had a hidden motive when I asked Bill about his advertising policy, because I had an idea for some fake ads. I suggested to Bill that he write a letter saying MAD didn't want to raise its rates but the only way to avoid that was to take ads, and to print the letter in the front of the magazine. Well, it's easier to show you than to tell you. I'll just say that Bill loved the idea, and in short order, this appeared in MAD:

Elsewhere in that issue were some of the ads selected by that "Blue Ribbon Panel". You can see them on the next two pages.

AN IMPORTANT ANNOUNCEMENT

FROM THE PUBLISHER

Dear MAD Reader:

Over the past few years, the cost of producing MAD has risen dramatically. Ink, paper, printing and shipping prices all have gone up. (In fact, just about everything connected with MAD has gone up, with the exception of the quality of the magazine!)

In order to avoid raising the price of MAD, I'm trying something in this issue that I swore I never would—running ads. I'm not happy about this, but I am trying to make the best of the situation out of respect to you, the reader.

Accordingly, I have established a Blue-Ribbon panel of experts who will carefully screen all companies who wish to advertise in MAD. In addition, every product advertised will be carefully reviewed and tested by this panel. You have my personal guarantee that only top-of-the-line companies and their products will appear in the pages of MAD. My foremost concern is that you, the reader, are satisfied. The "MAD Merchadise Mart" appears on pages 22 and 23 of this issue. Read the ads, judge for yourself, and let me know what you think!

If the response to advertising is good, we will try it again in future issues. If not, we will not use ads again and will maintain our "cheap" price as long as possible. Unfortunately, the low quality of the magazine will remain the same, no matter what you say!

William M. Gaines

BECOME A DEEJAY!
Newscaster/Announcer Extra/Flunkie/Janitor

NO PREVIOUS EMPLOYMENT NECESSARY!
NO FUTURE EMPLOYMENT GUARANTEED!

LEARN BY SITTING BEHIND AN ACTUAL RADIO AND TALKING THROUGH THE SPEAKER!

SOME OF OUR TRAINEES ARE ALREADY LISTENING TO CBS, ABC AND NBC AFFILIATES THROUGHOUT THE WORLD!

TAKE A BUSINESS-SIZE ENVELOPE AND SPEAK INTO IT IN LOUD, CLEAR TONES. SAY YOUR NAME, ADDRESS AND HOME PHONE NUMBER INTO THE ENVELOPE. ENCLOSE $20 SO WE MAY DETERMINE IF YOUR VOICE IS STILL IN THE ENVELOPE WHEN WE OPEN IT. IF IT IS, YOU HAVE THE KIND OF RESONANCE THAT WE REQUIRE. SEND YOUR ENVELOPE TO:

DJ/NEWSCASTER/ANNOUNCER/EXTRA/FLUNKIE/JANITOR SCHOOL
14 Rich and Famous Lane, Robin Leach, Nebraska

MAKE BIG BUCKS!
SELL BURGLAR ALARMS TO YOUR NEIGHBORS!

If they won't buy because they think burgler alarms are worthless, sell their addresses to shady characters and make big bucks anyway! You can't lose! Send for info. Enclose $2.00 postage and a large hacksaw. Mail to: Alarming Money-Making Plans, Cell 1717, Sing Sing, New York 10304

SONGWRITERS—
DON'T BE RIPPED OFF!

Others may steal your songs! Let us determine if your song is worth stealing. Send us all copies of your music and lyrics. (Send us everything! Don't leave a single copy lying around in your home to be stolen!) If we feel your work is not suitable for stealing, we will return it and you pay just $10 for our appraisal! If your stuff *is* worth stealing you won't hear from us again, but we guarantee you will hear your song on the radio! Remember, send all copies of your music and lyrics to: **Tin Ear Alley, 87 Lionel Richie Road, Sondheim AZ.**

They're Available In Dozens Of Shapes!
They're Available In Dozens Of Colors!
They're Illegal In Dozens Of States!
They're Responsible For Dozens Of Injuries And Deaths!

FIREWORKS

FIRECRACKERS! ROMAN CANDLES!
ASHCANS! SPARKLERS!

plus: **HAND GRENADES! LAND MINES! TORPEDOES! EXOCET & PERSHING MISSILES! NUCLEAR WARHEADS** & more!

For **FREE CATALOG**, send an unmarked five dollar bill (just to cover postage, of

I LOST 14 POUNDS THE FIRST THREE MINUTES...
41 POUNDS THE FIRST WEEK...
133 POUNDS THE FIRST MONTH...
(And I only started out weighing 127 lbs.!)**

**Actual testimony will be on file if this satisfied customer ever reappears!

ZZZZ

Yes, it's the incredible...

ABDOMINAL SNOWJOB SLEEP-AWAY-FAT DIET!

NO EXERCISE! NO PILLS!
NO NONSENSE! NO REFUNDS!

(But you must sleep during breakfast, lunch *and* dinner and snooze during between-meal snacks!)

ACTUAL DOCTOR'S TESTIMONY: "I've seen hundreds of diets in my life, but NEVER one like this!"

OUR TRIPLE GUARANTEE

We will send you **a diet guaranteed** to put three times your original weight back on if you decide you looked better before trying the **Abdominal Snowjob Sleep-Away-Fat Diet!**

This **incredible new diet plan** was discovered by a registered nurse who was trying to come up with a better paste for hanging wallpaper. But her **secret formula** can now be **yours!**

RUSH ORDER FORM

Abdominal Snowjob Diet Plan
10 Love Handle Lane
Fat Chance, Ill 225 +

Yes! Please rush my order so I can start losing weight immediately! I understand that if I don't hear from you in three or four months I may start losing weight anyway just from worrying about my order, so I can't go wrong!

- ☐ 4-Week Supply $19.95
- ☐ 8-Week Supply $45.98
- ☐ 12-Week Supply $72.35
- ☐ Calculator to check our math: add $12.95

NAME ____________

ADDRESS ____________

HOMEWORK PROBLEMS?

DUNCE

For only $5 we will complete one term paper on any subject. For $25 we will complete six term papers on any subject.

SAVE EVEN MORE!

Send us $100 and we'll send you a diploma! (Yearbook $10 extra.)

School of Higher Edukation
Box 100001
Aldorado, New York

Actresses!

We are looking for sincere talented girls to appear in an all-nude version of Shakespeare's "As You Like It." Here is your chance to be seen and handled by top agents and producers! Send nude photo (or a bunch if you have them) to: Shakespeare-in-the-Buff Festival Auditions, c/o The Wild Pussycat Strip Joint and Pizza Palace, Las Vegas, NV 12121

GENUINE FAKE I.D.'s

DRIVER'S LICENSE! MEDICARE CARD! SOCIAL SECURITY CARD!

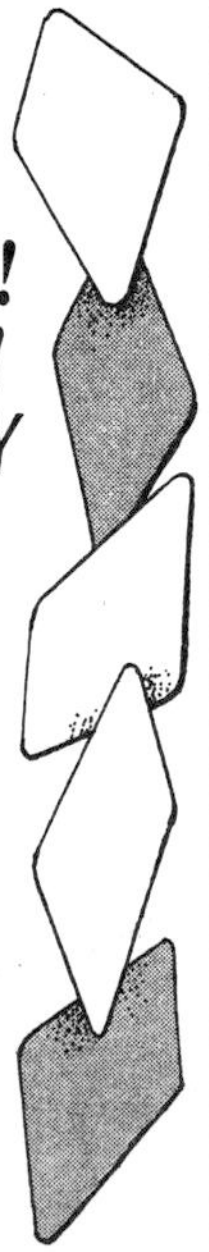

So authentic they will fool any government agency! Get on welfare roles! Receive unemployment checks! Use food stamps! Bilk the government out of hundreds of thousands of dollars! Obviously we offer these I.D.'s "For Fun Purposes Only." For complete catalog send your name, address and proof that you're not a federal agent to: Fake I.D., 21 Wedtech Lane, Bronx, NY.

Murry's House Of Health

VITAMIN SALE!

MULTI-ALPHABET VITAMINS!

BRAND NEW!

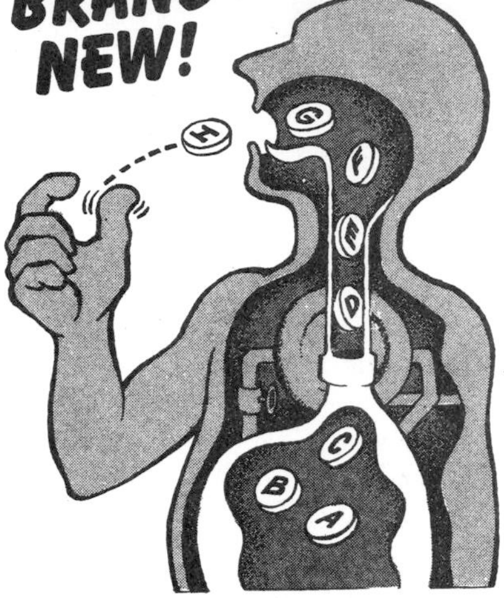
H
G
F
E
D
C
B
A

A to Z VITAMINS!
Released in Alphabetical Order!
100 tablets. $12.99

MULTI-ALPHA VITAMINS with EXTRA VOWELS!
More than 10 times your body's needs for vitamins A,E,I,O, and U!
100 tablets. $18.95

VITAMIN U TABLETS!
The much-needed vitamin if you want to use the other vitamins you take to spell dirty words!
100 tablets $22.95

HIGH FIBER SUPPLEMENTS!

FORGET BRAN, OATS AND THOSE OTHER "KIDDIE" FORMULAS! MURRY HAS...

OAK...TEAK...and now...MAHOGANY!...mix in cereals, juice, eggs etc. Or mix with Elmer's Glue and make tabletops, floor tiles, book shelves etc. Only $9.99 per pound (add $3.98 extra for building plans).

SPECIAL!

COD LIVER OIL ...$1.79/4 oz.
COD LIVER OIL w/ONIONS ...$5.99/4 oz.

VITAMIN E

E

(Can be taken face down as Vitamin M)
100 tablets. $15.95

HAIR VITAMINS!

30 Day Supply. $18.95
(Please state where you would like hair to grow.)

REMEMBER:

In the words of Murry, our founder, "Vitamins, they can't hurt and they just might help!" (And don't forget, Murry's next-door neighbor is a doctor!)

Murry's House Of Health

300 OUTLETS!!!

Unfortunately, they're all located at the same address! 4711 Gary Null Drive, Steroid, Arizona. Mail and phone orders accepted, except from government and FDA officials!

I don't want to say that some people didn't read carefully, or perhaps they didn't get the joke, but after that piece appeared, MAD got three letters from people asking us to please send MAD's advertising rate card!

BONUS #3

My Reader's Survey, which ran in MAD *years* before MAD ran a REAL Reader's Survey. It's one of my favorite pieces because about three dozen readers took the time to fill it in with crazy answers and send it back to MAD.

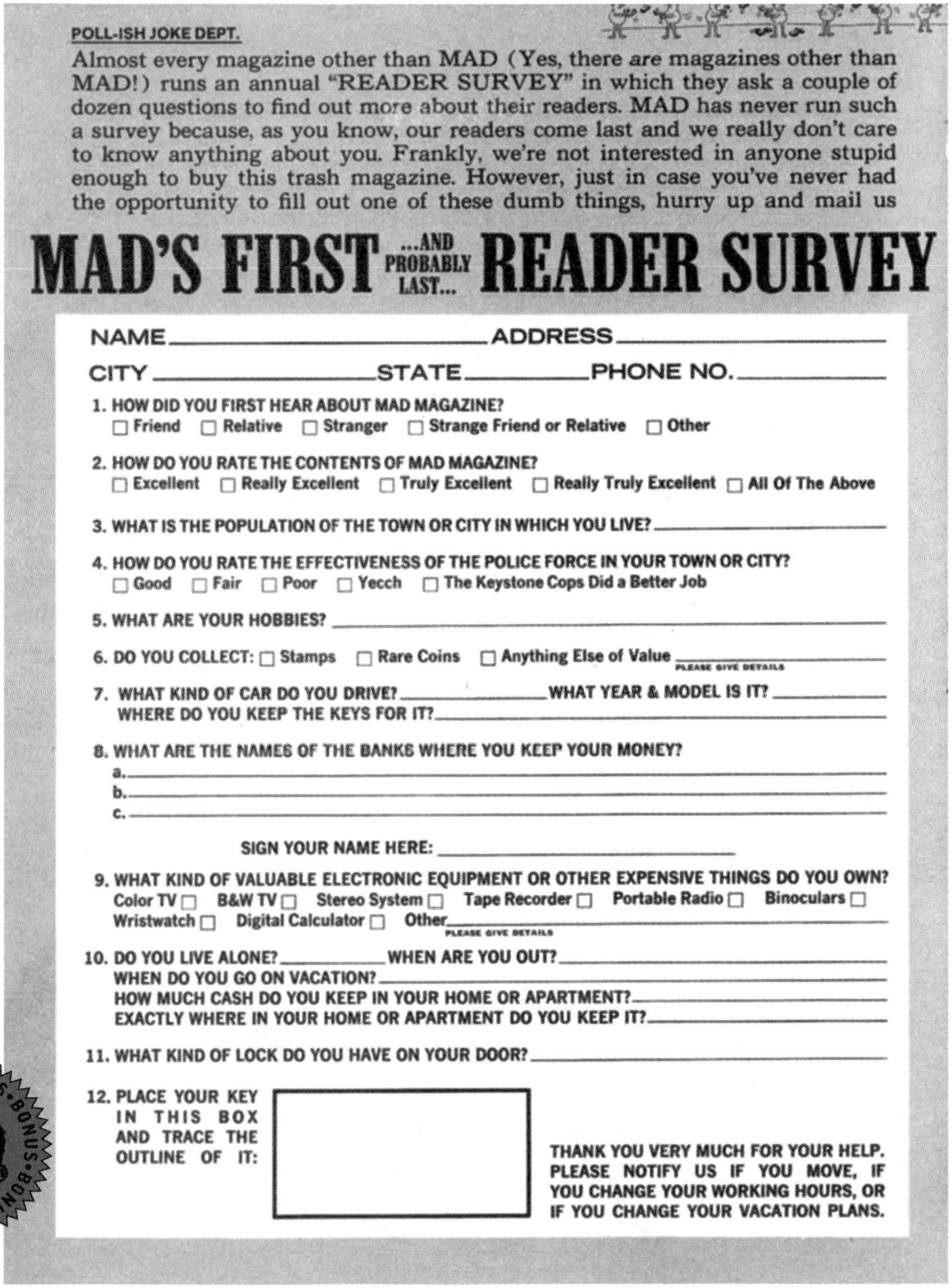

POLL-ISH JOKE DEPT.

Almost every magazine other than MAD (Yes, there *are* magazines other than MAD!) runs an annual "READER SURVEY" in which they ask a couple of dozen questions to find out more about their readers. MAD has never run such a survey because, as you know, our readers come last and we really don't care to know anything about you. Frankly, we're not interested in anyone stupid enough to buy this trash magazine. However, just in case you've never had the opportunity to fill out one of these dumb things, hurry up and mail us

MAD'S FIRST ...AND PROBABLY LAST... READER SURVEY

NAME ______ ADDRESS ______

CITY ______ STATE ______ PHONE NO. ______

1. HOW DID YOU FIRST HEAR ABOUT MAD MAGAZINE?
☐ Friend ☐ Relative ☐ Stranger ☐ Strange Friend or Relative ☐ Other

2. HOW DO YOU RATE THE CONTENTS OF MAD MAGAZINE?
☐ Excellent ☐ Really Excellent ☐ Truly Excellent ☐ Really Truly Excellent ☐ All Of The Above

3. WHAT IS THE POPULATION OF THE TOWN OR CITY IN WHICH YOU LIVE? ______

4. HOW DO YOU RATE THE EFFECTIVENESS OF THE POLICE FORCE IN YOUR TOWN OR CITY?
☐ Good ☐ Fair ☐ Poor ☐ Yecch ☐ The Keystone Cops Did a Better Job

5. WHAT ARE YOUR HOBBIES? ______

6. DO YOU COLLECT: ☐ Stamps ☐ Rare Coins ☐ Anything Else of Value ______ PLEASE GIVE DETAILS

7. WHAT KIND OF CAR DO YOU DRIVE? ______ WHAT YEAR & MODEL IS IT? ______
WHERE DO YOU KEEP THE KEYS FOR IT? ______

8. WHAT ARE THE NAMES OF THE BANKS WHERE YOU KEEP YOUR MONEY?
a. ______
b. ______
c. ______

SIGN YOUR NAME HERE: ______

9. WHAT KIND OF VALUABLE ELECTRONIC EQUIPMENT OR OTHER EXPENSIVE THINGS DO YOU OWN?
Color TV ☐ B&W TV ☐ Stereo System ☐ Tape Recorder ☐ Portable Radio ☐ Binoculars ☐
Wristwatch ☐ Digital Calculator ☐ Other ______ PLEASE GIVE DETAILS

10. DO YOU LIVE ALONE? ______ WHEN ARE YOU OUT? ______
WHEN DO YOU GO ON VACATION? ______
HOW MUCH CASH DO YOU KEEP IN YOUR HOME OR APARTMENT? ______
EXACTLY WHERE IN YOUR HOME OR APARTMENT DO YOU KEEP IT? ______

11. WHAT KIND OF LOCK DO YOU HAVE ON YOUR DOOR? ______

12. PLACE YOUR KEY IN THIS BOX AND TRACE THE OUTLINE OF IT:

THANK YOU VERY MUCH FOR YOUR HELP. PLEASE NOTIFY US IF YOU MOVE, IF YOU CHANGE YOUR WORKING HOURS, OR IF YOU CHANGE YOUR VACATION PLANS.

BONUS•BONUS•BONUS•BONUS•BONUS•BONUS

TOUR DE FARCE—A LOOK AT THE MAD OFFICES

Rather than try to explain the MAD offices to you, I'm going to take you on a little pictorial tour. The pictures on the following pages are from the "Backstage at MAD Magazine" slide show. I've performed "Backstage" all across the country, mostly at colleges, but I've even done it aboard the Queen Elizabeth 2. Now, a trans-Atlantic crossing on that ship costs anywhere from $1,500 to $8,000, and going to college can cost ten times that, but you're going to see some of those VERY SAME SLIDES here! (Now I think you're beginning to realize what a bargain this book is!)

MAD
BACKSTAGE
PEEK AT
MAD
MAGAZINE....

MAD's new $100,000 computer generated this exciting graphic. Notice, it looks hand written!

The "Backstage at MAD Slide Show and Office Tour"

MAD
1

2

MAD
3

1- When MAD Magazine became part of Warner Communications, we were one of the few divisions that did not move into the parent company headquarters. (It's not because they didn't want us there. When a Warner executive approached Bill about moving MAD into the Warner building Bill said, "If your parents called and asked you to move back home, would you go?")

2- Instead, we maintained our own small complex of offices...

3- ...complete with Meditation Garden to help inspire MAD writers and artists.

4- I, of course, have my own private office.

4
MAD

5

5- After I write a script, I take it upstairs to the editorial department.

6
MAD

6- There, I convince co-editor Nick Meglin...

MAD
9

9- Of course, now that Bill is gone, his wife, Annie Gaines, is pleased to make out my checks.

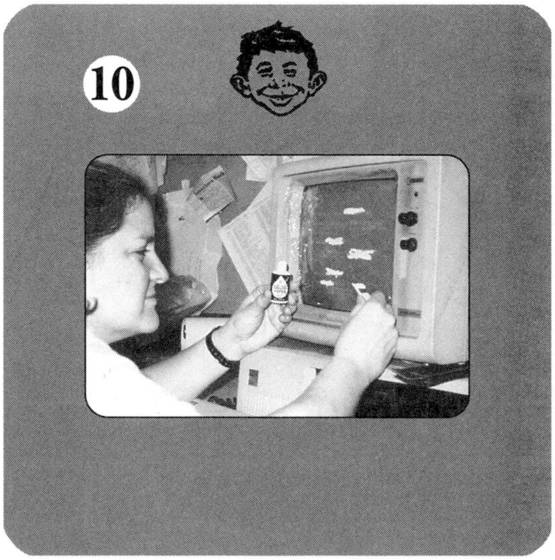
10

10- Being a computer whiz, Annie keeps track of all of our accounting records, making changes whenever necessary!

MAD
7

7- ...and co-editor John Ficarra, that the story IS indeed funny!

8
MAD

8- Once the script is accepted for publication, Bill Gaines gladly pays my fee.

MAD
11

11- Since we have no advertising, MAD is a lean, mean operation.

MAD
12

12- MAD doesn't accept advertising, nor does MAD advertise itself. We have to depend on the kindness of others, like Morley Safer at "60 Minutes"...

MAD
13

14
MAD

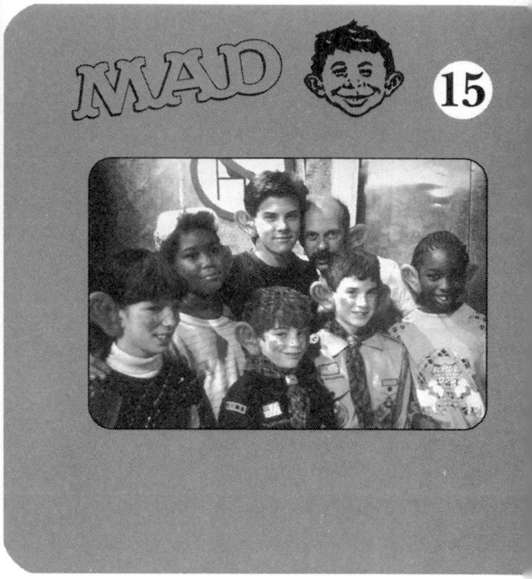
MAD
15

MAD
16

13- ...and Regis and Kathie Lee at "Live!" who always show the latest MAD Magazine whenever I appear.

14- When I appear on TV shows, I not only talk about life at mad Magazine, I olso do consumer reporting. Here on a TV show in Boston, I discuss the disadvantage of buying cheap herbal shampoo!

MAD
17

MAD
18
MAD
13

19
PLANT TOUR
PLANT TOUR

MAD
20

21

15- Highlights of my TV career also include the most appearances by a single guest on the Nickelodeon show "Don't Just Sit There." On this particular episode, I'm emceeing a look-alike contest—for a Ted Koppel look-alike, of course!

16- Here's my buddy Chic Glitz. Chic's appeared many times in MAD Magazine, and has an identical twin, Blink FunLove, who hosted "You Want It, You Got It," a game show on Nickelodeon's "Total Panic."

17- People often ask, Does MAD still accept outside submissions? Yes, we do, and they are treated with great care.

Now, finally, the "OFFICIAL MAD TOUR."

18- Take the elevator to the 13th floor.

19- Look for the "Plant Tour" sign.

20- On the tour, you'll see our boardroom...

21- ...and our boards.

22- There is no frontal nudity in the magazine, but there is in our office.

23- If you'd like to subscribe or buy a copy of MAD, the staff wouldn't object.

22
MAD

23

...Rare photo of much of the MAD staff all in one place at the same time.

As a MAD staffer, I'm often called upon to give a personal guided tour. Of course, as soon as people enter our offices, they ask for their favorite writer or artist. A typical question is, "Where does Sergio Aragonés sit?"

And my answer is, "At the end of this hall, and about three thousand miles to the right!" That's because Sergio works out of his studio—in California. In actual fact, none of "the usual gang of idiots" has a desk at MAD. Almost all the MAD artists work out of their own studios, and almost every one of these freelancers do other work. Sergio, who is famous for his "MAD Marginals," does his own comic book, *Groo*; Duck Edwing does a comic strip for the *Tampa Tribune*, the "Tribune Toon"; Mort Drucker does national ads and magazine covers; Arnie Kogen writes TV sit-coms; Frank Jacobs wrote for Stiller and Meara and is working on a new book. I don't have anybody's resume handy, but we all do a variety of non-MAD things.

Actually, if you want to see what we look like, look no further than Dave Berg's "The Lighter Side" MAD feature. "The Office" panels depict the gang that works in the MAD office. And then sometimes we are called upon to model for the photos that occasionally appear in the magazine, because we work really cheaply.

Since we do most of our work in our own studios or offices, for years MAD survived with just seven small, mostly windowless, offices. (Well, Bill's office DID have windows, but he covered them up! That way they never had to be washed.) Even so there was something about the set-up that was just perfect—or at least apt. I'll never forget a young woman's comment at the end of her MAD office tour. After the ten minutes it takes to see everything, she turned to me and said, "Thank God! This is just the way I pictured it! All the way here,

SKLITCH
DON MARTIN
BILL GAINES
AL FELDSTEIN
SERGIO ARAGONÉS
DAVE BERG
MORT DRUCKER
HARRY NORTH
ANGELO TORRES
DON EDWING
JOHN FICARRA
JACK DAVIS
TOM NOZKOWSKI
GEORGE WOODBRIDGE
PAUL PETER PORGES
RICHARD
WILLIAMS
ANTONIO PROHIAS
LEN BRENNER
NICK MEGLIN
BOB JONES
BOB CLARKE
PAUL COKER
AL JAFFEE

I was terrified I was going to find industrial carpeting, stainless steel railings, and stuffy furniture. This place is just the way it ought to be."

For years I shared a desk with MAD's accountant Rey Cruz—but just his desk top. I didn't have anything in any of the drawers; my file cabinet was two cardboard boxes. Then one day, when the commercial real estate market was at its lowest, the building management offered Bill more space in an empty suite of offices right next door. Bill took it. He called me into his office and told me I could have my own desk.

DICK: Bill, that's fine, but I would like three desks!

BILL: Why three?

DICK: Because I need one for me, and I'd like to put two desks back-to-back, so I can set up model trains.

BILL: That's a great idea! You can have the three desks!

So I got the three desks, now all we needed now were some model trains. About a month later, I was doing a TV spot about the new toys being shown at the Toy Fair, and I asked the people at Tyco if they would like to have their trains on display at the MAD offices. They said of course, and sent MAD a steam train set and a diesel train set. The trains were up and running for about a year until space got short again, and they had to go. But before they were dismantled, I did get "Entertainment Tonight" to come up and do a piece on MAD—with the trains running in the background.

Since people do drop by from time to time to take the tour, John Ficarra told me that we ought to have something for people to read while they waited for someone to show them around. I told him we should have "Rules and Regulations," like they sometimes have posted at the entrances to theme parks. John liked that idea, and writing them was one of my favorite assignments. Here's the result:

MAD

WELCOME TO MAD MAGAZINE

We hope your visit to MAD will be fun and even a little bit educational. There are just a few simple rules we ask that you observe. Failure to do so will result in cash fines, and repeat offenders will be jailed and tortured. You will not be allowed to call the American Embassy!

1. Keep your arms and hands inside the car at all times.

2. Do not stand during the ride.

3. Secure loose objects, glasses, hats, etc.

Opps, sorry, those are the rules from Space Mountain at Disney World! Here are OUR rules!

1. Do not place your fingers inside the cages of MAD staff members or feed them. They are very clever at begging and looking hungry. But we repeat: DO NOT FEED THEM!

2. Beware of pick pockets. The staff is not well paid and will try anything! Keep your eye on your camera, and all personal belongings!

3. Tipping is not necessary, but is appreciated! (We recommend 15 to 20% of your bill.)

4. Although there is no frontal nudity in our magazine, there is some frontal nudity in the office. Parental Guidance is advised. You may not take pictures of nude staff members. (But you may purchase the ones we have at the conclusion of your tour!)

5. We have back issues of MAD magazines, MAD Specials, and a few MAD items for sale on a cash basis. If you wish to use Visa or Mastercard, purchases must exceed $50,000!

6. Please sign our guest log. That way, we know who visited us, and we can use your name as a reference on loan applications.

7. Thanks for visiting MAD. Remember, there is NO SMOKING! Barfing is permitted in the designated BARFING AREA.

8. If you wish to stay-over, we have a sofa that converts to a bed. Rates are $85 single/$110 double. This is not bad for a place that's right on Madison Avenue! Check out time is 10 a.m., because that's when the office opens! PLEASE be washed and dressed by then!

thanks...

the usual gang of idiots

Every once in a while I'm asked if there is a dress code at MAD. My answer is, "Yes, and it's very strict! Some form of clothing must be worn at all times!!"

No one at MAD dresses very well, unless maybe they're meeting someone outside the office for lunch. In fact, Bill was about the worst-dressed of all of us. That's why one year as a gift, the staff gave Bill a shirt and tie encased in glass. It came with a little hammer and instructions: "BREAK GLASS IN CASE OF AN EMERGENCY BUSINESS MEETING."

Since Bill was such a lousy dresser, it was lucky that he liked to eat in expensive restaurants. They tend to be dimly lit, and in the semidarkness, Bill didn't look like such a slob.

One day Bill took me to a fancy restaurant. He had one of his favorite jackets on, one he would carefully press by sleeping in it the night before a big engagement. At the entrance to the restaurant, the maitre d' started the usual nonsense that drove Bill nuts. He really hated any pretense of formality.

MAITRE D': You need a tie.
BILL: I have a tie.
MAITRE D': I don't see it.
BILL: That's because it's in my pocket.
MAITRE D': Well, you have to wear it.
BILL: Well, you didn't say that. You just said I needed a tie!

At that point Bill pulled out a crumpled old tie and hung it in some fashion on his shirt. He was there to eat.

Many years ago, Al Jaffee, inventor of the famous "MAD Fold-Ins," gave Bill a T-shirt that had a fake tie painted on it. It even had real buttons sewn on its painted collar. This was long before that sort of gag T-shirt was being marketed. Bill just loved it. When he wore it under a jacket, Bill looked like he was pretty well dressed. He just hoped no one would tell him to relax and take off his tie!

Jaffee tells a story about the time he met Bill for dinner in one of Bill's favorite dimly lit food emporiums, and Bill said to Jaffee, "So how do I look?" Jaffee said, "Fine." Bill repeated the question, and Jaffee repeated, "Fine!" It wasn't until the third time Bill asked that Jaffee took a close look at what Bill was wearing. It was the T-shirt he had made! Jaffee had no idea that it looked that good and that realistic, when worn under a jacket. And neither did the Maitre D'!

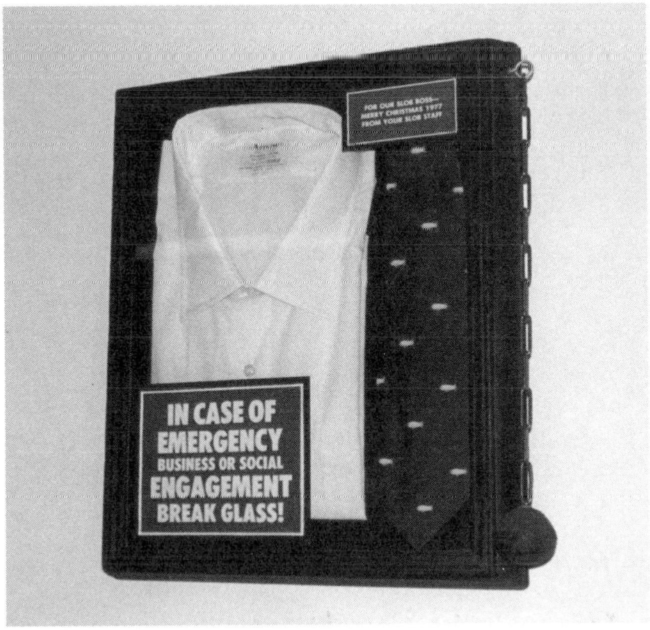
IN CASE OF
EMERGENCY
BUSINESS OR SOCIAL
ENGAGEMENT
BREAK GLASS!

Al Jaffee on Bill Gaines

Anyone who has dealt with Bill Gaines in business knows what an S.O.B. he could be. But what is little known is that in his personal dealings he was a giant pussycat.
I remember a time when he invited me to a wine tasting at a downtown hotel. I met him there and afterwards he offered me a ride home in his limousine. On the way he asked how I liked my new apartment. I told him my problem.

"I get no respect from the doormen," I said. "My fellow tenants are a spiffy lot. The men dress in suits and ties and the women wear the latest fashions to walk their poodles.

"It didn't take long," I continued, "to notice how the doormen bowed and scraped to the fancy folk and how their noses zoomed skyward when disheveled old I approached."

My sad tale ended as the huge black limo drew up in front of my building. Suddenly, before the chauffeur or doorman could move, Bill jumped out, opened my door, bowed low, and ushered me out. "I do hope everything was to your satisfaction, Mr. Jaffee, sir," said Bill in a warm, unctuous tone. As I walked past my doorman I knew Bill was rocking with laughter in the limo as it drove away.

Anyway, I never got dissed by the doormen again.

THE MAD INTERN PROGRAM

This is another part of the MAD Slide Show that I really love. People often ask, Does MAD have an intern program? The answer is, *yes!* It's a great place for a college intern to learn the rules of comedy writing.

MAD
1

2

MAD
3

1- For an intern to learn important editing techniques.

2- How to punch up a satirical article...

3- ...and how to use sophisticated word processors.

In actual fact, MAD does have an intern program. Interns are not normally paid, they do it for college credit, but Bill always offered them a small salary. *BUT* don't rush out and apply for the job, because when Bill passed away it was decided by someone at Time Warner that the interns could no longer be paid, because that was the policy in place at all the other divisions of the company.

FOREWORD *Number 7?!...*

BY ANDREW J. SCHWARTZBERG, ASSISTANT EDITOR, MAD MAGAZINE

When Dick DeBartolo asked me to write the foreword for his book, I was first dumbfounded, then elated and finally, I was dumbfounded once again. Why would a man associated with the world's most prestigious humor magazine for over thirty years ask the youngest and least influential member of the editorial staff to write the foreword to his book? It didn't quite add up, so I decided to explore the matter further.

Looking back on my relationship with Dick it occurred to me that I knew him long before I ever worked with him. As the youngest of three brothers, I was taught to regard MAD Magazine as gospel and to revere its creators as saints. This I did, and Dick was to me like St. Patrick would be to a devout Catholic. I even went so far as to get drunk and wear green every year on his birthday.

Upon entering college I decided to major in English, hoping that I could get a professor's keen insights into the intricate writings of Mr. DeBartolo. Unfortunately, NYU's inferior English department did not offer any courses that dealt with the work of this modern literary giant.

Dissatisfied studying the paltry writings of has-beens like Hemingway, Wordsworth, and Chaucer, I decided to more actively pursue my own literary goals. Essentially, this is where the heartwarming story of my glorious association with Dick DeBartolo begins.

When I first met Dick, I was a struggling young intern desperately trying to make it in the cutthroat world of comedy writing. Any bit of sage advice I picked up during my six-week intern stint at MAD was coveted like a shining pearl.

I remember spending countless hours dwelling on the hidden meaning behind Dick's words when he said to me, "You're a pathetic loser and you'll never amount to anything. Why don't you just go home and stop bothering me?" Indeed, his frequent pep talks have been a major contributing factor to my incredible success at MAD.

But my relationship with Dick has gone well beyond that of student and mentor into the realm of collaborators. After I toiled for several months tediously rewriting a satire of the television show "American Gladiators," the editors finally gave my script to Dick who finished it in two days, got a huge paycheck, and received top-billing for the article. He shared his bounty with me, keeping the dollars and giving me the cents. Our tender bond continued to grow.

As I recalled all of these fond memories it finally dawned on me why Dick would approach me to write the foreword to his book rather than any of the other editors who have been associated with MAD for so much longer than I. It has to do with a little thing called job security. Long after Nick Meglin, John Ficarra, Charlie Kadau, and Joe Raiola have retired, I will be at the helm of MAD Magazine deciding which scripts to purchase and which to reject. While this kind of power can easily be abused, Dick can rest assured knowing that I will always treat him with the same respect and kindness that he has shown me over the years—especially since he has chosen me to write this foreword.

FREQUENT FLYER FANATICS

The usual gang of idiots must have logged hundreds of thousands of miles on the MAD trips. And as you can imagine with our obsession with bargains, Bill and I were both frequent flyer mileage junkies (of course, Annie and I still are). I'll never forget the day I found out about the frequent flyer program... I was in the American Airlines terminal at JFK, waiting to board a flight to California, when a gentleman carrying a clipboard approached me and asked if I wanted to join American's frequent flyer plan.
He explained that in the plan you got mileage credit for flights you took, you could earn free travel, and there was no cost to join. I signed up in a second!

Then I got to thinking how bad the timing was on the part of American Airlines. I'd been working on a Mark Goodson TV show being produced in California, and was commuting between coasts every three weeks, and now, this was my final round-trip! I asked, but no way was there credit for PREVIOUS trips on American. Oh, well.

When I got back to New York, I told Billy about the frequent flyer plan, and of course he joined immediately. Soon after, the airline started to offer triple mileage, and Bill went a little nuts. He wanted the mileage, but he didn't want to do all that flying to earn it. So he went through the office, offering to buy anyone tickets to any place in the U.S., but most hopefully to California. Since it was 3,000 miles away, that meant a triple mileage credit of 18,000 miles! Bill's only stipulation was that they fly under his name, so he would get credit for the mileage.

One day I said, "Billy, I want to be there when there's a mid-air collision, and it turns out that you were killed on BOTH airplanes—but were still at home to take the condolence calls about your demise! That's going to take some explaining!"

Eventually Bill joined the frequent flyer programs of most of the major airlines and he racked up as many miles as humanly possible, using proxies, airline-linked credit cards, car rentals, and hotels. He took advantage of every mileage bonus offered. If it wasn't for computers keeping track of such things, perhaps Gaines would have tried to have all forty tickets written in his name when he took all the free-lancers on a MAD trip! But once I did help him get an extra 25,000 miles when I pointed out that the fine print in one of our frequent flyer programs said the organizer of a travel group would be awarded that many extra miles as a bonus!

I used to tell Gaines that he single-handedly drove Pan American and Eastern airlines out of business by cashing in too many frequent flyer miles at one time.

HAVING GAINES AS MY RUMINATE

Even though Bill didn't buy the material for the magazine—that was (and still is) left to Nick Meglin and John Ficarra—Bill was a great judge of material that would fit MAD. And even though he wasn't my roommate (that's what I was trying in the title pun) sometimes he was a captive audience, like when we were sitting next to each other on a plane and I'd do a bunch of one-liners to try to entertain him. If he saw possibilities in the material, Gaines would suggest turning the jokes into a MAD article. This happened several times.

And as it happens, one of my favorite pieces was developed while we were on a flight to one of the MAD trips. A baby was crying two rows in front of us, and I turned to Bill and said, "You know, instead of giving us free miles just for flying, they should reward us with free miles for things that annoy us when we fly! I mean, don't you think we deserve about five thousand bonus miles for having to put up with that crying baby?!" Bill laughed and laughed.

I continued: "Have you been in that restroom? Having to use that ought to bring in another three thousand bonus miles!" Gaines laughed again and said, "You know, you have a great MAD premise there! There are so many things people hate about flying!" So I took out my trusty pen and jotted down some notes. A couple of weeks later, I handed in the following piece, which eventually made it into print as:

BONUS #4

UN OCCUPIED
Baggage
48
BONUS
Flight 1313 Slight Delay
EXIT
"Ladies and Gentlemen, this is the Captain. Just wanted to report that everything is fine up here."
UTAH BACK ROADS
SPIDER DIGESTIVE SYSTEMS
CONFESSIONS OF MOTHER IN LAWS

For every inflight meal that you eat without barfing, you get a bonus of 10,000 miles.

For having to use a restroom in disgusting condition, you collect 15,000 bonus miles.

For every boring story told to you by the passenger sitting next to you, you are awarded 1,000 bonus miles.

For every one of your bags damaged, you collect 15,000 bonus miles.

DICK DePT.

Almost every airline flying today has a "Frequent Traveler Bonus Plan"—a system whereby regular passengers are given points for the miles they fly. Well, the folks here at MAD fly a lot, and often use airplanes to do it. But we don't think passengers should be given bonus points for the miles they fly, we think passengers should be given points for the hassles and aggravations they're forced to put up with! So, while we doubt this will ever get off the ground, here's

A FREQUENT FLYER BONUS PROGRAM WE'D LIKE TO SEE

ARTIST: JACK DAVIS WRITER: DICK DE BARTOLO

For every 10 minutes your flight is delayed, you collect 1,000 bonus miles.

For the movie being so bad that you walk out on it, earn 50,000 bonus miles.

For every boring announcement the Captain makes when you're trying to sleep, earn 500 bonus miles.

If "Utah Backroads" (or a similar publication) is the only magazine available, earn 5,000 bonus miles.

For being assigned a seat in the smoking section, when you are a non-smoker, earn 25,000 bonus miles.

For being assigned a seat next to a crying baby, earn 5,000 miles. (If you are a non-smoker and get assigned a seat next to a crying baby that smokes, earn 25,000.)

24 25

On another long flight, Bill and I were chatting while waiting for—what else—the food. (Yes, on a long flight, you *will* be served airline food.) Finally the stewardess came through and handed us menus. Wow, there would be a choice of bad food! As I looked over the menu I said to Billy, "Hey, they have devil food's cake—they call it that because it tastes like hell....And look, three kinds of bread—stale, staler, and stalest!"

Gaines handed me a pencil. "Don't waste those jokes on me, write them down! By the time we get served, you'll have a MAD piece!"

...Putting spit on mosquito bites can stop the sting.

From that menu came:

BONUS #5

Speaking of food gone wrong, once while Bill and I were out at a restaurant, someone at a distant table must have had a piece of food go down the wrong pipe. This guy started coughing and his companion patted him on the back to help dislodge the food. It must have worked because the man seemed to be all right after that. Bill turned to me and asked if I knew the Heimlich maneuver. I said I knew the first step from seeing all those signs in restaurants. Bill asked what the first step was.

"Find out what the victim is choking on—and do not order that dish for yourself!" I'm glad Bill wasn't eating at that moment because his laughter would have caused *him* to choke. He loved it and spurred me on.

"What's the second step?" he asked.

I thought for a second and said, "I'm not sure, but I think it's give the victim white wine if he's choking on fish, and red wine if he's choking on meat...."

HOW TO READ AN AIRLINE MENU

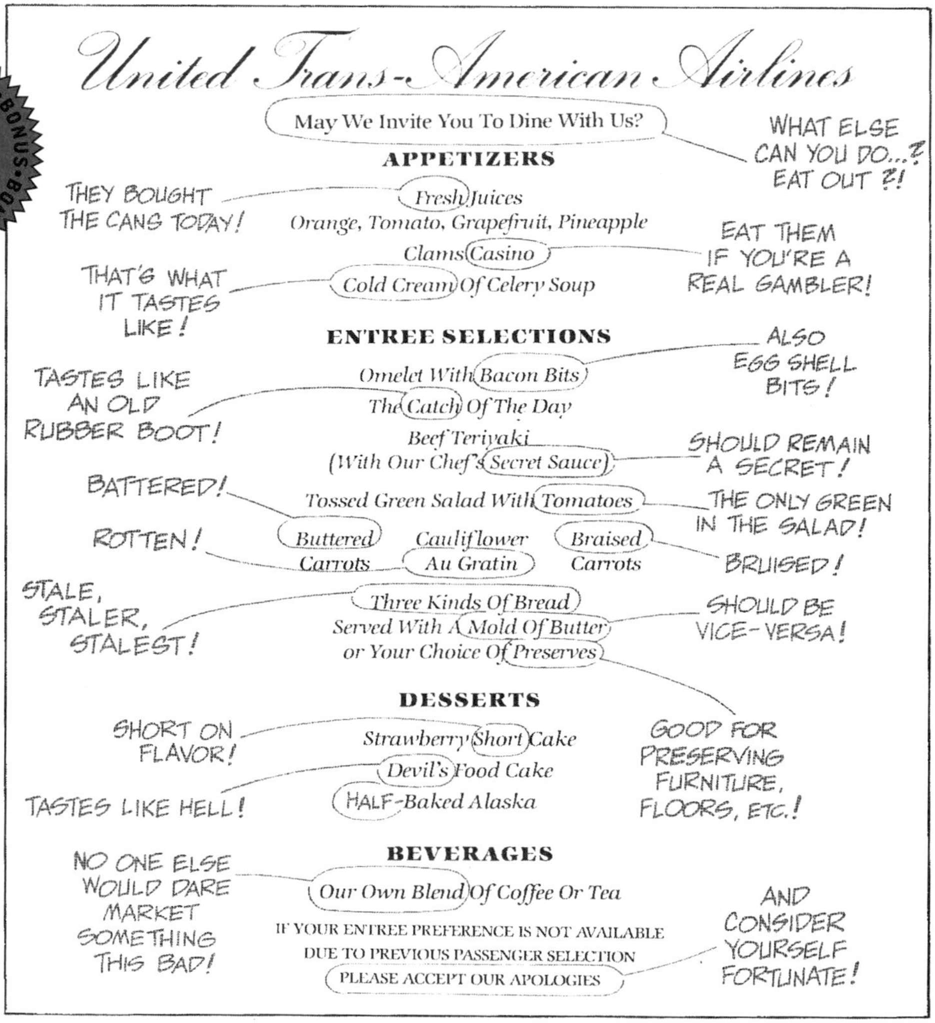
United Trans-American Airlines
May We Invite You To Dine With Us?
WHAT ELSE CAN YOU DO...?! EAT OUT ?!
APPETIZERS
THEY BOUGHT THE CANS TODAY!
Fresh Juices
Orange, Tomato, Grapefruit, Pineapple
Clams Casino
EAT THEM IF YOU'RE A REAL GAMBLER!
THAT'S WHAT IT TASTES LIKE!
Cold Cream Of Celery Soup
ENTREE SELECTIONS
ALSO EGG SHELL BITS!
Omelet With Bacon Bits
TASTES LIKE AN OLD RUBBER BOOT!
The Catch Of The Day
Beef Teriyaki (With Our Chef's Secret Sauce)
SHOULD REMAIN A SECRET!
BATTERED!
Tossed Green Salad With Tomatoes
THE ONLY GREEN IN THE SALAD!
ROTTEN!
Buttered Carrots
Cauliflower Au Gratin
Braised Carrots
BRUISED!
STALE, STALER, STALEST!
Three Kinds Of Bread Served With A Mold Of Butter or Your Choice Of Preserves
SHOULD BE VICE-VERSA!
DESSERTS
SHORT ON FLAVOR!
Strawberry Short Cake
Devil's Food Cake
HALF-Baked Alaska
TASTES LIKE HELL!
GOOD FOR PRESERVING FURNITURE, FLOORS, ETC.!
BEVERAGES
NO ONE ELSE WOULD DARE MARKET SOMETHING THIS BAD!
Our Own Blend Of Coffee Or Tea
IF YOUR ENTREE PREFERENCE IS NOT AVAILABLE DUE TO PREVIOUS PASSENGER SELECTION PLEASE ACCEPT OUR APOLOGIES
AND CONSIDER YOURSELF FORTUNATE!

Bill laughed loudly again and when he recovered he whispered those three little words I loved to hear: *Great MAD premise!* It only took a few weeks before I had the "MAD Choking Poster."

At first we had the posters made as a giveaway for retailers' conventions. Then Nick and John said it would make a great back cover for the magazine—they wanted it as a back cover so it would be in color, like the real choking poster. Its life didn't end there, either. Bill's 45th high school class reunion was held at the last remaining Horn & Hardart Automat in New York City. (That was the place with wall-to-wall vending machines. You would pick out your food by looking through the little windows and you'd put coins into the slots next to the windows to release your food.) In honor of the occasion, instead of buying an ad in the alumni souvenir booklet, Bill bought the back cover—and reproduced the MAD Choking Poster.

I don't want to say the MAD Choking Poster looks pretty much like the original from a distance, but I will tell you a story that illustrates the point.

I often had coffee and cake at a little Hungarian pastry shop on the East Side. The owner's son was a MAD fan, and I gave him one of the choking posters we had printed to give away. Well, the son forgot it and left it in the store.

A couple of days later, people from one of the city's billion regulatory agencies stopped in to do a check of the pastry shop. Since patrons could eat on the premises, the owner was told he must have a choking poster on display and they showed the guy what it looked like. The owner, who didn't completely understand English, remembered seeing that exact poster somewhere in his store. So, a couple of weeks later when the people from the city stopped back, he proudly pointed to the MAD Choking Poster—as proof he had complied with the law. Surprise!

Fortunately they had a sense of humor about it. They explained the difference to him and gave him another couple of weeks to get a REAL Choking Poster!

Your personal copy of the MAD Choking Poster appears in the color section.

Another great food premise was born while Bill and I were at one of the famous fast-food chains. (I won't tell you which one, lest the *chicken*-hearted *Colonel* get offended.) Anyway, we were waiting on this long line—the service was pretty awful. While looking around to pass the time, I saw they had the Employee's Pledge on the wall. The Pledge said things like, "We promise to serve you with a smile" and "We promise to give you the exact change." Things like that.

I said to Bill, "They ought to change that to read 'We promise to greet you with a grunt.' At least that would be a pledge they could live up to." Once again, Bill laughed and said that a satire on that pledge would be good for MAD.

I wrote it, MAD published it, and you get it in this book as :

BONUS #6

BONUS•BONUS•BONUS•BONUS•BONUS•

Bill and I both subscribed to and read *Consumer Reports*. We thought the information was very useful, but we joked about how serious they were about everything. (*Consumer Reports* is a little better now. Believe

OUR PLEDGE
TO YOU THE CUSTOMER

☞ You will be greeted with a grunt, a nod, or at least a "Yeah?"

☞ We will serve you promptly, providing we don't have anything nasty to say about the customer who has just been waited on.

☞ We will get three or four of the six items you order correct.

☞ We will pack your order with three times the bags necessary.

☞ We will pack the hot foods directly on top of the cold drinks—so the hot foods will be cold, and the cold drinks will be warm.

☞ When it comes to those little packets of salt, pepper, catsup, etc., we will give you none . . . unless you ask for them . . . in which case we will give you ten times the amount you can use.

☞ We promise to put the napkins we give you on top of your drinks so when you get to your table, they'll be soaked and unusable.

☞ We promise to put all the soft stuff on the bottom of your bag and all the hard, heavy stuff on the top, for obvious reasons.

☞ We promise to ring up and charge you for every item you ordered, even if we forget to put some of them into your take-away bag.

☞ We will smile and shrug when we give you the incorrect change.

☞ We promise to supply crowded tables, hard chairs and intensely brights lights . . . so the "fastest" part of your experience will be your desire to eat quickly, and get the heck out of here.

BONUS•BONUS•BONUS•BONUS•BONUS•BONUS

me, it was once a lot more stodgy!) One day while glancing through the new issue, Gaines looked up and said, "You know, you ought to poke some fun at these guys! Shake them up a little!"

I wondered whether they would get the joke, or if they would be upset.

Gaines said, "Who cares! It's the PERFECT job for you! You know products, you know the *Consumer Reports* style, and you know how to write satire! It should be fun for you, and I might even pay you a few dollars if we actually run it!"

Well, it turned out to be a very complicated writing job. By the time we ran it, it had become a six-page piece satirizing all the various features in the magazine. (But not only did the *Consumer Reports* people like it, they called and asked if they could reproduce parts of it for their Christmas card.)

CONDEMNER REPORTS
OCTOBER 1969 / MANUFACTURERS HATE US SO WE GET / NO ADVERTISING / 50 CENTS
Razors and Blades
Use-Tested by a special 500-Man CR Panel
Styptic Pencils
Use-Tested by the same 500-Man CR Panel right after the Razors and Blades tests
Electric Hot Plates
Almost all models had poor insulation and none had adequate, heat-resistant handles
Burn Ointments
An unscheduled report necessitated by the tests of those %&$#@¢!! Electric Hot Plates
Mixers and Blenders
Our special 26-Man Team tests most brands
The New Long Ties
A special CR Report shows why men who use mixers and blenders should not wear them
Fire Extinguishers
None of the Fire Extinguisher Units that we tested could adequately control a fire
New Construction
CR examines new building construction as it searches for a new home after making those %&$#@¢#!! Fire Extinguisher tests

BONUS #7

Another magazine satire I really enjoyed doing was the take-off on *Outdoor Life,* called "21st Century Outdoors" magazine. I liked it even more after I got a letter from some congressman, saying that he had read my article into the *Congressional Record* as an example of how satire could be used to help educate people. In this case, he said, I used satire to point out the way we are wasting our natural resources. Unfortu- nately, that was many years ago, so I don't know who that kind person was. While I don't have the congressman's letter, I do have the first page of the article that prompted him to write it.

BONUS #8

Writing about my send-up of *Outdoor Life* reminds me of an incident that took place some years ago. My buddies and I were touring Florida in an open cockpit race boat and we planned on spending a night in the Everglades. When we tied up in the small marina, a park ranger walking by noticed our sleeping bags. He told us that we shouldn't plan on sleeping on board because we'd never make it through the night after the mosquitoes came out at dusk. But even that far into the Everglades, there was a small motel within walking distance, so our lives would be spared.

...Lucky you! This book contains 100 pages MORE than a 205 pages book!!

At the motel desk I was met by a pleasant young lady. I asked if they had rooms available—they did. I asked if the rooms had hot and cold running water—they did. I asked if the rooms had air conditioning—they did. I asked if they had a restaurant; it was small and it closed at 8 p.m., but they did. Then I said, "I know we're fifty miles from the nearest town, but by any chance do the rooms have cable TV?" They did. "Color?" They were. Finally, the lady behind the desk had a turn to ask a question: "Are you on vacation?"

"No," I replied, "I'm here on assignment. I'm writing an article on roughing it in the Everglades for *Outdoor Life*." She gave me one of those "are you nuts or what?" nods and didn't ask another question.

I actually did get a story out of it, but I wrote it for *Powerboat* magazine, whose readers would expect me to have air conditioning and cable TV and in my room!

The next piece didn't develop from personal experience. It didn't develop from a conversation with Bill, either, or have any input from him. But it's one of Bill's favorite MAD pieces, so I'm including it as a Bonus. Once I asked Bill why he thought it was so funny and he told me, "It's funny because

December 2003
50c
(In Plastic Coins)
21st CENTURY
OUTDOORS
MAGAZINE
HOME PROJECT: Duplicate every variety of flower still growing in New York State in a 1′ by 3′ window box.
EXCLUSIVE PICTURES!! Taken in January when the debris-ridden HUDSON RIVER caught fire and burned to the bottom!
Proper care for a lush crabgrass lawn, the "Better Than Nothing" solution!
WEATHER SECTION SPECIAL: How you can tell FALL without a calendar!
TRAVEL EXPERT Sid Ascher tells how "You can save a fortune DRIVING FROM THE U.S.A. TO EUROPE by following my specially prepared map of heaped-up garbage routes!"
FELLED 1965
BONUS
LET'S SAVE OUR GIANT REDWOOD STUMP PARK!!!

you don't drink, you don't smoke, you don't do drugs, and yet it reads like you were really tripping out when you wrote it!"

I said, "Bill, I *was* tripping out. I had two Pepperidge Farm mocha cakes AND a package of Oreos just before I wrote it. It was written under the influence of a sugar high."

BONUS #9

After being in every issue of MAD for five years, I was about to miss being in one because the article I had written conflicted with something else being published. I was heart broken. Then the scare about Cycladmates and MSG hit the headlines and every product was quick to claim in didn't contain this things. I sugested to Gaines that MAD should make similiar claims. Since it was such a timely news story, the issue being printed was stopped, and my cover idea was used instead!

No. 133 March '70
MAD
35¢ CHEAP
NO LONGER CONTAINS
CYCLAMATE
OR
M.S.G.
(Monosodium Glutamate)
ONLY
PURE, UNADULTERATED, FAT-FREE
HUMOR

BONUS #10

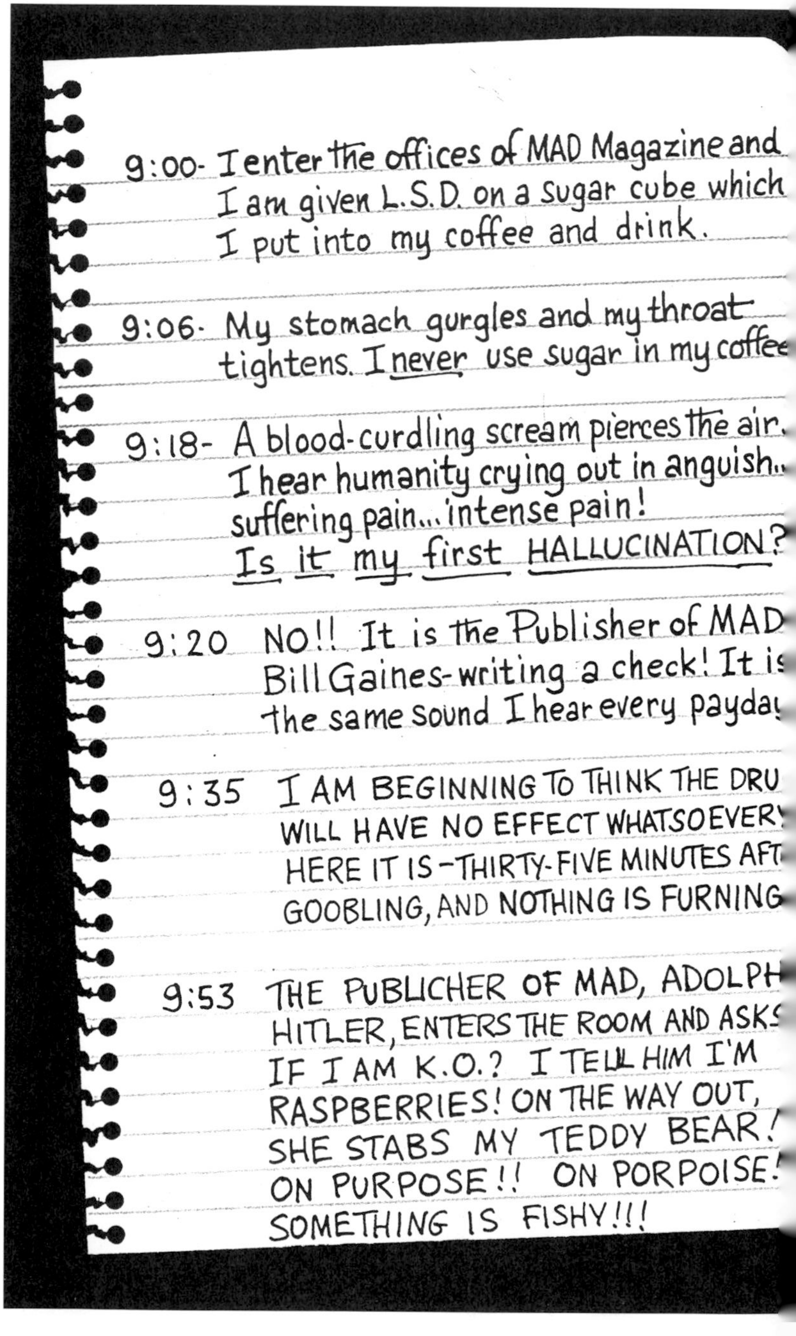
9:00- I enter the offices of MAD Magazine and I am given L.S.D. on a sugar cube which I put into my coffee and drink.
9:06- My stomach gurgles and my throat tightens. I never use sugar in my coffee
9:18- A blood-curdling scream pierces the air. I hear humanity crying out in anguish... suffering pain... intense pain! Is it my first HALLUCINATION?
9:20 NO!! It is the Publisher of MAD Bill Gaines-writing a check! It is the same sound I hear every payday
9:35 I AM BEGINNING TO THINK THE DRU WILL HAVE NO EFFECT WHATSOEVER HERE IT IS-THIRTY-FIVE MINUTES AFT GOOBLING, AND NOTHING IS FURNING
9:53 THE PUBLICHER OF MAD, ADOLPH HITLER, ENTERS THE ROOM AND ASKS IF I AM K.O.? I TELL HIM I'M RASPBERRIES! ON THE WAY OUT, SHE STABS MY TEDDY BEAR! ON PURPOSE!! ON PORPOISE! SOMETHING IS FISHY!!!

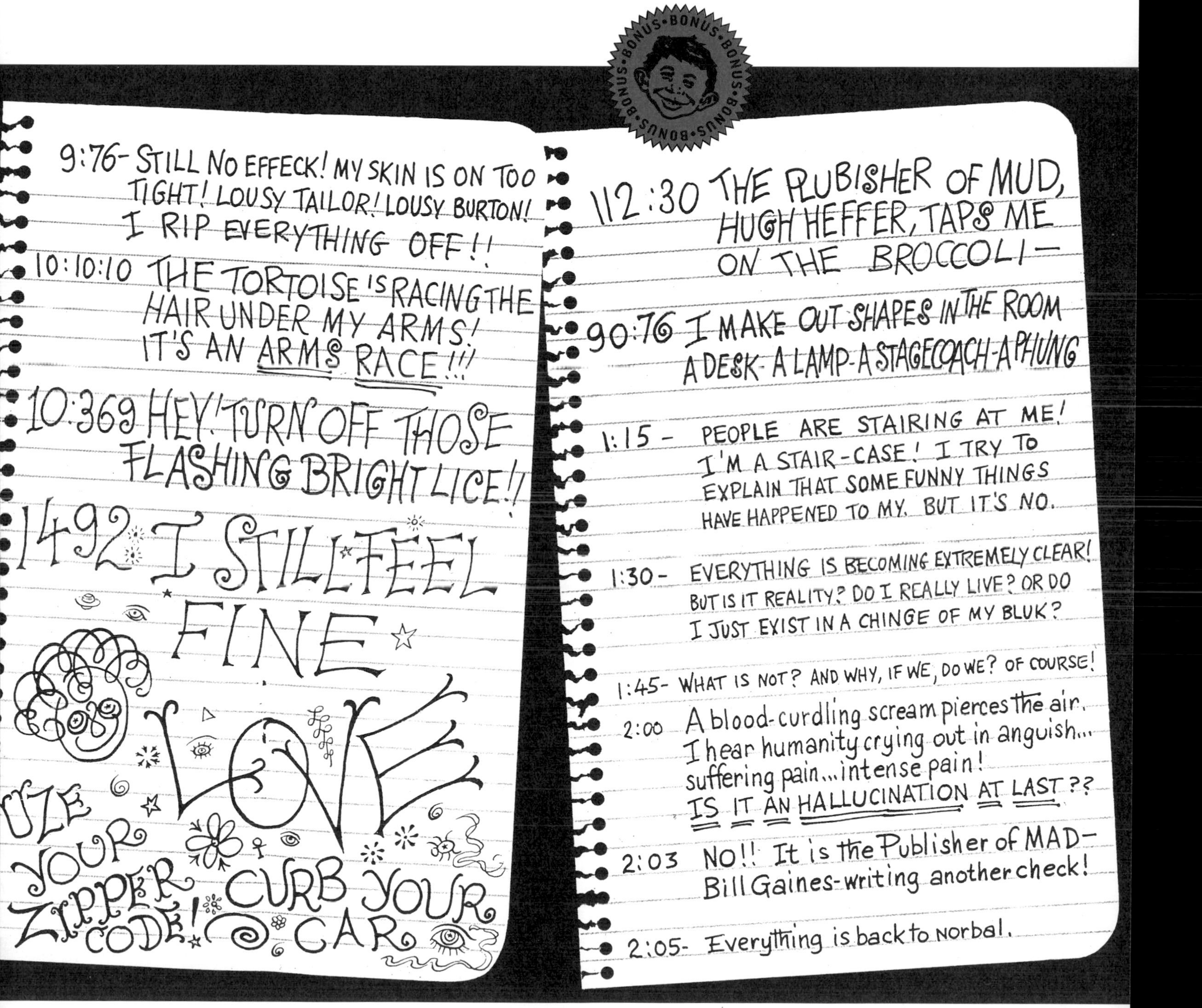
BONUS · BONUS · BONUS · BONUS · BONUS · BONUS
9:76- STILL NO EFFECK! MY SKIN IS ON TOO TIGHT! LOUSY TAILOR! LOUSY BURTON! I RIP EVERYTHING OFF!!
10:10:10 THE TORTOISE IS RACING THE HAIR UNDER MY ARMS! IT'S AN ARMS RACE!!!
10:369 HEY! TURN OFF THOSE FLASHING BRIGHT LICE!!
1492 I STILL FEEL FINE
LOVE
UZE YOUR ZIPPER CODE!
CURB YOUR CAR
112:30 THE PLUBISHER OF MUD, HUGH HEFFER, TAPS ME ON THE BROCCOLI—
90:76 I MAKE OUT SHAPES IN THE ROOM A DESK - A LAMP - A STAGECOACH - A PHUNG
1:15 - PEOPLE ARE STAIRING AT ME! I'M A STAIR-CASE! I TRY TO EXPLAIN THAT SOME FUNNY THINGS HAVE HAPPENED TO MY. BUT IT'S NO.
1:30- EVERYTHING IS BECOMING EXTREMELY CLEAR! BUT IS IT REALITY? DO I REALLY LIVE? OR DO I JUST EXIST IN A CHINGE OF MY BLUK?
1:45- WHAT IS NOT? AND WHY, IF WE, DO WE? OF COURSE!
2:00 A blood-curdling scream pierces the air. I hear humanity crying out in anguish... suffering pain... intense pain! IS IT AN HALLUCINATION AT LAST??
2:03 NO!! It is the Publisher of MAD— Bill Gaines-writing another check!
2:05- Everything is back to Norbal.

FOREWORD
Number 8?!...

BY MICHAEL GELMAN, EXECUTIVE PRODUCER, "LIVE! WITH REGIS & KATHIE LEE"

After a recent appearance on "Live! With Regis & Kathie Lee," Dick turned to me backstage and said, "Michael, why don't you write the foreword to my new book?" Quite frankly, I was surprised, because I prefer Dick to call me "Mr. Gelman" or "sir." But, I pretended not to notice his breach of respect, and agreed to write the foreword, assuming I could knock it out in under five minutes, I'd get a free copy of the book, plus $5 a word. I assume he was desperate for someone to write the foreword, because he agreed immediately! So here goes—the clock is running. I'll try to be fast, wordy, verbose, long-winded and redundant where possible. Hey, it's five bucks a word!

Dick is one of the most eclectic, good-looking, smart, intelligent, brilliant, well-rounded, off-beat, hilarious, multi-talented people I know. He's a gadget freak, a consumer reporter, a comedy writer, a boating enthusiast, former disco king, and a creator of material for popular game shows. I've advised him on many occasions to select **one** profession and "try to be good at it," but Dick insists on the buckshot approach to making a living.

Now he's adding to that list another occupation—author of a nonfiction hardcover book. Isn't he spreading himself **too** thin? Too lean? Too slim?

I could go on being complimentary like this for pages, but there's only ten seconds left to the five minutes I'm devoting to this foreword

I also hit Dick's maximum payment of $1,500. Which means I have only nine more words left so—**Enjoy reading GOOD DAYS AND MAD!** If you can.

DAY MORNI
8:30
9:00
9:30
10:0
banking; 2715
American Jrnl 83425
Hard Copy (r) 19338
Joan Ri
in the work-
Jane Whitney Bullies 58425
Leeza
Montel Williams (r) 92883
Paid prg 54086
Culinary) 73609
Regis and Kathie Lee Dick DeBartolo 87951
Rolond (r) 5211

P.S. I hope Dick does well with this book, so he can afford electrolysis to remove that one humongous hair that keeps growing back right into between his eyebrows! Quite frankly, I feel so strongly about this, I've ignored the fact that I've gone over the $5 per word limit, and I am *donating* these important words of advice to Dick!

MAGAZINE PROMOTION—THE MAD WAY

Bill liked to travel for pleasure, which translated into "going to a place where one could get a three- or four-star meal." And when he went to such a place—always accompanied by Annie—it wasn't unusual for him to have lunch at a three-star restaurant and dinner at a four-star restaurant. If he was someplace on a restricted time schedule, and there were several three- and four-star restaurants in town, Bill would have an early dinner, and then a late dinner!

But Bill wasn't much for public speaking—or hotel food—and since conventions and hotel food often went together, he was happy to send me in his place. I enjoy getting up in front of audiences, and my only gastronomical requirement is that the coffee shop be open 24 hours day—so it was a perfect arrangement.

One of the events Bill would send me and Dorothy Crouch to was the publishers' convention. A few words about Dorothy Crouch: She's listed on the masthead as "resident suit." Although like me Dorothy only comes in part-time, she always looks respectable—no sneaks and jeans for Dorothy. The rest of us keep jackets and ties stashed in the office in case of an attack from Time Warner executives, but Dorothy's worked directly for Warner for years, and she just feels comfortable dressing corporate. And then there's traveling with

Dorothy—it's like traveling with a Girl Scout leader. We've never been anywhere together when I've said, "Gee, I wish had so and so," that Dorothy hasn't been able to produce it. You know, things like a knife, an umbrella, a flashlight, scotch tape, a magic marker, blank index cards—Dorothy is ready for any emergency.

So she's a great traveling companion, especially when we attend the Warner's publishers' convention, which is held every few years. This meeting is a major event which showcases the entire line of Time Warner magazines. It's at this meeting that the publishers of the magazines tell the top retailers and distributors how they plan to spend megabucks promoting their magazines, and how that would translate into increased profit for them. Years ago Bill asked Dorothy to attend the conventions with me because she handled all sorts of circulation deals for MAD and she really knew her facts and figures. So we would appear at these conventions, taking on the same roles as Bill and I would—Dorothy would give the real answers, while I'd make up the goofy ones.

Most of the magazines at this event go all out, dropping big bucks on wooing the audience. The folks from *Playboy* put on a show with their bunnies; other publishers hire cheerleaders or hand out impressive gifts. And everyone always puts on a slide show, showing dozens of slides outlining their plans to pour money into print, radio, and TV advertising campaigns. MAD, however, has never really had a public relations budget. We were never able to match the big guys, so the only way we could make an impression was by taking the completely opposite approach.

"...We were doubling our circulation mailings: we had sent out two solicitation postcards in 1986, and planned on sending out four in 1987."

For example, one year we told retailers that we were doubling our circulation mailings—and we followed that up with a slide that showed we had sent out *two* solicitation postcards in 1986, and planned on sending out *four* in 1987. (Of course, in reality we sent out NO solicitation postcards!) While some magazines gave away Cross pens with their logo on it, **we** gave away bubblegum. Not only that, we taped it to the bottom of their seats, telling them if they wanted their gum, it was stuck under their seats! (Which it was, but it was in a sealed pack. We wanted to be amusing, not gross.) Another year, we gave out 3-D glasses. On the envelope the glasses came in was the claim that when you wore the glasses, you would see everything in *Incredible 3-D*. And the glasses worked—mainly because they were cardboard frames without lenses. The instructions that came with the giveaway suggested that you have someone heave a cream pie at your face while wearing the glasses, so you could judge for yourself how realistic it looked coming toward you!

We really drew a lot of attention with our gimmicks. Normally, publishers or publishers' representatives are not allowed to see the presentations of other publishers because competitors don't want each other to know how much they are spending on advertising and what sort of promotion they are planning for the coming year. Since MAD doesn't advertise or do much promotion, we just went to give our distributors some bare-bones facts—and some laughs. And it really worked. So many publishers asked for special invites to our presentations that we finally just opened them up to everyone, not just distributors of MAD.

One of our best convention giveaways was the MAD gift certificates, which entitled the bearer to free gifts at any store in the nation that would accept it.

BONUS #11

GIFT CERTIFICATE
AMOUNT $
REDEEMABLE AT
Alfred E. Neuman
AUTHORIZED SIGNATURE
GIFT GIVER'S NAME
BONUS•BONUS•BONUS•BONUS•BONUS•BONUS

We even made and gave away our own cash machine cards.

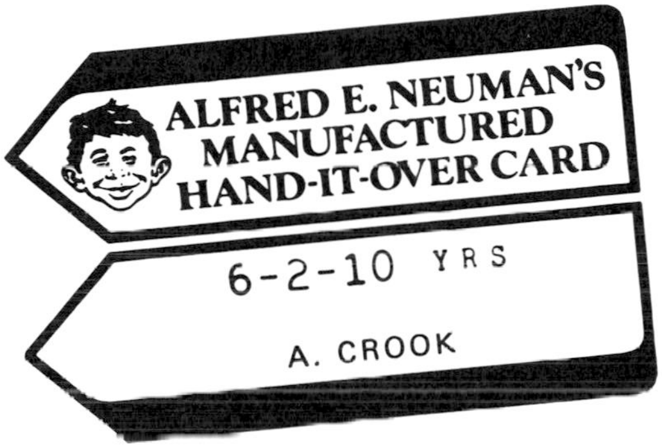
ALFRED E. NEUMAN'S
MANUFACTURED
HAND-IT-OVER CARD
6-2-10 YRS
A. CROOK

OKAY, MACHINE . . .
HAND OVER
THE CASH!

Out of all the slide presentations we did at the conventions, there are two that I remember especially fondly. In one, I asked why other publishers felt it was necessary to tell the audience something, and then put a slide on the screen that merely repeated what had just been said. I said my feeling about this was that it told the audience they weren't very smart, and they had to be treated like children. Of course, as I spoke, everything I said was repeated verbatim on a slide on the screen.

Another time, we did have some real facts and figures about MAD's circulation that we had to present to the group. So I asked the audience if they would please pay close attention to what I had to say. They all promised they would listen carefully. Then, instead of showing slides that repeated the info I was giving them, we presented slides of a MAD vacation in Puerto Rico, while I reeled off the stuff they needed to hear!

FOREWORD

Number 9?!...

BY JOHN CALDWELL

When Dick DeBartolo asked me to write the FOREWORD to his book of memoirs of 33 years with MAD and Bill Gaines, I was beside myself with delight. The honor of being associated with a project of this magnitude more than made up for the fact that I would not be compensated for my work.

When I think of all the great people Dick's worked with over the years, I couldn't believe he chose me for this prestigious task. Perhaps this was some sort of karma payback from a past life or maybe I once, inadvertently, gave Dick a winner at Aqueduct or a commodities tip of Hillary-type proportions. Who could say? All I know is I was excited to have the opportunity to be involved.

After the initial glow that came from the prospect of taking part in a project slated to be wrapped in a glossy dust jacket, I sat down to contemplate the task at hand. It wasn't long before panic set in. I realized that, although I've read lots of books (yes, *Cliff Notes* and *Classics Illustrated Comics* count), I had no idea what the difference was between a FOREWORD and an INTRODUCTION. I dreaded the thought of handing in my finished copy to Dick, only to be chastised for penning an INTRODUCTION rather than the FOREWORD I had been assigned. It wouldn't take long for word of my offense to spread throughout the chic literary crowd. I'd be the laughingstock of the belles-lettres circuit. What to do?

My initial solution took on a plagiaristic bent. I found an out-of-print edition of *The Stained Glass Windows of France* and began copying the FOREWORD word for word substituting Dick DeBartolo for DeGaulle, William Gaines for Voltaire, and MAD Magazine for any reference to the Cathedral of Notre Dame. I thought it read very well and submitted it to Dick, who returned it immediately explaining that he didn't speak French and would I mind retyping it in English. So much for that cheesy ploy. After several more honest but feeble attempts at something resembling a FOREWORD, I was close to throwing in the floppy disk. However, thanks to the support of my wonderful wife and a cadre of dear friends, to whom I owe a great debt of gratitude, I was encouraged to type on, overcoming every unwieldy grammatical obstacle that lay (lie?) in my path. Though I'm still too proud to admit my ignorance in the area of FOREWORD/INTRODUCTION, (while we're at it, I'm also a bit foggy in matters concerning APPENDIX/GLOSSARY as well as INDEX/TABLE OF CONTENTS) I decided to forge ahead, ignore Dick's original directions and flesh out a part of the book he may have overlooked. No way this would ever be mistaken for an INTRODUCTION.

ACKNOWLEDGMENTS:

A FOREWORD/INTRODUCTION of these dimensions is by no means a one-man task. The author would like to express his sincere thanks to all those whose efforts contributed greatly to the completion of this tome. To Phyllis Folger, for lending me the MEMOIRQUIK software. To Ray Passinella, who kept the donuts coming. To Dorothy Katzwein, thanks for the free rhumba lessons, Dot. To Jimmy "Mule Kick" Wiggins, for delivering a bouncy score even Bill Gaines would have danced to. To the human spell checker, Royce Bonenfant. To Bob Weiss, hold that elevator, Bobbo! To Wanda Van Zandt, a great temp with an even greater perm. To the Giesenhoff quintuplets, Larry, Donna, Joey, Floyd, and Denise, for their kind thoughts and complimentary wardrobe. To "name and address withheld," for the inspirational and moving letter to *Penthouse* magazine. To Sammy Guagliardo, owner and operator of the biggest little office supply store in a Pontiac trunk in Bergen, New Jersey, thanks for all the carbon paper, Sam. And lastly, to Arthur and Ramona Lembauer, who took time aside, sat me down, and tried, though in vain, to get me to understand what the hell a PREFACE was and when to use one.

Well, there you have it. Although it's not a FOREWORD, I hope it stands to serve Dick's purpose. Which, now that I've had some time to think about it, was probably to (A) fill out the book and save himself any extra work, (B) cash the big advance, and (C) be squired around like royalty on a twelve city publicity tour. If that was his intent, he should be ashamed of himself! And I should be ashamed for buying into the whole premise! But no one should be more ashamed than you. You heard me, You should be ashamed of yourself! Just look at you! What do you think this is, a library?!? Either put this book back on the shelf right now or march yourself up to the counter and hand the nice clerk your credit card. If I've gone to all this trouble for zip, nada, a big zero, then I'd like to see this baby sell zillions. After all, once Dick is rolling in gravy, I figure he'll be ready to show his appreciation for my efforts. I'm not greedy, but I'll settle for nothing short of a surf and turf lunch at The Palm with my gracious host, the gadget guy himself. Yo, waiter! Another bottle of Chateau Neuf du Pape '67 if you will. This one's for Bill.

THE "MAD MINUTES"

YEK

As I said, MAD didn't have a budget for promotion, so we did very little of it. But occasionally, if I came up with an idea Bill liked, and if it was cheap enough, Bill would give me the go-ahead. That was the case with the "MAD Minutes" radio spots. The "MAD Minutes" were one-minute long bits of silliness that Sara Fowler (a MAD associate editor with a wonderful sense of humor) and I recorded. The promotion part came in with the opening and closing lines, which mentioned MAD Magazine.

The "MAD Minutes" were sent free to disc jockeys around the country, and in no time we had about eighty disc jockeys who played them—or claimed they played them—on the air. A small article in *Billboard* about the "MAD Minutes" got us our initial mailing list of d.j.s, and from time to time we added to it by running a sentence or two about the program on the letters page of MAD. In fact, the "MAD Minutes" were even picked up by Armed Forces Radio. (Yes, they were played for OUR armed forces—not used as torture for the enemy!)

Some of the "MAD Minutes" were adapted from the pages of MAD, but since MAD is such a visual medium, much of the material didn't translate to just being heard, so I ended up doing a lot of writing for the spots. Valentinos, the studio where we taped them, was famous for its sound effects library, so I concentrated on writing material for the ear, rather than the page. Of course, I worked in sound effects whenever I could. And to top it off, we had original organ music written by Dennis Wunderlin, little sixty-second pieces he played softly under the "MAD Minutes." (To keep in tune with the "quality" of the "MAD Minutes," the organ Dennis used cost a whopping $199!) Dennis composed a whole range of music to use as background—"soap opera themes," "fanfares," "busy people themes," "hard-sell ad themes," and "light themes," and after we had done the "MAD Minutes" for three years, we had enough music to jokingly release a CD: *100 Themes from the MAD Minutes*. On top of that, Sara Fowler and I got some extra work while up at the studio. And now, enshrined in Valentinos' CD sound effects library, are Sara and I—screaming, moaning, laughing, and yes, even burping! Hey, it's a *complete* sound effects catalog! (By the way, Sara Fowler also joined the MAD staff via the mail. Like Annie, she was a college student who started to correspond with Bill. Bill asked her to come by the MAD offices, and before long Sara was on staff.)

Anyway, here are a few samples of the "MAD Minutes." To get the full effect have someone hide behind your radio and read them aloud through the speakers!

BONUS•BONUS•BONUS•BONUS•

BONUS #12—THE "MAD MINUTES"

MAD MINUTES #1

Hi, this is Dick DeBartolo, MAD Magazine's Maddest Writer, with Sara Fowler and another MAD Minute.

SFX: (Organ fanfare, then Dennis' background music continues softly under the entire MAD Minute)

DICK: The Frankly Mint is proud to announce the "Toxins from Around the

World" collection!

SARA: That's right, poisons and dangerous chemical substances from around the world can all be yours! It's a collection *to die for!*

DICK: Start with our first offering, nuclear waste.

SARA: Much has been written about nuclear waste, but so few people actually *own* nuclear waste.

DICK: What fun it will bring to your home! After touching it, you can watch various parts of your body glow in the DARK!

SARA: Be amazed as you can actually see THROUGH your pet cat!

DICK: Put some in the garden and watch giant mutant mushrooms as big as beach umbrellas grow overnight!

SARA: Nuclear waste must be handled carefully, so we pack each shipment in triple plastic bags-and put on not one, but *two* of those heavy duty tie wraps.

DICK: Request your first selection of Toxins from Around the World, today.

SARA: Just dial 1-800-WASTE.

DICK: Till next time, this is Dick DeBartolo, MAD Magazine's Maddest Writer with Sara Fowler and the MAD Minute.

MAD MINUTES #2

DICK: Hi, this is Dick DeBartolo, MAD Magazine's Maddest Writer with Sara Fowler and another MAD Minute.

SFX: (Fanfare)

SARA: Here's great news from Turbulent Air and Turbulent Seas, America's cheapest airline and cruise line.

SFX: (Lower music and play throughout)

DICK: Now you can take advantage of our new Land and Sea package vacation. Go one way by Turbulent Air...

SARA: Return by Turbulent Seas.

DICK: *Two kinds* of motion sickness for one low price!

SARA: Every Saturday morning our ship sets sail for sunny Bermuda.

DICK: And depending on the wind, arrives there, or some other place, within a couple of days!

SFX: (Music out, splashing water in)

SARA: All the way there, you'll take part in wonderful shipboard activities—like bailing your cabin.

NC13
STOCK SHOTAIRLINES

DICK: Fishing for parts that fall off the ship as she pitches and rolls.

SARA: And remember, your ship is just like a hotel.

DICK: Except if you step outside to hail a cab, you drown.

SARA: It's a trip you'll never forget. No matter how much you try.

DICK: Call Turbulent Air, today. Dial 1-800-FEAR. This is Dick DeBartolo and Sara Fowler on the MAD Minute!

SARA/DICK: Bye!

MAD MINUTES #3

Hi, this is Dick DeBartolo, MAD Magazine's Maddest Writer with Sara Fowler on the MAD Minute.

SFX: (Begin with "Sappy Wunderlin Theme" and play low throughout entire Minute)

SARA: Are you lonely, would you like to talk to nice people on the telephone?

DICK: Well, here are some money-saving tips from the MAD Minute. Other phone services charge you up to one hundred dollars an hour to connect you to people to talk to.

SARA: But here are ways to talk to people for just the price of a local call.

DICK: Lonely? Why not phone your local post office and ask how much it would cost to ship a package, third class, to Manila, insured for twelve hundred and fifty-three dollars.

SARA: You'll be switched to dozens of different people.

DICK: And the hours will pass quickly as you speak to folks from many foreign lands.

SARA: But suppose it's midnight and the post office is closed. Here's another great way to talk to friendly folks.

DICK: Call any airline and ask, "How do I get that eighty-nine dollar fare to London?"

SARA: Then just sit back and listen. By the time you've heard all the restrictions,

you'll almost be best friends.
DICK: That's it, money-saving tips from the MAD Minute. Till next time, this is Dick DeBartolo with Sara Fowler on the MAD Minute.
SARA/DICK: Bye!

The "MAD Minutes" were very successful, and they ran for over seven years. Every six-and-a-half weeks we sent out a new cassette of nine "MAD Minutes," a time frame that sort of coincided with the eight-times-a-year publishing schedule of MAD Magazine.

Somewhere along the line, Bill was approached by a company in Hollywood, asking if he would like to try syndicating the "MAD Minutes." This company hoped to get a national sponsor and then perhaps do a thirty-second "MAD Minute" with a fifteen-second commercial at either end. It sure sounded good to me, because I had already written about 400 "MAD Minutes" and Bill had told me I could do what I wanted with the ones that weren't based on material from the magazine. That left me free to sell them to this company. As a matter of fact, Bill wanted a clause in the contract that would make me a consultant on the project and give me approval of any additional MAD minutes written by others. The company had no problem with either of those provisions. They produced a demo version of several "MAD Minutes" and sent them over. I loved them! Instead of using my voice, they had hired a professional announcer. (I believe it was Gary Owens from "Laugh-In.") Instead of that pathetic two-hundred-dollar Casio organ playing in the background, they had an orchestra and a chorus! I thought they sounded great! I couldn't wait to play them for Bill.

"...Hmmm, wait a minute. Bill is gone, I still own 400 original MAD Minutes. Where did I put that Hollywood producer's phone number."

Bill listened, and then he said something that threw me for a loop! "I don't just not like them, I hate them! They're too slick, and too professional, everything MAD isn't! I like *your* voice and *Sara's* voice! I like that tinny organ sound and the simple 'Mickey Mouse' kind of music Dennis composes and plays in the background. *Your* 'MAD Minutes' sound cheap and hokey, and that's the MAD feel!" So there were no syndicated "MAD Minutes," and my dreams of striking it rich faded. Then into the seventh year of the "Minutes," Sara Fowler left to get married and have a child. And it seemed like a good time to end the project. Actually, I think the only reason Sara got married and had a child was so she could stop doing the "MAD Minutes" without offending Bill or me. (Hmmm, wait a minute. Bill is gone, I still own 400 original MAD Minutes. Where did I put that Hollywood producer's phone number—)

It wasn't until the paper shortage in the late 1970s that I really understood how strongly Bill felt about MAD's "cheap" image. Our printer called to say he was having trouble getting the newspaper stock that MAD traditionally uses, and that even though it would cost him more, he would print MAD on slick paper and take the loss. Bill wouldn't hear of it! "MAD belongs on cheap stock," he said, "and I want cheap stock!" So the printer had to go shopping for the kind of paper Bill demanded. Bill said it probably cost him more than using the paper the printer had on hand, but he would NEVER let MAD be printed on slick paper!

I learned something from Bill, and I carried that same "cheap" philosophy over into this book. Ninety-nine percent of all the photos here are reproduced from MAD staffer snapshots, or stuff either Annie or I shot with our totally automatic 35mm "idiot" cameras. The thought of hiring a professional photographer had entered my mind, but then I thought, "Professional photos will stand out too much—and make ours look worse then they are!" So in that "wonderful 'cheap' MAD tradition," this book is full of amateur photos, with two exceptions: The photo of Regis, Kathie Lee, and me was shot by Steve Friedman, the official "Live!" photographer. Steve's work has appeared in *People*, *TV Guide*, the *New York Times*, and other prestigous places like that. Having something published in this book should lose him some valuable clients. A few of the other photos in this book were shot by MAD's official photographer, Irving Schild. Since his work is in this book, he'll probably get some valuable clients!

FOREWORD
Number 10?!...
BY GEORGE WOODBRIDGE

I couldn't believe that Dick called to ask if I would write the foreword to his book. He usually just calls to ask for free artwork. This is the first time he's called to ask for free script!

More than anything in the world, I wanted to write the foreword for Dick's book, because I consider him a close friend and a talented writer.

Unfortunately, a series of medical problems has prevented me from doing so. First it was that pesky hangnail. Just as that was healing, I got an awful splinter in my foot, which made writing difficult, as you can imagine.

After a three-month recovery period, I was about to start the foreword, when a severe case of razor burn reared its ugly head.

Since the deadline for Dick's foreword is about an hour from now, I don't think I'll be able to write it. But I'm sure his book will be *so* good, it won't need a foreword!

SPECIAL BONUS PAGE OF PHOTOS!!!

(Actually we had these photos and we wanted to use them some place!!!)

WARNING!: THESE PICTURES WOULD SHOW TOTAL NUDITY IF THE PEOPLE WEREN'T DRESSED.

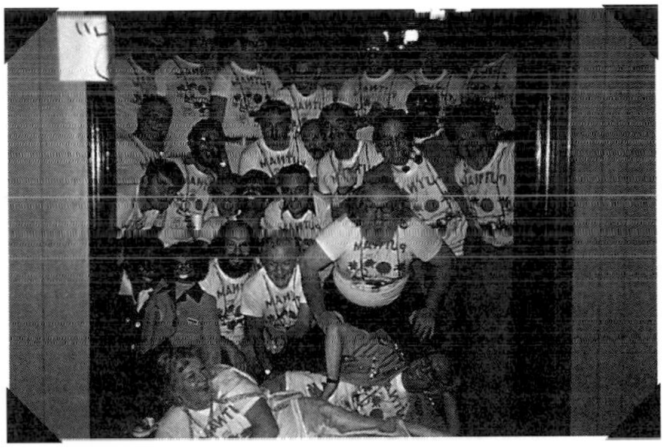

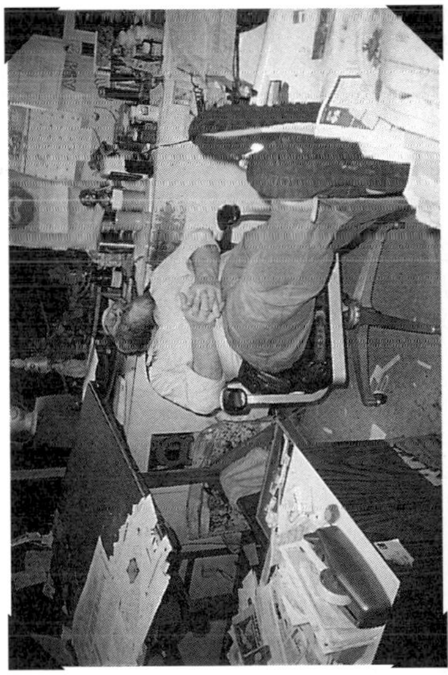

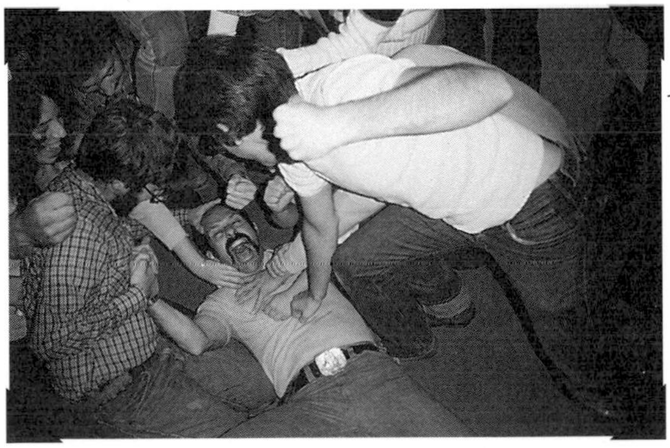

"The book was worth the price, wasn't it?"

THE "60 MINUTES" EXPERIENCE

Although Bill didn't do much merchandising, he did put out a few items. So when Bill's son Chris worked in the MAD mailroom, he took it upon himself to try to sell those items and he started a mini mail-order business called "MAD Stuff." He even produced a catalogue (Did I say "catalogue"? I mean two sheets of paper photocopied on both sides), which was really helpful because MAD merchandise was often hard to find. (Actually, that's changing now that we're under DC Comics' supervision. And the Warner Stores carry some MAD merchandise now, too.)

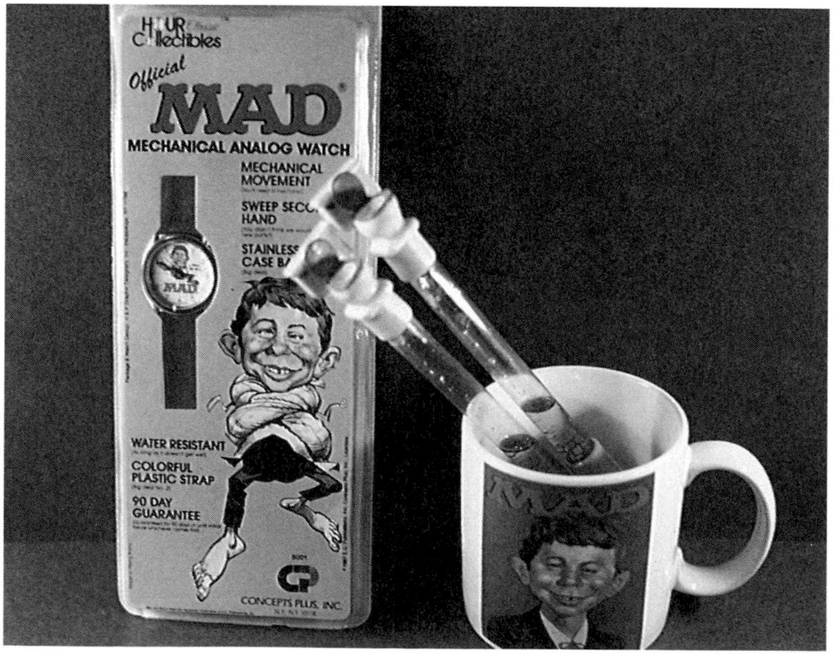
Official
MAD
MECHANICAL ANALOG WATCH
MECHANICAL MOVEMENT
WATER RESISTANT
COLORFUL PLASTIC STRAP
90 DAY GUARANTEE
CONCEPTS PLUS, INC.

One really popular item was the Alfred E. Neuman wristwatch. It showed Alfred all tied up in a straightjacket, so for the watch's hands, we had to use Alfred's feet. Then there were mugs and pens...

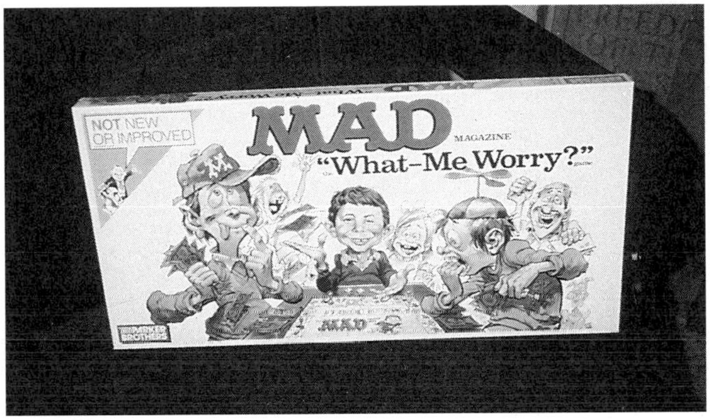
NOT NEW OR IMPROVED
MAD
MAGAZINE
"What-Me Worry?"

...and the MAD Game.

MAD had a very big hit with the MAD Game from Parker Brothers. Millions of units were sold. I particularly liked the way Parker Brothers advertised the game. For example, when it was re-released for a second Christmas season nothing about the game was changed, so the box proudly stated, "NOT NEW or IMPROVED!"

But I really loved the game because, in the true MAD spirit, it was a satire of one of America's most famous games—Monopoly. In the MAD version, the winner was the first person who could go bankrupt. So in the MAD Game, you wanted to get **rid** of all your money! And that made playing the game real fun. You'd land on "Chance" and win $5,000 and cheer because that's what you were used to doing in games, but then you'd remember this was the MAD game, and you'd just won $5,000 that you'd have to get rid of!

I did the MAD Game media tour for Parker Brothers, traveling to various markets to do radio, TV, and newspaper interviews, and it was great fun. On tour with me was Roy Brunett, a publicist from the Rowland Company, which was the public relations agency for Parker Brothers at the time.

A publicist goes along to do last-minute rearranging of the schedule if necessary, and to add new interviews if the opportunity arises. And in case they are traveling with a temperamental celebrity, the publicist is there to cater to the celebrity's bizarre needs. I'm easy to travel with, not one to make any unusual demands....Oh, okay, so I have ONE demand! I must have chocolate chip cookies in my dressing room...and there must be EXACTLY seventeen chocolate chip cookies on a plain white plate. A china plate, not a paper plate. And each of the seventeen cookies must contain thirty-seven chocolate chips. And the chips can't be near the edge of the cookie where they'll melt, or get broken. And the cookies must be baked so they're EXACTLY the same color brown as Sherwin Williams Desert Sand Tan. So, outside of having to carry a gallon of Sherwin Williams Desert Sand around with him, I made no unreasonable demands on Roy.

Actually, Roy and I hit it off really well. We had great long meals together because there was often a two-or three-hour gap between interviews. But, as these things go, when the tour ended, we lost track of each other. Then one day, it was a couple of years later, the phone rang, and it was Roy. "I left the Rowland Company," he said, "and you'll never guess where I work now. I do publicity for '60 Minutes.'"

I was not only excited for Roy, but right away I thought, maybe "60 Minutes" would care to something about MAD. I told Roy that MAD had satirized "60 Minutes" a dozen different ways, and I sent him copies of everything I could find. Being a good PR guy, Roy knew every story needed "a hook," and nothing I sent him seemed to have one.

A hook is what gets a story on TV. You never interview a teacher. You interview *the world's best teacher, the world's oldest teacher, the world's most corrupt teacher, the world's only trans-sexual Buddhist teacher* (but probably just for "Hard Copy" or "Inside Edition"—but you get the picture). Every story needs one, and for years, we never found the hook for MAD Magazine. Then one summer day I called Roy and said, "I've got the hook, and it's a natural! Next February MAD will be thirty-five years old! Here's a magazine that has survived thirty-five years without advertising itself, and without taking ads! Now, if that isn't a hook, what is?"

Roy agreed that this was at least something he could submit to the powers that be at "60 Minutes," and over the next few months the suggestion for a story about MAD Magazine chugged along. Then Don Hewitt, the long-time genius behind "60 Minutes," said he liked the idea; I was ecstatic.

But suddenly, I stopped dead in my tracks. I had never asked Bill if it was okay for MAD to be on "60 Minutes." Basically, I hadn't wanted to tell anyone about "60 Minutes" in case we never found the suitable hook. Besides, "60 Minutes" does only three stories a week, and they probably get thousands of suggestions a week, so it was the longest of long shots.

I went to see Bill, and popped the question: "Do you want to be on '60 Minutes'?"

Bill became animated. "I *love* '60 Minutes.' The question is, do they want us on '60 Minutes'?"

I told Bill how Roy and I had been pursuing it for a number of years, and that now we had a real shot at making it. Bill said he would be very excited to participate in a "60 Minutes" piece.

Then I asked Bill if there was a dark side to MAD I didn't know about, because "60 Minutes" is very thorough, and they'd find it. Bill assured me—as I had guessed—that there were no skeletons in MAD's closets. (Hell, our offices are so tiny, there are hardly any closets, period!)

After another couple of months, Roy called to say that Morley Safer had said he would like do the piece, and that David Teracamo would be producing it. David came up to the office to do some preliminary interviews and set up a filming schedule.

When they came to film, the staff was told to do whatever they would normally do, and that the crew from "60 Minutes" would be like a fly on the wall—observing everything, but staying out of the way. They filmed for several days and left.

Some weeks later I called Roy to ask how the footage looked. Roy said they liked the piece so much, they were going to save it for the fall premiere, rather than air it in the one or two remaining new shows that spring. I told Gaines and said I thought that could be interpreted two ways: The first was that they hated the footage, and they figured by the fall we would have forgotten about it. The second was that they REALLY did love the footage, and *were* saving it for the fall premiere. The latter turned out to be true, and it was a wonderful fourteen-minute puff piece for MAD!

The power "60 Minutes" has is incredible! Bill told me we picked up over $150,000 in new subscriptions right after the program aired—that's $150,000 **over** the normal number of new subscriptions! "60 Minutes" received hundreds of letters, many of which they forwarded to us, thanking them for paying "a long overdue tribute to MAD Magazine" and for "bringing back such fond memories of MAD." Just about everyone I'd ever met while on media tours or at comic book conventions has a favorite thing they remember from MAD Magazine, but I didn't realize the range, the *numbers* of people out there who have been touched by MAD. Men who were in the service overseas said MAD helped keep them in touch with what was happening back home. An eighty-year-old woman wrote in to say she was a subscriber, and they should have shown older people reading the magazine on "60 Minutes." The mail was truly wonderful.

But there was one letter that really stood out. On the piece there was a short interview section with Morley Safer asking questions of Bill, Nick Meglin, John Ficarra (on drums), and me. Morley asked what was the hardest thing about putting the magazine together. No one said anything. So after a long pause, I volunteered, "Stapling it!" Everyone broke up, including Morley, which you don't get to see very often. Then, among the letters sent to CBS was one from "ACME Stapling Company." (I may have the name wrong, but I'll never forget the content.) It said, "On a recent '60 Minutes' program, a gentleman indicated that they were having trouble stapling MAD Magazine. Our company is one of the world's largest manufacturers of stapling equipment, and I'm sure we can solve any problem they have!" Okay, so not everybody understands MAD humor!

"...You won't find this quote in the text."

For weeks after the piece, Bill got congratulatory calls from all over the country, and subscriptions stayed above normal for a couple of months. Bill told me that the "60 Minutes" segment was the nicest thing that had ever happened to MAD Magazine, and since I had pursued it for such a long time, he wanted to buy me something VERY special.

BILL: So, what do you want?

(He really was serious...so I thought, what the heck, I'll ask.)

DICK: A new boat!

BILL: How much is a new boat?

DICK: One hundred thousand dollars.

BILL: That's a little more than I wanted to spend!

DICK: Fourteen minutes of airtime on "60 Minutes"??? If you'd *paid* for it, it'd be about nine million dollars! And you won't buy me a crappy little hundred-thousand-dollar boat??

BILL: Can't you be happy with a more modest boat? Something around fifteen thousand dollars?

(I really think he would have bought me a $15,000 boat—but hey, I loved seeing MAD on "60 Minutes," too!)

DICK: Billy, I'm not asking for a boat, but if you'd really like to buy me some thing, I'd sure like a new computer.

BILL: How much?

DICK: About twenty-five hundred dollars.

BILL: Go buy one, but make sure you get something you really like, and if it's a little more than that, that's okay, too!

So I did buy myself a computer, and I sent the bill to Gaines, which he paid promptly. I thanked him, but since he liked it much better when I nagged him, I bitched and moaned every time a more powerful computer was released. I would storm into Bill's office with a fistful of computer ads, and wave them in his face while I ranted and raved!

DICK: Thanks for buying me that piece of crap!

BILL: *You* picked out that piece of crap!

DICK: That's all you can get for twenty-five hundred dollars—crap!

BILL: Are the new computers that much better?

DICK: Well, for one thing, with the new computers you don't need a hamster inside to generate the power.

BILL: You love animals. Be happy you got one that came with a hamster!

DICK: All right, *so I'm happy!* Someday, I'll send you a thank you note. But a twenty-five hundred dollar computer isn't powerful enough to generate a thank you note!

I'd slam the door and leave, and Bill and I would both be happy.

FOREWORD
Number 11?!...

BY SAM VIVIANO

Is Dick DeBartolo funny, or what? Don't ask me. After all, I have illustrated only a handful of the hundreds of thousands of stories, articles, parodies, and monographs Dick has written for MAD Magazine over his long career. And, to be honest, I was much too busy trying to get my drawing finished to read any of it. But I do know this: Dick DeBartolo is an amazing person, whose skills are not limited to crafting words for the printed page. Author, adventurer, scientist, sailor, public advocate, television personality—all are terms that could only begin to describe him. Indeed, it is no exaggeration to call Dick a "Renaissance Man"—he has told me this himself many times, as I sat entranced at his feet listening to him recount his exploits.

MY HERO
©SAM VIVIANO 1994

Of course, we all know how Dick emerged victorious from the late-night talk-show wars to wide and lasting public acclaim, but how many of you are aware of his earlier film career as Errol Flynn's stunt man? And while his heroics in the battle of Panmunjom are well-documented, his behind-the-scenes shuttle diplomacy in the Middle East went largely ignored by the press. Moreover, the full story of his involvement in the Second Vatican Council has yet to be told. While these adventures could fill several books, they pale beside the most amazing untold tale in the life of Dick DeBartolo: how he single-handedly created the most successful humor magazine of our century, MAD. Ever the paragon of modesty, Dick has never publicly acknowledged that he was the mastermind behind this enterprise, even to the extent of installing an innocent from Queens named Bill Gaines as its nominal publisher.

MY HERO
©SAM VIVIANO 1994

This saga has left me spellbound the many, many times Dick DeBartolo has cornered me in a hallway and made me listen to it. So it is with a kind of dizzy glee that I accept the honor of writing this foreword to the book that will finally tell his story to the world.

And when you finish reading it, perhaps you can tell me: Is that Dick DeBartolo a funny man, or what?

FLY BABIES

One of the most famous MAD stories—and the one about which veteran MAD staffers are constantly asked, "Is it true?"—is the MAD trip to Haiti story. It *IS* true, and if you haven't heard it already, you will at least read about it now. Just about to his dying day, Gaines read ALL the subscription mail. So when our one subscriber in Haiti did not renew his subscription, Bill knew. Unlike other magazines, MAD sent only a single postcard to inform subscribers that their subscription was about to expire. (Now we do even less; we just put a note on the magazine's brown wrapper.)

Other magazines start sending renewals along with your first issue—and they send follow-up letters YEARS after you've let a subscription lapse. Not MAD! You'll also notice that our single renewal card was unlike *anything* those other magazines would send out.

The point is, we don't pester our subscribers with mail. But when Gaines noticed that MAD's Haitian subscriber did not renew...well, he felt we should have at least one subscriber in Haiti. So, as one of the world's most expensive practical jokes, he took the entire MAD staff to the guy's house to beg him to renew! Surprise! The guy *does* renew! (And, as I tell this story, I always add that two months later a second person in Haiti subscribed—doubling our Haitian subscriptions for an outlay of a mere $20,000 or so!) Some years after the trip, Bill told this story on "Later with Bob Costas," and Bob asked Bill if the man still subscribed. Bill said he'd lost track of the guy, but that if he happened to be watching, he should get in contact again. Shortly after the program, the man, a lawyer named Paul Tomar, called Bill. (The power of television is awesome! Now all I need is a talk show spot, and maybe Paul Tomar will buy this book.)

It is a great story, but the real reason the expedition to Haiti will go down in history is that it was the start of the famous MAD trips, which have been going on for over thirty years. There's been only one trip since Bill died in June 1992, and with lots of changes going on at MAD, I don't know what the deal is going to be on future trips. (That last trip was to Monaco, but I didn't go because you had to dress up; and besides, Bill wasn't going to be there.)

But while Bill was alive, he organized and paid for all the MAD trips. Staffers were invited to come based on a complicated formula devised by Gaines, which in turn was based on the number of pages of material you had sold to MAD in a given twelve-month period. For example, one year the base to be eligible for the trip might be 26 published pages. If you had sold MAD that much material, you were eligible to go—*maybe*. Knowing Gaines, it wasn't quite that simple, and for various reasons, the number of pages you'd had published might be multiplied by .03, or .077, or whatever. Gaines once explained his rules to me, but I never understood them. I just felt lucky to have sold MAD enough material to qualify for all but the first couple of MAD trips. Altogether, I've been on twenty forays with the usual gang of idiots to the far reaches of this planet: Bora Bora, Moscow, Kenya, Paris, Rome, Monte Carlo, even New Orleans.

One thing that made these trips special was that they were the only time—once a year in the past, then starting in the mid-eighties, about once every two years—that the

"...Our single renewal card was unlike anything those other magazines would send out."

MAD 485 MADison Avenue, New York, N.Y. 10022

Dear Reader:
Boy are you lucky! Your subscription to MAD expires with this issue! But just in case you're the type who never profits from past mistakes, here's your chance to re-subscribe!

In the U.S.A.—8 issues $13.75, 24 issues $33.75, or 40 issues $53.75. We cannot be responsible for cash lost or stolen in the mails. CHECK OR MONEY ORDER PREFERRED!

Outside U.S.A. (Including Canada)—8 issues $17.75, 24 issues $43.75, or 40 issues $69.75. Payment must be made in U.S. Funds by International Money Order or check drawn on U.S.A. bank.

We will not supply your name to list-renter mail-order advertisers, and we will not annoy you with additional re-subscription literature. This will be your only notice!

NAME (please print) ____________________

ADDRESS ____________________

CITY __________ **STATE** ______ **ZIP CODE** ______

entire staff was ever in one place at one time. (You took the MAD office tour earlier, right? You can see that the reason the MAD staff has to meet in other countries is that our offices are so tiny, so terribly cluttered, so noisy, and chaotic. Like, for example, every phone rings in every office. Whoever's annoyed enough by the ringing answers the phone, and leaves the message under a pile of clutter. Consequently, you won't get your message until it's found. So while your chances of getting a message are good, you probably won't get it in the same week as the phone call. You can see that it's an impossible place to work—which is why I love it so much!) Most longtime contributors work as freelancers, and consequently do 98 percent of their work in their own studios, which are all over the country, anyway. MAD is largely put together via fax machines and Fedex packages. So when the entire staff does get together there's a lot to talk about. That's why the MAD trips became so important.

Basically, we began with a series of Caribbean excursions; then Bill concentrated more on planning trips to places that excelled in great food—and even better wine. What Bill did on the MAD trips was eat, drink, and read. He read a lot, and rarely left his room at the hotel. To Bill, sitting around in his underwear reading a book was the perfect way to spend the hours between meals, and the perfect vacation. Then, after a number of MAD trips, Bill felt he'd run through all the usual vacation spots, so he began to pick diverse locations like Hong Kong, even Africa.

...If laughter is a good medecine, is this book tax deductible as a medical expense?

About the only downside to these trips was the fact that we were all assigned roommates. The roommate was, of course, another MAD Magazine talent—respected, maybe even revered—but mutual admiration didn't necessarily translate into being good roommates. Sometimes a smoker ended up with a nonsmoker. Or a nondrinker with a drinker. I don't smoke or drink, but I like to stay up very late. And get up late. And listen to a Walkman to fall asleep. That was fine for some of the MAD folks, but not for others.

For one trip my roommate was Paul Coker. Now Paul draws "Horrifying Clichés," one of my favorites of the features that appear in MAD from time to time, and he's illustrated a few of my satires, but we do not make good roommates. For one thing, Paul likes to go to bed at about 9 p.m.! On the trip where we were roommates, I pointed out to Paul that we were on

I'M SICK.
I LOST MY PASSPORT.
When do we eat?
I have to pee.
Where's IRVING?
I WANT to call my BROKER.
Not another SOUVENIR stand?!
ROME
MOSCOW
MARRAKESH
ATHENS
MEXICO CITY
PARIS
NAIROBI
HONG KONG
LONDON
MADRID
TOKYO
PAPEETE

vacation in a foreign land, out to have a good time and enjoy the nightlife! So he extended his bedtime to 9:15 p.m. I found out on that trip that Paul also likes to get up early, like ridiculously early, like 6 a.m.! I am catatonic at 6 a.m., even at 9 a.m., so it was not a match made in Heaven.

On this trip we were visiting different cities, so we changed hotels two or three times. I discovered that Paul and I have very different packing techniques. I like to wait till the last minute, put my suitcase in the middle of the floor, take each drawer from the bureau and turn it upside down, spilling the contents into the suitcase. It's quick, and I never forget anything I've put in a drawer. But Paul likes to start packing a day or two before we're set to leave. To keep things wrinkle-free he likes to put cellophane in all his pants, his shoes, his shirts, and I guess even his underwear; so, many mornings I awoke at 6:15 a.m. to the sound of crinkling cellophane. And I *prayed* to God that the airline, or the bell captain, would lose Paul's luggage! A great artist, but Paul is not my kind of roommate.

But that was only one trip. For years and years, I roomed with artist Don Martin, and that worked out

MAD
JACK DAVIS

MAN OF MANY HATS
AND FOOD.

fairly well. Don and I have done a lot of work together. He illustrated one of my MAD paperbacks, and I wrote many of the stories he used in his MAD books. It was from Don that I learned how the artist's mind differs from the writer's mind. When I was writing "Bullets over Broadway," a musical satire, I would say to Don something like, "In the opening panel, we see fifty girls in a line kicking..." and Don would talk aloud as he made notes: "Four girls in a line kicking." I would ask, "Why not fifty?" and Don would say, "Because I have to draw them!"

Although Don draws funny, he's very quiet in person. You could knock yourself out trying to break Don up, and maybe get him to smile. The only time I was really able to break Don up was when I least expected to, or wanted to. We were on the MAD trip to France and we were walking down a street in Paris, when I stopped to pet a tiny little poodle. Now I love dogs and usually they love me—in fact, just days before, I had impressed Bill with my ability to tame a stray—but as I held up my hand, this poodle leaped at my face, growling and baring his teeth. I fell over backwards and Don was convulsed! When he finally composed himself, he said, "Bill told me you had a way with dogs. Now I see what he means."

I'll tell the story of the OTHER French dog later on, but for now, here are some other fond memories from various MAD trips. (Although we didn't take the trips in alphabetical order, I've arranged them that way. People don't die in alphabetical order, yet the newspaper arranges them that way, so it seems like a good system.)

AFRICA

One of the funniest lines on the African trip was delivered by Al Jaffee. We were at some jungle camp, sitting around a roaring fire so the animals wouldn't attack us, when a young couple joined us. They asked what the staff of MAD Magazine was doing at such a remote location and Al answered, "We're on a tour of Bermuda, booked by a Polish travel agent!" (I guess that line is politically incorrect now. But it's still pretty funny. And while I can't recall the background of our travel agent, as you'll learn later on, the possibility that we would be booked to Africa by way of Bermuda wasn't really so far-fetched.)

For two days of the tour we stayed at a resort called Treetops. I'm not too particular when I travel, but I sure do want a place that has hot water, a shower, and a toilet you can flush. When Bill mentioned that Treetops was a resort built—where else?—on the tops of trees, I became concerned.

DICK: Do we go up there for a few hours, or what?

BILL: We go up there for two days!

DICK: If it's built in the trees, what are the facilities like?

BILL: What do you care?? You love animals. You'll see animals, plenty of animals!

DICK: I mean, do we have separate rooms?

BILL: No. It's in the trees. You'll have a cot.

DICK: And what about eating? How do we get our food?

BILL: A truck comes once a day with picnic baskets.

DICK: We're going to picnic for two days and nights?

BILL: I'm sure they'll bring some cookies or something. Stop complaining, it's a once-in-a-lifetime experience.

DICK: All right, one last question. Is there running water?

BILL: I don't think so. There'll be buckets for you to wash in.

DICK: I'm talking about going to the bathroom.

BILL: Well you can't have a toilet in a tree! They probably have an outhouse or something you climb down to!

I was excited about the African trip, but I sure had concerns about staying at this Treetops place. It sounded so crude. I packed plenty of candy bars and boxes of cookies. I bought a portable radio. As we approached the resort,

I mentally prepared myself for the worst. While we climbed the stairs, game wardens stood by with guns, and I felt like we were being sent to prison. But once inside the place, I started to look around...and, hey, there were actual bedrooms. It's two guys to a bedroom, but they were pretty nice. Small, but clean. And there's a sink, and running water—even toilets that flushed! Then I asked one of the innkeepers about meals, and he told me hot meals were served in the dining room. And I can tell you, the food was delicious!

"...Gaines, stretched out on the couch, emitting ungodly snoring sounds that were loud enough to scare the elephants away!"

All in all, the place was really comfortable. About the only thing that was a little crowded was the dining room. Everybody sat at very long tables with their backs just about to the walls. Since there was no room for waiters to move about, the food was served on a moving board that was loaded with food then pushed along the center of the table toward the end. People served themselves as the plates moved by.

After I took a tour of the place, I sought out Gaines. "You son-of-a-bitch! I thought you said there was no running water? No hot food? No toilets??" Bill just smiled and said, "I really had you going for a few weeks, didn't I!"

Once everyone was inside Treetops, the stairways were raised so the animals could roam freely under our digs. Everyone wanted to see the herds of elephants that were said to come late at night and a dozen or more of us sat up until two or three in the morning, our cameras at hand. But the elephants did not come. Finally, almost everyone turned in. About 4 a.m., we heard the trumpeting we were waiting for, and Sergio Aragonés ran through the halls, waking up all the MAD guys. Bleary-eyed, but with cameras at the ready, we dashed out to the open terrace—*surprise!* There were no elephants, just Gaines, stretched out on the couch, emitting ungodly snoring sounds that were loud enough to scare the elephants away!

RZORZZZR
ROWAAU"

But we did see elephants—I can prove it.

MAD
1

MAD
2

1- We visit the elephants.

2- The elephants visit us.

AMSTERDAM

Amsterdam is a clean, quaint city, with lots of small, picturesque canals. But as I recall, there wasn't a lot to do at night, so writer Lou Silverstone (who no longer works at MAD) and I were forced to visit the city's famous red light district. We roamed up and down the narrow streets until we came upon a giant porno store. The sign above the store listed the sort of books and films it sold, and the list was pretty inclusive:

S & M SEX
GAY SEX
LESBIAN SEX
BONDAGE SEX
ANIMAL SEX
CHILD SEX
UNUSUAL SEX

Lou read the sign from top to bottom, then he turned to me and said, "God, I'd love see what the 'unusual sex' is!"

CASABLANCA

Do you have a favorite joke, or one-liner, that breaks you up, or at least makes you smile, *every time* you hear it, even if you deliver it yourself? I'll tell the one that never failed to put Gaines away—but it only worked on MAD trips.

We were in Casablanca, and had just gotten in from the airport. As we were getting off the bus in front of our hotel, hordes of locals literally surrounded us. They were selling anything and everything—necklaces, earrings, postcards, perfume, ashtrays, wallets, clothing, food, pictures, trays, glasses, vases, you name it. And with each step we took, a new person would appear, pushing their wares in our faces. I was next to Gaines and as we struggled to move I turned toward him and said, "God I can't believe it! We come all this distance—you would think there would be someone selling some sort of souvenirs or little trinkets to bring back home....I'm really disappointed."

Bill loved it, and he laughed every time I used it—or one of its many variations. You know, like in Rome: "Bill, if you see a church, let me know. I'd love to see an Italian church."

Or in Tahiti: "Bill, if you see any nice scenery, let me know. I want to take a picture. I'm especially looking for a scene with a palm tree."

Or in Paris: "Bill, do you think there's any place in this city that might sell postcards with—oh, maybe a picture of the Eiffel Tower on it?

ITALY

Duck (Don) Edwing breaks me up. And fortunately, I have the same effect on him, so when we're traveling, we hang out together as much as possible. We're also both coffee freaks—we can drink coffee any hour of the day or night. But when we were in Italy, we found that it's difficult to get coffee as we know it here in the U.S. It's not that we didn't like Italian coffee—we just wanted *full* cups—not the little demitasse cups. One day we were in this little Italian cafe and we ordered coffee. Duck tried to indicate with his hands that we wanted large cups of coffee. The waitress seemed to understand because she nodded her head and said, *"Grande."* We repeated that word still making

gestures of giant cups. Ten minutes later, she brought our coffee, but once again in those tiny cups. Duck drank his in one gulp and said, "I've been in Italy for four days, and so far I've only had three tablespoons of coffee!"

One time on that trip we were sightseeing in this huge church when Duck nudged me and said, "Do you want to know the latest news?" I didn't know what he meant, so I said, "Yeah!" Duck pointed to the Latin phrases carved in marble and running along the upper wall of the church. Then he said, "Oh, it stopped!" That really broke me up. It took Duck's weird mind to connect those Latin phrases carved centuries ago with the moving "News of the Day" sign in Times Square!

Al Jaffee was kind enough to remind me of a couple of my one-liners that he remembers fondly from Italy. On one museum tour, after roaming through fifteen or twenty rooms filled floor-to-ceiling with priceless art, I turned to Jaffee and said, "God isn't dead. He just afford the upkeep anymore!"

Another time we were at the Vatican and our tour guide was showing us the Sistine Chapel. She told us it took Michelangelo fifteen years to paint the ceiling. "Yeah, but it was TWO COATS," I informed her.

Everyone broke up and later on, Dave Berg asked if he could use that line in one of his "Lighter Side" features. Of course I said, "Sure." But I couldn't resist adding, "But why break your long running streak and put something really funny in your feature?"

JAPAN

On each MAD trip there are one or two dinners that the entire staff attends, but for other meals, the MAD crew splits up into small groups, each going off to seek its own restaurant.

One night when we were in Japan, four of us went to this one restaurant where it turned out almost no one spoke any English at all. Of course we had to order from menus printed entirely in Japanese, and of course we had no idea what we were ordering. When the food arrived and the waitress put it down in front of us, we all just stared. Even though we were seeing it in person, we still had no idea what anything was, and no one felt like eating any of it! What the heck were we going to do? Just then, I spied Lenny Brenner and Bill walking down the street. We were sitting at a window table, so we waved frantically, trying to get their attention. They came over and pressed their noses against the window. We pointed to the food and asked, "Do you guys want to eat our dinners?" And they did. Bill and Lenny had just finished eating **their** dinners, but since they had walked a **full** block, they had worked up an appetite, and were ready to eat again! As we got up to leave, the workers in the restaurant became very concerned that we were just walking out, so I tried to explain that we merely *ordered* food. After it's on the table, these two BIG people—Lenny and Bill— come and eat it!

PUERTO RICO

On one of our Puerto Rico trips, a lady of the night approached Arnie Kogen, one of the most athletic-looking of the MAD writers. Arnie has a really dry sense of humor and when she told him she would do anything he wanted for $50, Arnie thought about the offer for a moment. Then he asked, "How much for just heavy petting?"

The next day, a group of us were sitting on the beach when Arnie came out from a dip in the ocean. One of us asked him how the water was. Arnie's reply? "Needs salt"!

On another MAD trip to Puerto Rico, Sergio Aragonés and I happened to approach the single unoccupied lounge chair by the pool at the same time. Acting on instinct, we got into an argument over who saw it first, and then we started some gentle pushing. Under his breath, Sergio asked if I happened to know judo. Surprise, I did! He told me to throw him over my shoulder onto the lawn that surrounded the pool. I did, and I got the chair! I assume I looked real macho to the innocent bystanders because I'm five feet, eight inches and Sergio is over six feet. Sergio didn't mind being "the fall guy," and we used that same routine several times on that trip. To be honest, we did it anytime we saw new people at the pool that we thought we could sucker into our "fight."

Sergio and I were also pretty good at falling down flights of stairs—of course, carpeted stairs were preferred. At one hotel we stayed at we worked up a fairly elaborate routine. Sergio would fall down the stairway from the mezzanine, landing on the hotel lobby floor. Meanwhile, I would stay up on the mezzanine hidden from view. Sergio, lying there on the lobby floor, would call for a doctor. I would appear, say, "I'm a doctor," and then I would fall down the stairs, landing on top of Sergio! Seconds later we would announce it was a joke. We didn't want anyone calling for a real doctor, or worse yet, calling an ambulance!

Unfortunately, Sergio and I only get to fall and fake fights on MAD trips. Since he lives on the West Coast, we meet face to face only about once a year.

RUSSIA

One trip I wasn't particularly fond of was the trip to Russia. It was impossible to get comfortable there. I thought perhaps my hotel room was bugged, and I think a lot of the other guys did too, because it was the quietist MAD trip I ever went on. Not too much joking around. And the food was *terrible*—even the soda. I don't like wine or beer with a meal, I like soda. But in Russia I don't think they ever washed the bottles, so the soda was somewhat grainy. I even tried ordering my soda "without sticks or stones," but it didn't help. (Shortly after the MAD trip, Coca Cola started shipping to Russia; unfortunately, too late to do us any good.)

At the hotel where we stayed, breakfast was served at 9 a.m., whether or not you were in the dining room! And I mean at 9 a.m. *sharp*—plates of eggs and "bacon" (not even our VIVID imaginations could let that chunk of wood pass for bacon) were placed on all the tables and stayed there till lunch. If you didn't get downstairs till 11 a.m., breakfast was still waiting for you! While the food was bad, the service was *awful.* Once the waiter left, it could be hours before he returned. After our second day there, Gaines caught on and ordered the entire meal at one time.

...This is printed here only for decoration.

Arnie Kogen on Bill Gaines

It was the MAD trip to Suriname, South America. Bill Gaines and I were alone on the veranda of the hotel. The other MAD staffers were out doing their thing. Some had gone off to taunt the natives about their country's GNP. Sergio Aragonés was coming on to a rubber tree. Al Jaffee was giving a snappy answer to a one-armed beggar. "Sir, can you spare any change for a starving cripple?" "No, I'm saving all my spare change for the ruling aristocracy."

Nick Meglin was following Sergio...wanted to know if the rubber tree had a friend. Bill was on his fourth Chivas with a little umbrella. I was slugging down ramos fizzes. We were both kicking back. Bill was loose. He was talkative. He told me some details about his life. Personal stuff he never told anyone before or since. I got to know the real Bill Gaines. He revealed intimate details. Such as:

On the first day of autumn, he liked to dress up in below-the-knee Anne Klein skirts.

He once paid $50 for a night with Eleanor Roosevelt.

He thought Bogart sucked in *Casablanca, Citizen Kane* was overrated, but thought that Tony Curtis was mesmerizing in *The Vikings.*

His passion was not gourmet foods and fine wines, but Appalachian clog dancing.

He regretted that he was too old to turn pro.

He once sued the Pillsbury Dough Boy for unauthorized use of his physique.

He was one-quarter Cherokee.

Bill made me promise to keep all this a secret. Never to tell anyone. I promised. Bill's dead now. He'll never know.

Since I'm an avid shopper I went to GUM, the biggest department store in Moscow, but there weren't very many high-tech gadgets to look at, and one didn't bring clothes back from Russia, at least not then. While I was in the sporting goods department, I noticed a small outboard motor. It was selling for $389, about the same price it was in the States, which surprised me. It seemed really cheap, until I learned that the average salary in Moscow was $7 a month, so there wasn't a lot left over for recreational sports! But I did get to visit a boat club—yes, they had boat clubs in Russia 25 years ago, but there was one slight difference. The club's 115 members owned one boat! (I don't recall seeing much sunshine in Russia, and I'm not quite sure how you divide what at best would be 17 sunny weekends among 115 sailors.) But they really thought I was putting them on when I told them *I* owned a boat—all by myself. One lady kept asking, "You mean you can take the boat out whenever YOU want?" What a concept!

Because conditions there were so bad, we didn't see much smiling among the citizenry either. It seemed like everything in Russia was under construction, and grimy and gray. (Except for the subway system which, I must admit, was spotless. A far cry from the New York City subways I was used to.) One night, I decided to take a bath at the hotel. I filled the tub with water, but the water was so filthy I was cleaner by not taking a bath. After that I stuck with showers, because it's harder to tell how dirty water is when it comes out in a spray!

To help make our stay even more pleasant, some of the dourest people we saw were the hotel matrons who let us into our rooms. They were right out of bad Hollywood women's prison movies! Each floor in our hotel had one: a large, heavyset woman all dressed in black carrying a huge set of keys. *No* communication was possible. So you can imagine how incongruous it was (or maybe just plain hopeful) that Frank Jacobs insisted on treating them like he would the people at the front desk of a friendly hotel back in the States. I'll never forget the night Frank came bouncing up the stairs, grinned and inquired of the matron, "Any messages for Jacobs?" She was not amused! As a matter of fact, I'm sure she didn't know what the hell he was talking about. But 25 years later, *I* still smile when I think about it.

THAILAND

Bill and I rarely had sex together—oh, suddenly you're starting to read with more interest??? Okay, so Bill and I NEVER had sex together! I think it was because neither one of us smoked, and we wouldn't know what to do after sex was over. Besides, I want to stay at MAD because of my writing talent, not my body!

But on the Thailand MAD trip, Bill told me that indirectly we DID have sex together. That really puzzled me, and I asked him to explain. But he merely said, "YOU figure it out!" I finally did. It's not a very long story, so follow along.

While in Thailand, a bunch of us went to a special "massage parlor." The MAD guys didn't all go together, there would have been too much laughing for anyone to perform, but each night a few of us went. One evening, Sergio Aragonés and I ventured over to the parlor to have our muscles relaxed. After paying our admission at the front door, we were shown a selection of beautiful women—behind glass, no less—and they each wore a number. The numbers had to be pinned on *very* carefully because they were wearing very little. We were told that we were looking at the girls through a two-way mirror; we could see them, but they couldn't see us. However, Sergio started making faces and drawing on the glass and the ladies started laughing—well, so much for the two-way mirror. Sergio and I picked our girls and paired off to separate rooms.

But I was feeling bad that it wasn't really a two-way mirror, because I was sure the girl I had picked would have much preferred Sergio instead. Sergio was the handsome, six-foot football player-type. (Today he's a handsome, six-foot, retired football player-type!) When we got to the room, though, the girl said, "I'm so glad you picked me. The other guy had too much hair here!" She pointed to the top of her head. "Yours is much sexier!" Rubbing my scalp, she continued, "Men with falling hair are much more desirable here! Very sexy!" That was great news. After that encounter, I didn't feel self-conscious about my rapidly thinning hair, and I didn't bother wearing my baseball cap for the rest of the Thai trip! In fact, I exposed my pate to every pretty woman I saw!

But to bring this story full circle, Sergio talked to Gaines and described the women we had picked. It turned out that the night before, Gaines had been with the same woman I had. So you see, in a strange way, we did have a sexual encounter in common. It was a threesome, but only two of us were there at a time! For a while, I felt sorry for our girlfriend at the massage parlor. She liked men with a small amount of hair on their head, and Gaines had a heck of a lot more than me! Maybe she fantasized about Yul Brenner while she was with Gaines. But then I thought, knowing Gaines, he left a much large gratuity than I did, so it was a nice variety for the lady in question. She had an overweight, hairy, generous guy one night, and a sexy, balding, cheap guy the next!

TRINIDAD

I'm a little wacky about animals, especially dogs, and I found an ally in Lou Silverstone, who is as much of an animal lover as I am. In Trinidad there were dozens of mangy, hungry dogs on the outskirts of town. Lou and I tried to buy dog food to give to them, but no one seemed to understand what we were talking about. We finally learned that in Trinidad there was no such thing as commercial dog food—people fed dogs leftovers and table scraps. So Lou and I would collect the "good stuff" left over from MAD dinners, and we'd go into luncheonettes and order ten or twelve different dishes to go, and then we'd take a cab to the edge of town and feed as many dogs as we could. We wished we could feed all the hungry strays we saw, but we did the best we could.

Paul Peter Porges on Bill Gaines

Bill Gaines was a fantastic eccentric, and a most loyal friend. He had a wine cellar in the middle of his living room that had the most extrodinary wines; and on the other hand, he had only one jacket. One lousy jacket, that looked like it came out of a flea market. He never owned an overcoat, and he was a multi-millionaire! But what really sticks in my mind about Bill was his love of greasy foods! My connection with him was mostly through food. Once interviewed by Al Goldstein, one of his good friends, he admitted one of his passions was greasy food. My most remembered adventure with Bill was on the MAD trip to Austria, which is, after all, where I was born and raised.

Bill had an obsession with Austrian Viennese sausage, which are truly unique. Actually, he adored **any** kind of sausage, even frankfurters. But on the MAD trip to Austria, he had his mind made up he that he must have the Austrian sausages that were sold at little stands throughout the city. They're like the frankfurter stands we have here in America. So we arrive in Vienna early in the morning, and as we board the bus Bill says to me, "I want to take everybody to eat those Viennese sausages at one of those stands, where they have choices of different mustards and different rolls." I could see his mouth was starting to salivate. I said, "Bill, it's eight o'clock in the morning, and we're going to be traveling on a highway! No way will we find a place like one of those stands!" Bill didn't want to hear it. He told me that we were in my native homeland, and that I WAS RESPONSIBLE for finding Viennese sausages! I asked the driver if there were any Würstlstands—which is what they are called—open at this hour. The driver looked at me like I was void of any sense! So we go on a superhighway where we'll have to drive for four or five hours to get to our destination. All during that time, Bill's mood got darker and darker, because he had made up his mind he wanted to go to a Würstlstand! He called me to his seat again! "Hey you, fuck! Where are those Würstlstands??? This is your home!! I hold you personally responsible!"

Bill made me tense, so I went to the driver and said, "The big man **has got** to eat!!" The driver told me what I already knew, there were no Würstlstands on the highway. But, he said, there was a food stop, sort of an Austrian version of a stop on the New Jersey Turnpike. Actually, it turned out to be much better. It looked like a little guest house. I found the owner, and told him that big man must have Würstls. The owner said, "Würstls, who do you think we are? But I'll tell what we do have. Goulash soup." So I told Gaines he was going to have something special, and that when they served it he was going to love it!

When Gaines tasted the goulash soup, he had tears in his eyes! It fulfilled all his desires! It was greasy, it was rich, and it was cheap!

FOREWORD

...OH, SURE ... I WAS AT MAD 15 MINUTES BEFORE De BARTOLO AND HE GETS A BOOK!! DOESN'T SENIORITY COUNT FOR ANYTHING?...AND IF THAT DOESN'T BEAT ALL... LISTEN TO THIS... WHEN I FIRST MET "DICK"... HIS FULL NAME WAS ZICK Zee ZARTOLO!!

HE EVEN CHANGED THE LETTERS FROM "Z" TO "D" SO HE WOULD BE FIRST ALPHABETICALLY!

GAINES ALWAYS SAID TO ME...

...WHAT CAN I TELL YOU, SCUMBAG, CHANGE YOUR NAME TO ADWING OR SOMETHING!

DUCK EDWING

AMERICANS EXPRESS (THEMSELVES)

Here a few of the other fun things that happened on MAD trips. Which MAD trips they occurred on really doesn't matter—it was just the MAD guys being MAD guys! Whenever a group of us would go out to eat, we would divide the check up equally at the end of the meal. Naturally no one checked the arithmetic of the person doing the dividing, and Al Jaffee, in particular, never had any idea of what the amount owed would be. Even when Al was told, he might still be confused. If the amount each of us owed was $15, Al would still have to ask, "Did he say we owe *fifteen* dollars—or *fifty* dollars??"

I don't know who hatched the plan to take advantage of Jaffee's bad math sense, but this was it: Since Al seemed willing to pay any amount he was told to pay, whoever divided up the check at the end of the meal would add at least $10 to the amount Al was told to kick in. If everyone's share for a dinner was $25, we'd tell Al to put in $35. Al's overpayment was kept in a separate kitty, and over the period of a ten-day trip, Al was overcharged something close to $200. At first we didn't know exactly what to do with the money we'd collected, but after some discussion it was decided that we would sneak into his room and put the money (in small bills) in his luggage...and never mention it again! We figured that all those hours Al spent wondering where that wad of money came from would drive him nuts, and that he would NEVER suspect it was really his own money!!! (Hey, Al...I guess you know now! And by the way, a bunch of us bought a dozen copies of this book to save money. If you want a copy at the bargain price, your share is only $41.20!)

John Putnam, the original art director of MAD, taught me a wonderful game that we always played on MAD trips. It worked best on captive audiences, like people in elevators. Here's the setup: John would already be standing in an elevator full of strangers, waiting for it leave the first floor. Then I would walk into the elevator, and immediately John would start an ad-lib conversation. I would jump right in with wild replies. Here's my favorite.

(John is on the elevator as I enter.)

JOHN: Excuse me, but aren't you Nick Manus, the famous architect?

DICK: Yes, do you know my work?

JOHN: Didn't you put up that forty-story skyscraper in Chicago?

DICK: Yeah, I put it up, but it fell over!

JOHN: Oh, my God! Was it faulty plans?

DICK: I didn't have any plans! I've put up two dozen twenty-story skyscrapers, so I know what I'm doing. Then I find out the firm that drew up the plans for my twenty story buildings wants eighty thousand dollars to draw up a set of plans for a forty-story building! I told them to forget about it. I figured I'd just put up two twenty-story buildings, one on top of the other. You would expect them to stay up, wouldn't you? (John nods vigorously) But they didn't! What a mess!

(Arriving at our floor, we would exit the elevator together, continuing the conversation till the elevator leaves with its stunned occupants.)

John's favorite was this one. I am already on the elevator when John enters.

DICK: Dr. Putnam, the famous surgeon?

JOHN: Yes, have you read my books?

DICK: No, just the excerpts in the *Reader's Digest.*

JOHN: I was not pleased with those excerpts. They left out some of the most

"...I'd just put up two twenty-story buildings, one on top of the other. You would expect them to stay up, wouldn't you?"

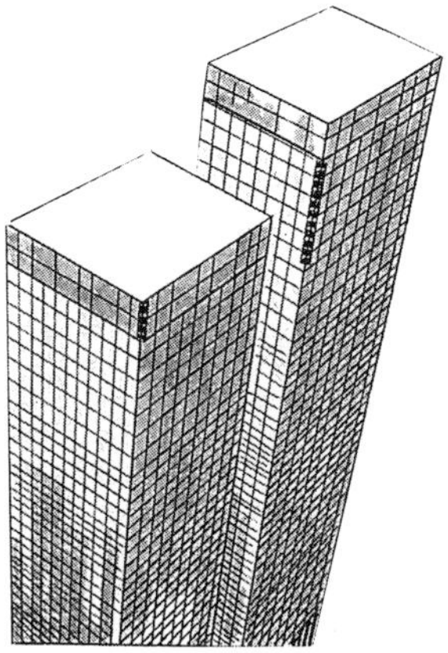

"...The last MAD trip Bill made was a cruise to Bermuda."

important parts of the operations. I hope you didn't try to perform any of them.

DICK: No, I leave that to a true professional like you. What are you doing here in (location of MAD trip)?

JOHN: I'm looking for a new source of leeches. They get harder to find every year.

DICK: Doctors still use leeches?

JOHN: I don't care what other doctors do, I use them. Plenty of them! (Exit. When alone, explode with pent-up laughter.)

John also concocted a neat practical joke to play on Gaines, but unfortunately, its cost made it completely impractical. He thought it up when Bill, whose weight ranged from overweight to grossly overweight, was going on one of his periodic diets. John suggested we take a tailor to Bill's apartment and alter all his clothes! He wanted to make them all smaller, so that no matter how much weight Gaines lost, all his clothes would still be too tight. But alas, we didn't do it because Bill had such a large amount clothing. A *large* amount of clothing, but not much variety. When Bill bought a shirt or a pair of pants, he bought it in many sizes. That way no matter which way his weight went, he could still wear his favorite things.

John was a truly unique spirit. His office shelves were lined with handmade model trains. When I told him how much I loved trains, he built me a model passenger car with my name on it. He also built futuristic 3-D model cities under glass, and he was a great photographer. Bill liked that especially, because that meant there was free photography in-house for quickie jobs. John had health problems which eventually claimed his life, but he worked for MAD until the very end. When John passed away, longtime associate art director Lenny Brenner took over, and today, Lenny is still MAD's art director. By the way, Lenny has given me NOTHING over the years! (This is just a reminder, Lenny.)

The last MAD trip Bill made was a cruise to Bermuda in the fall of 1991. By that time, the MAD trips had been opened up to include spouses for part of the tour, and on this trip, about forty MAD staffers, friends, and family members set sail on *The Horizon*. One evening while walking on deck, I was talking to a ship's officer, who said he was proud to have the MAD staff aboard. But he was especially proud, he added, that William M. Gaines was among us.

I recognized an opportunity, so I asked if he would like to play a practical joke on Gaines. He was very willing. I told him how much Bill loved the Marx Brothers and how he especially loved the overcrowded cabin scene in *A Night at the Opera.* I said I wanted to fill Bill's cabin with at least a hundred people. The officer asked me what I needed, and I told him, "About four ship's mechanics with tool boxes, a half-dozen waiters with big trays of dishes, a lot of cleaning people with mops, brooms, vacuums..." et cetera. He agreed.

Now all this had to be carefully orchestrated, because you only get *one* chance to do something this elaborate! We got everyone assembled one deck above Bill's cabin. Annie had made sure that Bill was awake and was at least wearing underwear. (Thank God, he was!)

For openers, Duck Edwing and his beautiful wife, Cluck (yes, Duck and Cluck), entered "just to visit." Then about every ten seconds, someone knocked on the door and went in. After about ten MAD staffers were inside, we started sending the maids, engineers, and other ship's personnel, interspersed with more staffers. It took about two minutes for Gaines to figure out what was going on, and from that moment on, he laughed every time a new person came through the door. That night I managed to cram Bill's stateroom with about 150 people—including a couple with a crying baby! Bill claimed this was his favorite practical joke ever, even though it was played on him.

ENEMY

Later that night, Bill phoned my cabin.

BILL: That was the best practical joke anyone ever played on me! Thanks, honey!

DICK: I'm glad you enjoyed it! Can I have a raise?

BILL: No! (Click! Dial tone)

Dave Berg on Bill Gaines

Bill Gaines was the strangest boss in the world. Some of his employees were his best personal friends, such as Dick DeBartolo, Lenny Brenner, Joe Orlando, and myself, amongst others. When I was new on the team, Bill came in one morning and all the MAD employees began to shout awful things at him. Bill just smiled. In shock I asked, "How can they say such things to the Boss?" Nick Meglin said, "If we don't, he thinks we don't love him."

For years, we turned out a special book for him, called "Fuck You, Bill Gaines." Believe it or not, it was a "thank you" book for all the MAD trips he so carefully planned!

While on a MAD trip to Mexico City, we all went for a ride on a lake which had boats that were beautifully decorated with flowers. Sergio Aragonés snuck down before we all arrived and did his dirty work. On Bill's boat, the flowers read, "Fuck You, Bill Gaines." Those boaters who could read English were shocked. Bill enjoyed the notoriety.

On a MAD trip to Paris, after a dinner boat ride on the Seine, Bill got into his waiting limousine. Sergio began to pound on the car rooftop, yelling, "CAPITALIST PIG! WARMONGER! YANKEE, GO HOME!" A group of English teenagers nearby joined in pounding and yelling. Bill, who had drunk much champagne, slept through the whole thing. The rest of us were rolling on the cobblestones, hysterical with laughter.

Bill told me this story about himself. As a kid, his teacher asked him how old this planet was. Bill said, "God only knows." The teacher said he was right and passed him. Yet Bill said, "I swear to God there is no God."

In my feature "The Lighter Side," I depicted Gaines as a mean old boss. He thought it hilariously funny, because he wasn't a mean old boss. All this was good public relations. It showed we don't just laugh at the world, we also laugh at ourselves even louder.

Gaines looked like Michelangelo's version of God. This gave him a Father image to go along with his making the MAD people feel like they belonged to a very exclusive family, with "GOD" Gaines at the head.

NOT A HAPPY CAMPER

The earliest MAD trips were short, usually four or five days in Puerto Rico. One thing I liked about these trips was that you could actually earn money on them. Bill not only provided airfare, hotel, and transfers, he gave us money for eating and drinking. I don't drink, so I'd come home with more money than when I'd gone! Another reason why I liked Puerto Rico is that I like to stay in touch with the folks back home and in Puerto Rico there were phones *everywhere!* Also, the flight was short and there was no language barrier.

But when the longer trips started—ten days to two weeks, which was the way Bill could get bargain airfares—I only went so the other guys wouldn't talk about me behind my back. (Okay, I admit it. I know this because WE talked about the guys who weren't there!) Actually, the longer trips *were* hard for me because I had to arrange to leave all my other jobs, and find someone to take care of my dogs—and hey, I missed my dogs!—and I didn't speak any foreign languages, and it was often difficult to call the States. (I guess you get the picture—I get homesick.) Of course there was Africa, where we saw incredible wild animals, but I mean, how many people do *you* know who would leave a free trip to Italy and fly home three days early at their own expense? Well, I did. And Duck Edwing left with me, too. I left because there weren't enough TV channels to watch late at night and Duck left because he couldn't get enough coffee.

So I'm just not a fan of international travel. As you know from reading the trip highlights in the previous chapter, it wasn't traveling abroad that was memorable, it was getting together and doing stuff with the MAD guys that was. Heck, after awhile I even stopped asking Gaines where we were going, and would just ask, "Should I bring clothes for warm weather or cold?"

Of course, a big reason why I went was to please Bill, but I wasn't going to let him off the hook that easily. I'm not sure when it got started, but at one point I began to take the attitude that NOTHING Gaines did about these trips pleased me. (It slowly evolved into complaining about EVERYTHING he did, but it did start with the trips!) For instance, the year he told me we were all going to Rome, instead of beaming about his choice, I bellowed in rage: *"Rome, the culture-starved capital of Italy??"*

BILL: Only YOU wouldn't want to go to Rome!

DICK: Gaines, wake up! Take away the food! Take away the wine! Take away the churches, the art, the statues, and the Italian women—and what do you have?? Paramus, New Jersey! We can go to Paramus for twenty dollars a person! What are you blowing a wad on Rome for?!

BILL: Because I like Rome.

DICK: Well, you're in the minority! If Rome was such a great place, we would have seen it in the movies, and we'd have read about it in books.

BILL: You're right, but I'm going anyway!

DICK: Count me out! I'm going to Paramus! And if you offer the rest of guys that option, they'll pick Paramus, too!

BILL: I know! That's why I'm not offering them that option....They either go to Rome, or they don't go!

DICK: What a little bastard!! FORCING people to go to Rome! And it's probably for more than a day.

BILL: It's for eight days, seven nights!

DICK: You despicable creep!

SCENE: BORA BORA.

Put her down in the first clearing you see, Duke.
I'm so glad you let me come on this expedition, Dad. Imagine! The **first** people ever to set foot in this territory!
ON THIS SITE WILL BE ERECTED A NEW JOHN'S BARGAIN STORE

The MAD group is there, in what must truly be the most idyllic place on earth. Gaines and DeBartolo are sitting on a dock built out over the ocean. The water is so crystal clear, you can see thirty feet to the bottom. Tropical fish are gliding through the coral formations. The sun is sitting behind some glorious clouds, shooting out rays, and the effect is like a fantastic fireworks display.

DICK: Another fucking hellhole you dragged me to!

BILL: Bora Bora—a hellhole...?

DICK: So, finally, you admit it! But it's too late, because we're here! If it wasn't for you, I could be in Riverside Park right now—cleaning up after my dog. But oh, no! Mr.I-Can-Drag-the-MAD-Staff-Anywhere-I-Want makes us come to Bora Bora. I'm only going to take these rotten trips for a limited number of years, Gaines!

BILL: You're going to go on every rotten trip I plan! And I'm going to make them two weeks next time!

DICK: Fucking sadist!

YOU ARE READING THE WORLD'S FIRST DE-CAFFINATED COFFEE TABLE BOOK!

MAD

George Woodbridge on Bill Gaines

Bill, Dick, and I were big W. C. Fields fans. One of my favorite memories from the MAD trips was Dick and I sitting behind Bill, and imitating the irritating mother and daughter from the film *It's a Gift.* Here we were on a free trip to Italy, touring in an air-conditioned bus, but this is what Gaines had to listen to—delivered in an annoying sing-song fashion just like in the W. C. Fields movie:

DICK: I didn't want to come to Italy.
GEORGE: I didn't either.
DICK: Then why are we here?
GEORGE: Because some big fat man said we had to come here.
DICK: Well, I'm bored.
GEORGE: I'm bored too, and I'm also freezing.
DICK: Then let's go home.
GEORGE: I wish we could, but we can't.
DICK: Why can't we?
GEORGE: Because we have cheap airline tickets and we can't leave the group.
DICK: Then we'll just have to complain like this for two solid weeks!

Gaines' reaction? What else—just laughter, from the beginning to the end! He was a wonderful laugher, and one hell of a special person!

LOYALTY*

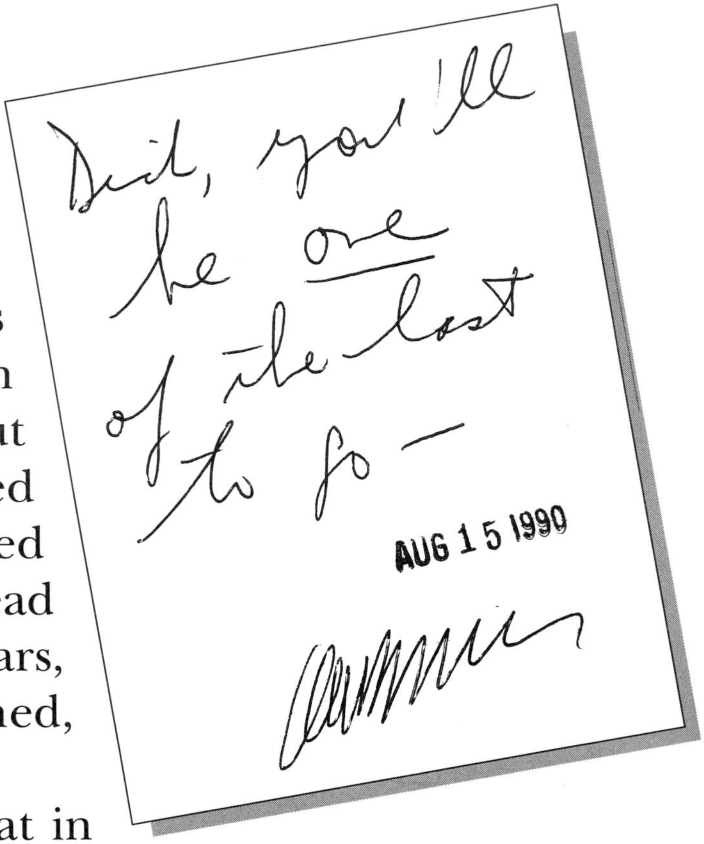
Dick, you'll
be one
of the last
to go —
AUG 15 1990

Bill was loyal to people he dealt with over the years, and that was reassuring. I was not on staff when MAD became a part of Warner, but I was there when Warner merged with Time and I became concerned that all the changes in MAD might lead to staff cuts. When I told Bill my fears, he said that no matter what happened, I'd be among the very last to go. "Really?" I said. "I'd like to see that in writing!" So naturally, Bill got out his date stamp and pen, and I *did* get in writing!

But Bill's loyalty also created problems, and one of the biggest problems was with the travel agent he insisted on using. She was the one who booked all the MAD trips, and it couldn't have been an easy job. At first only the guys went on the trips. Then, like I said, the trips opened up to include mates. But of course it wasn't quite that simple. Bill set it up so that the first part of the trip was only for MAD staffers. Then the mates could join us for the second part of the trip. I'm sure that making these arrangements was not a travel agent's idea of fun, but on the other hand, it did mean writing fifty or sixty tickets that some times ran close to $1,000 apiece.

---

*Author's Note: When I read books, which is EXTREMELY RARE, I love it when I suddenly come across a short chapter, so this is a fairly short chapter

However, the problem with the trips wasn't the logistics. It was that this travel agent didn't always know the shortest routes. Let's face it, if you're flying from New York to Puerto Rico, the plane shouldn't have to make a stop in Rome, Italy. Now if frequent flyer plans had been in place when Bill was using her services, flying via Rome would have been great, but this was prior to that perk.

It sounds like a minor complaint, but many of us really were upset with the bizarre flight arrangements this travel agent made. We often had to endure six- and eight-hour layovers, when we could have gotten through service on another airline. But when Bill heard us complain, he'd just say that he had been with this travel agent for 29 years, and he'd get a new one when she left the business. Bill claimed he didn't mind the extra hours of flying, but one time I really got him when I told him about a fare that was $200 cheaper than the one he had been given by this travel agent. Bill made her re-book our flight—heck, 32 tickets at a saving of $200 each came to $6,400—but he didn't stop using her! And whenever MAD staffers asked him why, Bill would always repeat: "Because I've been using her for twenty-nine years, and I'll stop when she stops!" Sure enough, it wasn't until she retired that Bill got a new travel agent!

Bill's loyalty extended to restaurants, too. There's a seafood restaurant called Little Charlie's. It's down on the Bowery in New York City, and when MAD's office was just a few blocks away, at 225 Lafayette Street, Bill often ate there. Well, just because the office moved uptown didn't mean Bill would abandon Little Charlie's. He managed to get there pretty regularly, often bringing Lenny Brenner with him. For years the MAD Christmas party was held there, one party as recently as three years ago.

Now, Little Charlie's is not your dimly lit romantic restaurant, like Gaines usually goes for. It's brightly lit, tablecloth-less, and fairly sterile, but the owners took good care of Bill and Lenny, mainly with extra garlic. I liked to joke with Bill about his loyalty to the place, and I'd tease him that it was the only restaurant I was ever in where the sign in the men's room said, "EMPLOYEES

I always thought that Bill never knew who I was. Then one day I tap danced and he knew. And he liked me! I think?

—Rick Tulka
1994

...Did you buy this book, or are you just reading this margin notes in the store?

DON'T HAVE TO WASH THEIR HANDS IF THEY DON'T FEEL LIKE IT!"

Another place Bill liked was the Hudson House, which sits about twenty feet back from the Hudson River in Cold Spring, New York. Dennis Wunderlin and I discovered it ten years ago, when we were on a boat trip up the Hudson River. We had roamed in looking for breakfast and we were told that we were their first customers at their first Sunday buffet. It was great! Pancakes, waffles, French toast, breads, muffins, and the like filled three separate tables. That week I told Bill about it, and two Sundays later a group of us were in his car, driving up to have the buffet.

Bill was so impressed he had the MAD Christmas Party there one year. But not just a Christmas party, it was a weekend Christmas party. Hudson House was also an inn, and Gaines had booked rooms for everyone to stay overnight. People went up Saturday afternoon, had dinner at the inn, and then on Sunday, there was a giant brunch. It was well, MAD!

The only thing that surprised us was that the inn really wasn't decorated for Christmas. There was a wreath on the door and a Christmas tree inside, but that didn't seem like enough. So Annie and I went shopping and bought some mistletoe, some lights, and some Christmas balls. When we finished decorating, the place looked great! Later that evening, after dinner and a few drinks, Dennis Wunderlin took out his little Casio organ, and we all sat around a huge fire—which was conveniently located IN a fireplace—and sang Christmas carols, doing a MAD version of *Holiday Inn.*

PRANKS FROM MY MEMORIES

Over the years we played dozens of pranks on Bill, and these were often elaborate and ingenious, but there was one particular "theme" prank that I really used to enjoy. Whenever I found out that Bill had an appointment he couldn't break—like being best man at a wedding—I would arrange for five or six of the MAD guys to call, offering him an extra ticket for a hit show and other spectacular (but nonexistent) events we knew Bill was dying to go to, but would not be able to attend. Here's how one of those pranks played out:

DICK: Bill, I know you love zeppelins, so I have an incredible surprise for you!

BILL: (with great interest) Yeah???

DICK: There's going to be a semiprivate auction of dinnerware, silverware, and other items from the Graf Zeppelin! (Bill's favorite)

BILL: I can't believe it! How did you find out about it?

DICK: One of the researchers on "To Tell the Truth" saw it in some local Jersey paper. The auction's going to take place in the hangar where the Graf used to land in Lakehurst, New Jersey.

BILL: This is unreal!! I'll get my calendar and mark down the date! When is it?

DICK: Saturday, June twelfth, at two p.m.

BILL: Oh Christ, I can't believe it!! I have to go to a wedding that day!

DICK: Certainly you can get out of it.

BILL: I'm best man.

DICK: Oh, Bill, I'm heartbroken. Well, I'll go and buy you something crappy that I wouldn't want for myself!

Then two or three other guys called Bill with tickets for hit shows—all for Saturday, June 12th, at 2 p.m. Boy, we were mean!!

Of course picking the EXACT number of guys to call Bill was crucial. We knew we had picked one guy too many when Bill would ask the caller, "Let me guess, this free submarine ride wouldn't be on Saturday, June twelfth at two p.m., would it?"

Bill could dish it out, too. One time he filled the water cooler with white wine, and he sat behind his almost-closed office door, laughing into his fist as he watched the reactions of the unsuspecting water lovers.

Then, just before the MAD trip to Africa, as Bill gave each person their malaria pills he said, "You must take the first one—RIGHT NOW!" As we swallowed our pills, he pretended to get a call from the doctor explaining they had gotten the pills mixed up.

"Don't take the pills!" Bill screamed. "They're poison!"

But one of Bill's best and longest-running practical jokes was played on the new kid in the mail room. Legendary MAD artist Mort Drucker explains the prank in his remembrance of Gaines.

THIS BOOK CONTAINS MANY OF THE SAME WORDS FOUND IN BOOKS COSTING $10–$20–$50 MORE!

MAD

MORT DRUCKER

MORT DRUCKER ON BILL GAINES—

ONE OF MY FAVORITE STORIES CONCERNING BILL GAINES WAS TOLD TO ME SOME YEARS AFTER I HAD BECOME A CONTRIBUTOR TO MAD MAGAZINE.

IT WAS ONE SUMMER IN THE EARLY 1950S AND A YOUNG MAN HAD SECURED A JOB IN THE MAIL ROOM OF THE MAD OFFICES. BILL HAD DECIDED TO HAVE FUN WITH THIS YOUNG MAN AND HAD ONE OF THE STAFF MEMBERS INFORM HIM THAT BILL GAINES HAD AN EVIL TWIN BROTHER, AND TO TRY TO STAY OUT OF HIS WAY AS MUCH AS POSSIBLE.

ON SOME DAYS DURING THAT SUMMER BILL WOULD COME TO THE OFFICE AS HIS USUAL, LOVABLE, JOVIAL SELF. HE WOULD BE CHARMING TO EVERYONE AND IN PARTICULAR TO THIS YOUNG MAIL CLERK.

MAD

On other days he would come to the office as the evil twin brother, wearing a thin mustache, a Panama hat and a scar down one side of his face. He would intimidate everyone and in particular, the young man in the mail room.

Bill pulled off the charade that entire summer and to this day that young man is probably telling his grandchildren of the scary and chilling events of that summer job at MAD in the early 1950s.

Mort Drucker

AND NOW, BACK TO OUR CHAPTER ON PRANKS

Then there was a prank that Bill and I pulled off together. Not only was it a success but it actually served a higher purpose—deflecting anger before it had time to explode.

Every year at the MAD Christmas party, we were given our bonus checks. A contributor's bonus was based on the number of pages of work MAD had published in that year, and my name was usually near the top of the list.

For a long time, the bonus checks were for very substantial amounts, but one year, just days before the party, Bill called me into his office.

BILL: I'm warning you ahead of time. The Christmas bonuses this year are very low. I'm telling you now, so you won't be too disappointed at the party.

DICK: How low?

BILL: It's not even four figures.

DICK: Is that with or without the decimal point?

BILL: It's under a thousand dollars.

DICK: Christ, how much money did you embezzle this year?

BILL: Obviously a lot! So you're been warned.

DICK: Thanks.

(I turned to leave, but then I had a thought....)

DICK: Bill, I have a great idea! At the party, hand me the check, I'll look at the amount and have a fit! I'll call you a cheap bastard, tear up the check, and throw it in your face!!

BILL: Fantastic idea! Let's do it...this is great!

And at the Christmas party I gave a sterling performance. I looked at the check and screamed at Bill—"All the work! All the promotion!! This check is a joke!! Right???"

Gaines sheepishly admitted that it was the real check. I tore it up, threw it in his face, and stalked off to a table to be by myself. Duck Edwing came over to console me, telling me that his check was tiny, too, and to take heart. I whispered, "Duck, it's a joke!" He was really impressed! He said everyone in the room was truly freaked out. What great fun!

This space for rent

Mort Drucker

Forward to Book—

I have had the good fortune and great pleasure of being a regular contributor to MAD magazine for thirty eigh years. For those unfamiliar with my contribution, it has been as a free lance artist illustrating, to the best of my ability, the very best satirical concepts of the very best humorous writers in America, the world, with the possible exception of Albania.

One of those writers is Dick DeBartolo. I have illustrated so many of his concepts over the years that his humor and satire have totally confused me. It is this ability that has made him a favorite national TV personality.

Wherever I happen to be, one of the most pressing and often asked questions is, "What is

DICK DEBARTOLO REALLY LIKE?"
FOR THE RECORD, HE IS INTELLIGENT, KIND, FUNNY AND AN EXTREMELY TALENTED WRITER. I THANK HIM FOR THE OPPORTUNITY OF BEING PART OF THIS IMPORTANT AND CONFUSING BOOK.

AS FOR BILL GAINES, I LIKED HIS EVIL BROTHER MUCH BETTER.

MORT DRUCKER

MORT DRUCKER

BILL, DICK, AND DOGS

I've always loved animals, and have had pets ever since I moved out on my own. At one point, I had four dogs—three of them from the same family. Today I have the granddaughter of that litter and I hope she will have pups and carry on the line. But a love of animals was not something Bill and I had in common. It wasn't that Bill didn't like animals, he just never spoke about them, and as far as I know, he never had a pet.

Yet in spite of his lack of interest, Bill became involved—much as he didn't want to—with the care and feeding of a huge number of dogs and cats.

It was years ago when I read about Betty O'Meara, a woman in Athens, Georgia, who took in any and all strays. Betty lived on a farm where she cared for about a hundred dogs and a lesser number of cats, but unfortunately, she had suffered a heart attack that left her financially unable to care for them all. The story moved me, and I started sending her money—for food, vet bills, and for fencing, so the animals wouldn't roam off the farm, and so the females could have separate quarters when in heat. It wasn't long before I was sending her a good amount every month.

While Bill well knew that MAD wasn't my only source of income, he took a paternalistic interest in my finances, from how much I was getting from my other freelance jobs to how I was spending my money. I don't know how I happened to tell Bill about Betty O'Meara but I did, and he became concerned that I was sending her too much money every month. But I was determined to keep doing it because caring for all those animals must have been one heck a job! Since I wouldn't stop sending money, the only thing Bill could do was send something to Betty every month, too.

Well, Betty was thrilled and she wrote wonderful, moving letters of thanks, and Bill kept contributing for more than a dozen years. Now Bill didn't believe in God, and I often told him that because of that he was going to burn in Hell for 2,000 years. But, I said, this charity was going to go onto his permanent record, and he should be cheered to know that because of it, he would be released from his 2,000-year sentence six days early! I added that he could get off a month early if he'd send MORE money, but he didn't buy that.

...It is said that chemicals in bananas repel allergies, unless you're allergic to bananas.
Joan Wilen & Lydia Wilen

After some years, Betty's husband Jack passed on. She cut down on the number of dogs she was taking in, found good homes for many of those she had adopted, and then she moved to a smaller place closer to town. And to this day, Betty still takes in dogs, and I still send money to Betty. I think it's a perfect arrangement. She has the time and space for the animals, and I have the resources to make sure they're fed.

Of course, caring for so many animals has been a terrible burden on Betty, but I didn't realize how big a burden, until one time when she told me that in thirteen years, she had never been away from her place overnight. I reported this to Bill, and we hatched a plan. We'd fly Betty to New York and have a special party in her honor. Of course if Betty knew we wanted to do something for her, she'd never come. So when Bill called her, he told her there was going to be a special party for me, to celebrate the release of a new paperback book I had written. Bill and I sent her an airline ticket, and I sent her money for a dog sitter. She came...and was she surprised! At the party, when Bill announced that we had all gathered to honor Betty O'Meara, she laughed and laughed. "Oh, Bill," she said, "you're always clowning, you know we're here to celebrate Dick's new book!"

Now it was my turn: "No, Betty, this party *is* really for you—and all you've done for the animals over the years!" Then to prove the point I presented a mini-slide show, featuring pictures of the various animals Betty had saved. Then Betty, moved to tears, knew the party really WAS for her. Betty still reminds me that it was a night she will never forget. Come to think of it, neither will I!

While Bill didn't share my love for animals, he started to understand my affinity for dogs when we were on the MAD trip to France. One morning, a few of us—Bill, John Putnam, and myself— rented a car and drove into the French countryside. We stopped at a beautiful inn for lunch, but when we went inside we were told that there was no room for us. Now this didn't sound too kosher (I say this even though this was a French inn), because only two of the twenty tables were occupied. John Putnam managed to come to our rescue by rattling off God knows what, in what I can only assume was pretty good French, because suddenly we were very welcome, and there was plenty of room. As a matter of fact, we were told to "sit anywhere we liked." We chose a table by an open door.

While waiting for the food, I saw a dog out in the woods, so I went to the door and started talking to him. When the waitress heard me, she explained in broken English that he was a scared stray who hung around the inn, but he didn't trust anyone—and no one trusted him. I stood there and talked to the dog some more, telling him I wasn't going to touch him or move outside the door. Between courses I kept getting up and going over to the door, trying to reassure the dog, telling him that I loved dogs and I had dogs at home that I missed. I don't know what Bill thought of this, but he didn't joke or make fun of me, or the dog. When lunch was finally over—after multiple desserts, of course—I put on my jacket and went back to the open door to say good-bye. I told the dog I was leaving, and that I had enjoyed seeing him. Well—and even I was a little taken aback by this—the dog looked around the garden, found a small stone, came up the three steps to the door, and dropped the stone at my feet! Then he ran off to what he considered a safe distance, and sat and watched.

Bill was astonished! "My God, no wonder you love dogs! You can talk to them," he said. Still amazed, he continued, "I can hardly believe it, I have Saint Francis on my staff!" And all the way out to the car, you could hear Bill muttering, "A totally mean, rotten stray that everyone hates comes up and gives Dick a present....It's Saint Francis all over again!" (I believe that it's St. Francis who's the saint of animals. I wanted to check it before this book was published, but I kept getting the Pope's answering machine!)

Of course, it was later on that same trip that I got ambushed by the Parisian poodle. But in the seconds following the attack the poodle apologized, and told me that she was really after Don Martin—but she'd missed. (This was a test! I hope you read the previous dog story carefully!)

BONUS·BONUS·BONUS·BONUS·BONUS·BONUS

BONUS #13

Is a reproduction of one of my favorite possessions—blank MAD stationery signed by Gaines. Read the details in the very next chapter!

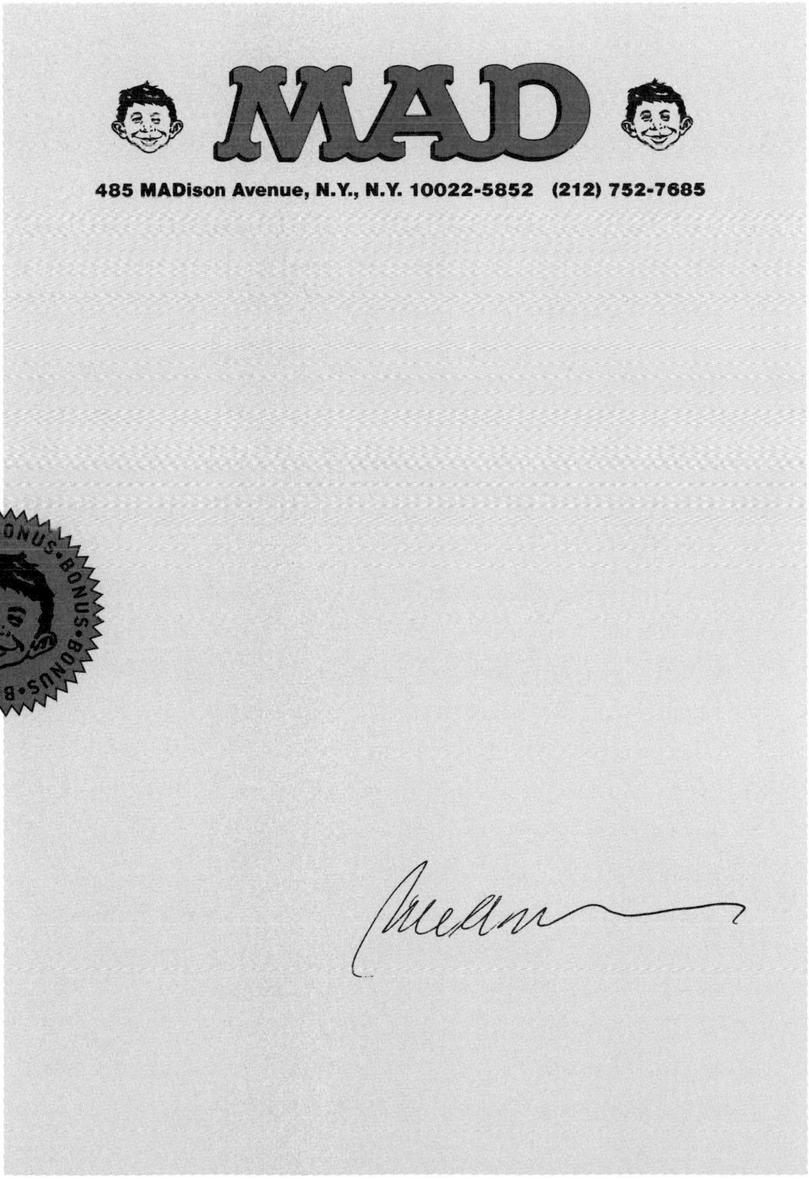
MAD

485 MADison Avenue, N.Y., N.Y. 10022-5852 (212) 752-7685

GET IT IN WRITING

Maybe it was because Bill was convinced I could communicate with animals, or maybe it was because I would sometimes talk to Bill about the power of the mind, that Bill decided I had a say in his dreams. One day he called me into his office.

BILL: Sit down.

DICK: Oh, Christ, what now? Paint your apartment?

BILL: No, I just want to thank you for last night.

DICK: Bill, I didn't see you last night. But you're welcome. You're senile, but you're welcome!

BILL: No, I had a wonderful dream, and you ran the entire thing!

DICK: Good! Can I go home early since I obviously worked late last night creating your dream?

BILL: No, you can't go home early, but listen! I dreamed you introduced me to two women. One was incredibly beautiful, and the other was just so-so. I whispered that I thought one of them was a knock-out and you said, "So, take the beautiful one." And in my dream, I did, and I had a fantastic time! You were so generous, I had to call you in to thank you!

DICK: Billy, *anything* you want in your dreams, I will gladly give you!

BILL: Great.

DICK: Now can I get something in return?

BILL: Sure, what?

DICK: How about giving me anything I want in reality!

BILL: Fine!

DICK: Yeah, but Bill, I'm not kidding.

BILL: Neither am I!

DICK: What a minute! **Anything** I want, you'll give me.

BILL: Anything. You're a dear, sweet man, and you can have ANYTHING you want!

DICK: Well, the first thing I want is this in writing!

BILL: Write it, and I'll sign it.

So, on a piece of paper, I scribbled: "Dick DeBartolo is a dear, sweet man, and he can have ANYTHING he wants!" I handed it to Bill. Bill took his date stamp, stamped it, and signed it. Then I began to wonder what the catch was.

DICK: So, if I decide I want to be paid TWICE what the other writers get, you'll pay it?

BILL: Of course! You've got my signed note!

DICK: So if I do a presentation for MAD at a publishers' convention and I want ten thousand dollars, you'll pay it?

BILL: Just give me a bill for ten thousand dollars.

DICK: I don't know what's going on now, but I'm sure something is.

I walked out of the room, tightly grasping the note Bill had written. About twenty minutes later, the picture became clear. I rushed back into Gaines' office.

DICK: You little son-of-a-bitch....Excuse me! You *fat* little son-of-a-bitch!

BILL: What's wrong??

DICK: I know why you gave me this note!! You know I'm too honest to charge you twice what the other writers make! And you know I would never charge you ten thousand dollars for anything. Even if it was worth ten thousand dollars!!!

BILL: Why else would I give you such a note???

DICK: I hate you!

I carried that note with me for years and years. Bill would often tell friends about the note and ask me to produce it. At first I kept it in my attaché case. Then Bill wanted me to show it so often that I started carrying it in my wallet. Over the years, the note fell apart. I didn't bother getting another one, because it wasn't worth the paper it was written on. But to tell you the truth, now that Bill is gone, I wish I had the note. (If I did, I'd go after Annie and try to collect on it!)

But I do have something else that shows how much Gaines trusted me—

it's several blank pieces of MAD stationery with Bill's signature already on them. Here's how I got them. One day while sitting at my desk, I thought to myself, "I haven't been in to shake up Gaines all day. I've got to do something to him!" Suddenly, *inspiration!* I brought a few sheets of MAD stationery into Bill's office.

DICK: Here, sign these.

BILL: Where?

DICK: Toward the bottom, on the right, where you would put your name, if you were signing a letter.

BILL: (signing) What is this for?

DICK: I have no idea right now. But I figure if I ever want to send out a nasty letter to someone and make it appear like YOU sent it, I would have your signature in the right place!

BILL: (grumbling) Oh great, I'll get beat up for nasty letters YOU send out!

DICK: Or, I might I write a note over your signature that says you're increasing my pay to twice what the other writers are getting.

BILL: You have that OTHER note you can use for that!

DICK: I need this as a backup. You're not all that trustworthy, Gaines!!

Gaines was a man of his word, but he often forgot what he'd promised, and he would ask me to repeat what he'd said. If he didn't remember the exact words, he DID know what he would, and would not promise. So he would either dismiss you with "I would NEVER say anything like that!" or he would whip out his checkbook and say, "That sounds like something I told you to do. How much do I owe you?"

MAD

Bob Clarke on Bill Gaines

Clarke

THE MAD ART AUCTION

Over all the years I dealt with Bill, he was fair, and I never had any complaints. Well, actually I do have one, and it concerns the sale in 1992 of our stockpile of original mad art. But by the time I realized that I felt there was something unfair about it, Bill was gone.

The arrangement between MAD and its contributors was that when MAD bought scripts and artwork, MAD bought all the rights. Consequently, MAD kept everything. So, after some 300 issues, the MAD vault was overflowing with original art and Bill thought it was time to start selling some of it. But even though MAD owned it outright, Bill made arrangements for the artists to get a share of the profits when their pieces sold. I don't know the actual figure, but it was rumored to be between 30 and 35 percent. I thought it was real decent of Bill to do that, since contractually he really didn't have to.

"...And in fact, this was the largest-selling issue of MAD in history—over two million copies."

There are many diehard MAD fans across the country, but I don't think anyone was quite prepared for the response to the MAD Art Auction held at Christie's. In fact, it wasn't until I attended that auction that I REALLY wished I still had my "ANYTHING he wants" note from Bill, and that Bill was still alive so I could execute it! While MAD is art driven and the script isn't much without the art, I sure had spent *many* hours writing copious art notes, describing in detail what the various panels in my satires should include. Again, my descriptions aren't much until they're art, but when I saw so many of the pieces I had written being auctioned off, I couldn't help thinking, "Gee, I wish I had some compensation." That feeling increased dramatically by the end of the auction. In four hours, the sale of the art had brought in over $600,000! Then I *really* thought the writers should have gotten something! Five percent, even one percent, but something!

Actually, I did come away from the MAD art auction with an unexpected bonus. I had gone to Christie's thinking that it would be nice to own one original MAD cover—but they were all selling for $5,000 to $7,000 which was a little too rich for me, so I didn't even bother to register. (In order to buy stuff at these auctions, you need to register. Then they give you a paddle with your official number on it, and you hold up the paddle when you want to bid.) Anyway, the cover I wanted to buy was the *Poseidon Adventure* cover. It had a lot going for it. It was one of the few covers that didn't have Alfred's face on it. Dear old Alfred was UPSIDE DOWN in his life ring, so we only saw his feet—but we all knew it was Alfred! And I especially wanted that cover because I had written the take-off on *The Poseidon Adventure,* called "The Poopsidedown Adventure." (Poop deck? Poop deck upside down? Get it?) My piece had been really well-received—Irwin Allen, the producer of the movie, had liked it so much he bought a hundred copies, enough for the entire cast and crew! And in fact, this *was* the largest-selling issue of MAD in history—over two million

TALES
CRYPT
S.S. POSEIDON

copies. So imagine my surprise when the bidding on the cover art stopped at $2,000. I couldn't believe it. But I didn't have a paddle, so I couldn't go to the next acceptable bid of $2,200. (There's some formula for bidding, I don't really understand it, but I think when the bid reaches $2,000, you can no longer bid just $100 higher.) Anyway, from somewhere in the room I heard "twenty-two hundred dollars." There was a long pause, and then going, going, gone! The cover had sold for $2,200, probably the lowest price a cover sold for that day.

Later I told Annie Gaines that I couldn't believe the "Poopsidedown" cover went for $2,200, and how disappointed I was. "Don't be," said Annie, "I was the one who bought it for twenty-two hundred dollars. I couldn't bear to see it sold for two thousand. And don't be sad, because I'll give it to you on permanent loan."

Pretty amazing, huh? Here's one MAD writer who did benefit from the MAD Art Auction, thanks to Annie! But I wish all the writers could have shared in the proceeds from that auction.

So, not benefiting from the sale of MAD art is one complaint. And, come to think of it, I do have one other. But this one, dear reader, **you** can do something about!

MAD does not have a retirement plan. Well, they do, but to be included you have to be in the office five days a week. While I am on staff, I do most of my work for them at home as a freelancer, so I'm not eligible. But...I've been writing for MAD for almost 33 years! It sure would be nice to have some sort of nest egg waiting at the end of the tunnel. (Is that where nest eggs wait?) Therefore, I consider **this book** to be my nest egg, my retirement plan, so to speak. So, you might ask, "How can I help, Dick?" Well...DON'T LEND THIS COPY TO ANYONE!!! Tell your friends you love it too much to let it out of your grasp and that they should buy their own copy!

"But," you say, "I'm too broke to buy a copy. Is there anything I can do?" I'll tell you: When you're at the bookstores, make sure it's displayed nicely. If it's not, put a copy at the front of the best-seller rack, where people can see it. Thank you!

...Why do people at the gym take the elevetor to the floor where they use the Stairmaster?

FOREWORD Number 14?!...

BY JEFF GINSBERG

I only had the good fortune of meeting Bill Gaines on a few occasions and those, unfortunately, were late in his life when his health and memory were already failing.

It's too bad too, because I always admired him and if I had gotten to know him better, I think I could have learned a lot from him—and maybe even been included in his will. But besides that, I respected Bill because he had a way of bringing out the best in people. He created an environment where creativity flourished, then he hired the best artists and writers (except for one and he knows who he is) and let them work their magic.

Maybe I feel a particular affection for Bill because before his father, Max, changed his last name to "Gaines," he—like me—was a "Ginsberg." Who knows, somehow we may have been related. On second thought, that affection probably has more to do with wanting to be named in Bill's will, if it's not too late. Anyway, when Dick asked me to write the foreword to this book, I couldn't resist. Considering the high-powered people Dick knows in publishing and broadcasting, for him to ask me was such an honor. He could have had people like Anne Gaines, Nick Meglin, John Ficarra, Dave Berg, George Woodbridge, Al Jaffee, and Sam Viviano to write the foreword, but instead, he asked me. And not only that, there was money involved...$1,500 to be exact. How could I refuse? Dick used to charge me much more than that just to let me write his MAD pieces for him, which he would then submit under his own name. Most people don't realize that since March of 1962 I have written all of Dick's stuff (including this book). But this time, at last, I can use my own name. And that's certainly worth $1,500.

P.S: Dick, enclosed you'll find a check for the first installment. Please don't deposit it until next Friday.

THE GADGET & GIZMO GUY

I've already told you a few stories about Bill's and my fondness for gadgets. Well, about a dozen years ago, this love of mine turned into an additional career. It began when I got a call from Barbara Griff, a friend of mine who was producing a show called "Saturday Morning Live" for a local TV station. Anyway, about a month before Christmas she called and said, "I'm trying to get away from the usual Christmas shopping spot where we show ties and sweaters and fruitcakes. I know you love gadgets...why don't you come on the show and do a spot about unusual gadgets people can give for Christmas? I think it would be fun for our audience."

As you can imagine, I had a great time making the rounds of all the places that specialize in the unusual type of gifts, like Hammacher Schlemmer and Sharper Image. The weirdest gadget I found that season was the "Ro-Butler." This was a remote-controlled robot hand that held a tray—it sort of looked like "Thing" from "The Addams Family." You were supposed to put a drink on the tray and deliver it to your guest via the remote control. (I guess it wasn't a big hit, because I never heard of it again.) I also had a great time on the program, demonstrating the gadgets I had found. Even though the show was live, I wasn't nervous and things went really smoothly.

A couple of weeks later, Barbara called to say the response to my spot had been good, and to gather gadgets for Valentine's Day. I did that segment, and a few weeks after that, Barbara got in touch again. No more holidays were coming, but did I want to be the consumer reporter for "Live"? I sure did, and my second TV career—this time in front of the cameras—got started. After about a year on "Saturday Morning Live," I got a call from one of the segment producers at "The Morning Show with Regis Philbin." She wanted to know if I would appear on that program. Barbara Griff wasn't thrilled with that idea, because she wanted me to be exclusive to "Saturday Morning Live," at least as far as appearing on morning TV. Since Barbara had given me my first big break as a consumer reporter, I thought her request was fair, so I didn't go on Regis' show right away. But when "Saturday Morning Live" went off the air, I immediately called "The Morning Show" and I started doing spots for them...and for Regis' cable show, "Lifestyles." Later, when "The Morning Show" became "Live! With Regis & Kathie Lee," I continued to be the show's consumer reporter; so far, I've racked up over a hundred appearances.

CONSUMER
① COUNTER REVOLUTION
③ "HEADHUNTERS"

I also do a Friday spot on CNBC's "Money Tonight," hosted by Janice Lieberman and Sue Herera. And, on most Wednesdays, I'm on The Nashville Network's "Country Today," hosted by Robb Weller and Lisa Foster. (Hey, Janice, Sue, Robb, and Lisa, when I plug my book on your shows, I can say that you're in it!) On CNBC and TNN my weekly gadget reports center on a particular theme—like gadgets for the beach, gadgets for the photographer, safety gadgets, travel gadgets, cutting-edge gadgets like a wristwatch that controls your TV and VCR, and on and on. The list is long, because I've been doing gadgets spots for *years.* I love gadgets and

I love being on TV and doing the two together is really a treat. Now, if someone would only give me my own show...

Actually, I had my own show for a while on TKR, a local cable station in New Jersey. The show was a weekly half hour called "Consumer U," and I did it for more than a year. It sure was a lot of fun, and a lot of work. Besides showing gadgets, I investigated mail order scams, and did some viewer-participation stuff. One very popular segment was the one where we invited viewers to the studio to take part in "taste tests." These things always amazed me—only rarely could people tell the difference between Coke and Pepsi and RC Cola. Or the difference between the most expensive bottled water we could find, and tap water from the kitchen faucet. Dogs, on the other hand, did much better. For example, I would have staff members bring their dogs to the studio to see if they could tell the difference between the dog food that costs 79 cents a can, and the stuff that costs 29 cents a can. They could!! The dogs smelled them both, and ate the 79-cent stuff. Then they ate the 29-cent stuff.

The money you earn working in cable isn't great. I only made $50 a week for my show, but I was nominated for an ACE (Award for Cable Excellence, which is given by the cable industry), for producing the "best informational local cable show"; and of course, that made all the work worthwhile. (This is the point at which people who are nominated but don't win, MUST add—"And being nominated for an ACE Award is just about the same as winning one!")

...Jeff Straze started my career at NJN, and he ends up in the margin.

I do one other fun TV spot, and it's on NJN—that's New Jersey's PBS station. Yes, I *am* on PBS, bringing cultural programing down a notch or two! The show I work on is called "Discover New Jersey," and I host segments that show viewers fun things to do in the Garden State—*New Jersey!* One spot I did was on Atlantic City, and at Bally's Park Place I won over $100! I think the key is *not* to know what you're doing! (Actually, the most important thing is to walk away as soon as you win!) I had never played roulette, but I just walked up to the table, bought $10 worth of chips, and dumped them on an assortment of numbers. I walked away with $90! I had never played blackjack before, either—the guy sitting next to me had to tell me what to do—but I won $30! On a different shoot for NJN, I went to wrestling school and became Daring

Dick Dangerous. I think I looked pretty good in the ring, but I still hurt from the experience. I also did a couple of boating spots: one piece on renting boats "down the Jersey shore" and another on sightseeing boat rides you can take in New Jersey.

The best part about shooting in the field is that you don't have to worry about a gadget screwing up on the air, which they are apt to do. In fact, I'm convinced that gadgets know "live" television from taped programs, because they fail to operate a much higher percentage of the time on live shows!

My office at NJN. Now you know how little money PBS stations really have!

Duck Edwing on Bill Gaines

BILL GAINES WASN'T A MAN.

HE WAS A MANU!

A MANU IS SINGULAR FOR MENU... AND BILL KNEW MORE THAN THE OWNER ABOUT ANY FOOD BEING OFFERED ANYWHERE.

ALL THESE TRIPS TO RESTAURANTS AROUND THE WORLD... AND I, AS A MAD TRAVELER, ONLY ATE VEGETABLES AND SALADS.

OH... I LOVE MEAT... AND GRAVY... BUT, WHEN SOME 300 LB GUY WITH COCKER SPANIEL EYES (AND IS PAYING FOR YOUR MEAL) IS EYEBALLING YOUR WINE DIPPED MONGOLIAN FRIED SAUSAGE... YOU TEND TO GIVE IT UP WHEN HE ASKS FOR A BITE!

SO... I FIGURE... WHAT THE HELL... AT LEAST I CAN EAT MY DESSERT.

DID YOU KNOW THAT DICK DeBARTOLO'S SOLE FOOD INTAKE IS DESSERT? DID YOU KNOW THAT BILL GAINES SYMPATHIZES WITH DESSERT DEVOTEES?

BILL GAINES WAS A MANU THAT GAVE YOUR DESSERT AWAY AFTER HE ATE YOUR MAIN COURSE.

ALL THESE RESTAURANTS AROUND THE GA!!A WORLD.. AND I AS A MAD TRAVELER, ONLY ATE THE GA☆!★G VEGETABLES AND GOD DAMN SALAD!

Duck Edwing

DUCK EDWING ON BILL GAINES

MY BROOKLYN CHILDHOOD

The only reason I'm including this chapter is that it will make it easier for some producer to turn this book into a movie. I visualize Macaulay Culkin playing me as a kid, and me playing me as an adult. (Actually, with the incredible things Hollywood makeup specialists can do these days, maybe I'll play myself as a kid, and Macaulay Culkin can play me as me now.)

When I was in grammar school, my mother always told me I should do whatever I wanted in life, but my father was much stricter. When he asked me what I wanted to do and I told him, "write and perform," he would argue with me, insisting that writing and performing was NOT an occupation. Plumbing was an occupation! Carpentry was an occupation! Not writing! Not performing! (You'll notice that my father did not write a foreword for this book. My brother, Joe, says it's because our dad passed away over seven years ago—but I say, if there wasn't that excuse, then it would be something else!)

At any rate, it was to please my father that I decided to go to a business high school. Central Commercial was one of the few trade schools in New York at the time, and it was really old and badly in need of repair. Shortly after I graduated from Central Commercial, it was torn down, and for years after, our class reunions were held in the parking lot where the school once stood. It was a nice improvement.

Since my father owned a business (making ornamental grilles and doors) I studied bookkeeping and shorthand so I could help out in the office. At least that's what I told him. In reality, I figured I could write comedy scripts in shorthand, and use my bookkeeping skills when I started gathering backers for the Broadway show I would write one day. (Hey, wait a minute! Maybe this book would make a better Broadway musical than movie.)

At Central Commercial I managed to do a lot of non-business things. I wrote for the school newspaper; I wrote all the school plays; I hosted all the events in the auditorium; and I generally had a good time. Actually, it was the perfect place for me to go to high school, because no one there wanted to get into show business but me! (Thank God I didn't end up going to the Performing Arts High School where, as I understand it, even the janitors have agents!) In Central Commercial I also started polishing my skills as a practical joker, and one of the really fun things I did took place in shorthand class.

Shorthand class consisted of the teacher dictating long letters, then calling on various students to read them back. I happened to notice that she really didn't listen to us read back our notes, but instead spent the time enjoying a novel she kept open in the middle top drawer of her desk. The only time she would look up from her book was when a student paused in the read-back...and that gave me an idea.

I would volunteer to read back the letters the teacher had dictated. I'd read the first sentence back straight, just as she'd dictated it, and then, as soon as I saw her eyes move to her novel, I would continue the read-back, but I'd make up the rest. As long as I didn't pause, I was on safe ground. My typical read-back went like this:

"Dear Mr. Jones:

"We are in receipt of your letter informing us that we overcharged you $20 on your last order."

(Teacher goes back to reading her novel.)

"You should consider yourself very lucky. We normally overcharge people $50! Therefore, you actually owe us $30! And we'd like it now, or we'll have the boys—Vinnie and Vito—come around and break your legs."

Then, to make it sound like I'd really been reading back the dictation, I would pause and ask the teacher what the first word of the fourth paragraph was. She would look in her notes, give it to me, and then we'd both go back to doing what we did best: She'd read her novel, and I'd make up stuff!

Most everyone in class was good at stifling their laughter so I never was

"..if I had been studious and become a shorthand expert, I probably would have gotten a job at a law firm instead of MAD, and then think how boring this book would be!"

caught. But as I write this, I realize what I really was in high school—just a wiseass kid. But if I had been studious and become a shorthand expert, I probably would have gotten a job at a law firm instead of MAD, and then think how boring this book would be!

Photo from Dick DeBartolo's private collection. Reprinted without his permission or knowledge.

BOATS AND BILL

When I moved from my parents' house in Brooklyn to the bright lights of Manhattan, I rented an apartment on the Upper West Side because it was very close to one of the two marinas in the city. And every day as I walked my dog past the boats I'd think, "One day when I'm big, I'm going to own a boat!" Then I realized, I was "big." So I bought a boat.

I had wanted an eighteen-foot runabout with a small engine. The eighteen-foot boat was available, but not the small engine, so I ordered the next larger engine. But that engine was on back order, too. As it turned out, the only way I could get the boat within a reasonable amount of time was with the largest available engine, so that's what I ordered. Back almost thirty years ago, my eighteen-foot SeaRay with its 225 hp engine was a hot boat! It did over fifty miles per hour—even by today's standards, it was no slouch. That boat got me interested in high performance boats, and into another mini-career.

When I got my SeaRay, I started reading *Powerboat* magazine, the bible of the go-fast set. In a way, when I first read *Powerboat* I felt about the same way I did when I first read MAD: I don't want to be *reading* this, I want to be *writing* this! So I wrote the publisher a letter expressing my interest in boats and in his magazine. I didn't hear back. Then after about six weeks, I called him and asked if he'd gotten my letter. He said he had and that he would love to have me write a monthly boating column. "So what's the problem?" I inquired.

"Well, you write for MAD, and I'm sure they pay well, and I'm embarrassed to tell you what we pay." He paused and then continued. "We pay fifty dollars for a column."

"That's fine with me! MAD pays me well enough so that I CAN afford to work for you for fifty dollars a month!" So I started writing a monthly column for *Powerboat*, and I'm still writing it today. I've been told by other scribes in the marine industry that it is possibly the longest-running monthly boating column ever—I haven't missed an issue in 25 consecutive years.

Not long after I got the boat, Bill became one of my regular boating companions. I thought he'd be wary because his dad had died in a boating accident, but Bill didn't turn down any invitations to go boating with me. One day we went down to the Statue of Liberty at sunset. The sun reflecting off the torch was a magnificent sight, and Bill was quite moved by it. He asked me to promise him that when the various publishers of the foreign editions of MAD came to town, I would take them for the same ride at the same time—sunset—and he would provide the money for gas. I was more than happy to do it because I loved seeing people's reactions to that close-up view of the Statue of Liberty, which you can only get from a private boat. After about a dozen of these trips, I made the experience even more dramatic by playing a tape of stirring music, including "God Bless America" and "America the Beautiful." I would really fake it up by cutting the engine and turning up the volume on the tape. When the engine noise died down, it was pretty moving!

"...One day when I'm big, I'm going to own a boat!" Then I realized, I was "big." So I bought a boat."

When Bill started dating Annie, I would take them on that same spectacular ride. Then one day, Gaines called me into his office.

BILL: Do you know how much that crappy little boat of yours cost me?

DICK: I thought you liked my crappy little boat.

BILL: I do, but so far it's cost me more than a hundred thousand dollars!

DICK: Bill, I know you pay for the gas, but for a hundred thousand dollars we could cruise around the world!

BILL: I've not talking about the money for gas—that's peanuts. I'm talking about the other money.

DICK: What **other** money?

BILL: Last time you took Annie and me out, we passed the Queen Elizabeth 2.

And Annie said, "Sweetheart, that looks like such a beautiful ship! Let's take a cruise." So, we're going on a cruise! That cost me two thousand dollars. And now I'm in love with the Statue of Liberty, and I've started buying the original models made by Bartholdi, the ones he cast before he decided on the final design.

DICK: You own models of the Statue made by Bartholdi himself?? Bill, they must have cost more than fifty dollars!

BILL: More than a hundred thousand dollars!! And it's all your fault.

DICK: When we go to the Statue, we pass the Empire State Building. Why don't you buy that, too? And blame me!!

BILL: I don't want to own the Empire State Building! But I will tell you something about the Empire State Building that I did do....I tried to rent the office on the seventy-ninth floor that that airplane crashed into in 1945. I thought it would be perfect for MAD.

DICK: So what happened?

BILL: The people who have that office have a very long lease. So I settled for the next best thing—an office on the thirteenth floor.

DICK: Bill, this is all very interesting, but I have to leave now before I cost you any more money. And I'll do you a favor, I won't take you and your horrible little friends to the Statue anymore.

BILL: **Please** take my horrible little friends to the Statue if I ask you.

DICK: Oh, okay!

While I'm talking about the boat trips, I'll mention something I did once that broke Bill up. We were passing the Queen Elizabeth 2 as it was heading toward the open ocean. Hundreds of people were lining the decks. We pulled up as close as we could in our tiny little boat, and I shouted up to the crowd, "Honey, you took the car keys!!" Bill loved it, and he requested that I do that shtick for guests anytime we passed an ocean liner when we were out in the boat.

Frank Jacobs on Bill Gaines

I spent many hours with Bill Gaines while gathering material for his biography, *The Mad World of William M. Gaines.* He being a large man, it seemed appropriate that his main after-hours interests, other than food and wine, were also of remarkable size.

His three main preoccupations, back then in 1972, were zeppelins, King Kong, and the Elephant Hotel. I asked him why he was a nut for zeppelins.

"Because they're a phallic symbol," he snapped. "Isn't that what you want me to say?"

"Come on," I persisted. "What's the reason?"

"Because they're big and you can't miss them."

At last—an admission that the girth of the objects he admired gave them their appeal....Or was it just a coincidence? Had I drawn a conclusion based on only three examples? Had I leaped too hastily to the premise that a large, noticeable man is drawn to things equally large and noticeable?

Not really. It was but a few years later that Gaines plunged into a new hobby—collecting any replica he could lay his hands on of the Statue of Liberty.

MAD

CARRYING A TORCH FOR BILL

After he had fallen in love with the Statue of Liberty, Bill often wondered what it would be like to get up into her torch. The torch had been closed for as long as I can remember (I'm not sure it was ever open to the public), but one day while doing research for one of Goodson-Todman's game shows, I met a guy who enabled me to fulfill Bill's most cherished dream.

Because NO ONE was allowed on the torch, I won't reveal this man's name! (And because it happened so many years ago I *can't remember* this man's name!) The whole affair was top secret from the word "go."

Our instructions were to take the ferry to the Statue, and then let the last boat leave without us. We were told where to hide so we wouldn't be seen when the park rangers made their last check for tourists on the island. For a few minutes we were frightened. Suppose we let the last boat go and it turned out to be a big, cruel joke! But after a short wait, "Mr. Big" (not his real name) met us, carrying a flashlight and a big ring of keys. We were all wildly excited and wildly nervous! We entered the Statue and walked up the stairs, stopping at the landing where the arm with the torch joins the body. After unchaining and unlocking the gate, we went through. And when we set foot on that ladder to the torch—well, we felt like we were in an Alfred Hitchcock movie!

It didn't take us long to realize why the arm was not open to the public. It was a *long* climb, and the ladder was *very* narrow, and it got even narrower where the arm bends...and that's where Bill got stuck!! Bill was a BIG MAN and the arm was far smaller than any of us would have thought. Since Bill had wanted to move at his own pace, Mr. Big, Annie, and I were well ahead of Bill when he had to stop. Bill called up to us to tell us what had happened, and he told us to continue climbing while he decided what to do. Annie and I were now both excited and worried. Excited because we were finally on the torch of the Statue of Liberty, and nervous because with Bill stuck in the arm, we might all die up there! Since we weren't supposed to be there in the first place, we couldn't call for help. We didn't want to starve to death, nor did we want to get Mr. Big in trouble. Then Annie went down to check on Bill. He told her to take plenty of pictures because he was afraid that if he pushed his way through that narrow spot, he'd never get down again!

"...nervous because with Bill stuck in the arm, we might all die up there! Since we weren't supposed to be there in the first place, we couldn't call for help."

Maybe Bill's getting stuck was God's way of telling us that Bill and his bulk shouldn't be up there. Not only was the climb narrow and difficult, it was a windy night and the torch was rocking all over the place. When we first got out on the torch, Annie and I sat on the floor until we finally worked up enough nerve to stand up.

Being so close to his dream...it was one of Bill's greatest frustrations. I actually think he went on a diet for a week or two afterwards, just in case we could convince our guide to let us have another try—but it didn't work. I don't know if the renovated torch they installed in 1986 is any stronger, but I don't plan on finding out any time soon!

RINGING IN THE NEW AND BILL'S WEDDING BELLS

Years ago for one of my *Powerboat* columns, I wrote a satirical piece on different ways to make your racing boat appear like it was going faster than it was—and how to do it without investing much money. One of these ways was an invention I called the "speed wig." It was actually a toupee stacked high with hair that was swept back and frozen in position with hair spray. If you wore it, well, even at 25 mph you would look like you were doing 50!

After the article appeared, some of my friends at OMC—the Outboard Marine Corporation—hired someone to make such a wig and they sent it to me as a Christmas gift. I was having the MAD gang over for a New Year's Eve party, and I decided that I would don the speed wig and appear at my party "disguised" as a new celebrity. Dennis Wunderlin suggested that I call myself "Chic Glitz," a name not unlike the chewing gum, Chiclets. (As it turned out, the name and the personality stuck, sort of like the chewing gum, and a whole alter-ego was born.)

When I decided that I would host the party as Chic Glitz, who was, of course, a very famous Las Vegas entertainer, I also decided that I didn't want to be alone in making a fool of myself. So I announced that everyone coming to the party would have to perform. They could sing, dance, tell jokes, recite poetry, but they **had** to do something! Surprisingly, just about everyone did.

Gaines did some magic, and he was pretty good. I can remember Chic's intro for Gaines: "Ladies and gentlemen, one of the most famous names in magic—recently he astounded a crowd at an Italian restaurant, where he made three plates of spaghetti and two pizzas disappear—please welcome William M. Gaines!"

After Gaines did his magic tricks, John Ficarra took off his shirt and jeans as he recited "Heaven Knows How I Love to Wear Women's Clothes." John was indeed wearing women's clothes underneath (and to this day, I still don't know if he was kidding, but in the office he does seem to adjust his clothing more than the other guys, even the women!). And Nick Meglin brought a guitar and sang "Try to Remember"—the title was all he could remember. There was tap dancing, puppets, a comedy monologue, and a parade featuring the Chicettes—Chic's show girls. NOT your typical party! But we had a hell of a good time, and for the next seven or eight years Chic Glitz hosted every New Year's Eve party, and everyone took part, whether or not they had talent.

And at all of these parties, Bill and Annie Gaines were the best audience, laughing uproariously in all the right places. In fact, they were such a good audience that when Bill felt it was too difficult to get around town anymore on New Year's Eve, I stopped having the parties. What fun would it be without our two best audience members?

Even though the parties died, Chic Glitz lived on. I was doing gadget spots on Nickelodeon's "Don't Just Sit There," when they put on a new show called "Total Panic." The producer of "Total Panic" wanted me to do spots on that show, but he wanted them to be "very different" from what I was doing on "Don't Just Sit There." I told him that I would not only do something different,

I would be a completely different person, and I brought in Chic's wardrobe to show him. In addition to the speed wig Chic had added a tuxedo, which was outlined in tinfoil and ringed with Christmas lights.

For my spot on "Total Panic," I hosted a game show written by Jeff Ginsberg (who also wrote "the" foreword for this book), called "You Want It, You Got It." I would bring out an item like a cream pie, and ask the audience of screaming kids what I should with it. Should I cut it up and serve it to the audience? Should I throw it into a paper shredder? Should I heave it at the camera? The kids voted with their applause—of course, they always picked the messiest thing. And that created an occupational hazard. Chic's tuxedo was AC, but he had to switch to DC for "Total Panic," lest he get electrocuted! Not that anyone would notice right away. With his hair and lights and tinfoil edging, Chic would pretty much look the same with or without 110 volts flowing through his body!

Chic has other TV appearances to his credit, too. He went on "Sally Jessy Raphael" to help Sally host a show on bad taste. And he lent his outfit to Ricardo'D, "editor" of *Cutting Edge* magazine. Ricardo'D appeared on "Live! With Regis & Kathie Lee" looking amazingly like Chic Glitz! They could be brothers, even the same person!

Of course, Chic is famous among MAD staffers. He's made several office visits and, from time to time, he even appears on the pages of MAD. But Chic is high-minded and only gets involved in totally respectable projects, so Chic is MAD's Dean of Words. Here, you can see for yourself:

Chic will soon appear in an upcoming MAD magazine touting another worthy venture: The Chic Glitz Home Study School of Specialization. For a few dollars more, people can sign up for The Chic Glitz Apartment Study School of Specialization!

But perhaps Chic's proudest moment came when he performed at Bill and Annie's wedding. They'd lived together for years before tying the knot—maybe it just took that long to plan the perfect party, or maybe it was because Chic's Vegas schedule was so tight he couldn't make it out before then...no matter, it was worth the wait.

Henny Youngman was also hired to entertain at the Gaines' wedding.

THE STAR
PHOTO FRAME

"...and then Chic came out! As soon as he entered the room where the formal dinner was, his fans leaped to their feet and mobbed him!"

Bill wanted Henny because he remembered being convulsed by him when he saw Henny perform at a Brooklyn theater when he was a kid. I don't know what Henny got paid; all Bill would admit to was that the fee was in the four-figure range. Chic, on the other hand—well, I **know** what Chic got. He got $12, plus carfare (two subway tokens). But, as you can see from the photos, some people were more excited about Chic's appearance than Henny's

Naturally, I wasn't present when Chic appeared. (To Chic's fans, he and I are like Superman and Clark Kent—we're never in the room at the same time.) Anyway, at one point I left the reception to go to the coat room...and then Chic came out! As soon as he entered the room where the formal dinner was, his fans leaped to their feet and mobbed him! Others, who didn't know Chic, were equally impressed. I understand quite a few wedding guests said things like, "Who the hell is that?" and "Is that guy for real?" Although no one was supposed to bring presents, Chic brought a large picture of himself, mounted in a blue plastic frame that had a big red plastic star glued on it. It's no wonder that "Mr. Tasteful" is one of the Chic's nicknames.

Bill and Annie's wedding was at Windows on the World, the revolving restaurant at the top of the World Trade Center. There was food for days (and *that* was just the hors d'oeuvres), and then there was a sit-down dinner. But for Bill, Annie had the waiter deliver to his table—what else?—a frankfurter!

The rest of us had to get by with sushi, prime rib, pasta, shrimp cocktail, salads, cheeses, breads, desserts, cookies, and wedding cake. But we made do.

One of the remarkable things about the wedding was that it was a MAD gathering, but we all played it pretty straight. There were a couple of reasons for that. Windows on the World is a very elegant place, and that intimidates the MAD staff. Second of all, there were dozens of non-MAD people there, and we didn't want to do any shtick that might backfire with guests who wouldn't understand that many of us are *really* off the wall. The only practical joke was Annie's, and the entertainment was provided by Henny and Chic only. (In fact, I even had Chic's agent clear Chic's appearance with Annie, but she insisted, so I passed that command performance invite on to Chic!) It was a sentimental occasion in the best sense of the word. Bill made a short speech to tell us that this affair was of great importance to him. First and foremost was his marriage to Annie. Second was MAD's 35th anniversary, and third was Bill's 65th birthday!

One thing that all the guests loved was that we were instructed NOT to bring gifts—and that was one instruction from Bill that every MAD staffer followed! My guess is that the "no gift" request solved many problems. Bill and Annie had everything they needed at home; they didn't have to worry about dragging tons of gifts from the World Trade Center uptown to their apartment; and Bill was kind enough to realize that shopping for the proper wedding gift for a couple like Annie and himself would be time consuming, and costly. Bill just wanted people to share in his joy, period. He even picked up the parking tab for those who drove!

Chic Glitz got married shortly after Gaines did, mainly because he got the leftovers from Bill's wedding and wanted to use them before they got too old. Now, I know what you're thinking—who the hell would marry Chic? Well, you're right. It *wasn't* easy finding a bride for Chic. But after much searching we found one right here in the MAD offices—we drafted Sara Fowler of "MAD Minutes" fame for the role. Sara said she'd do it, but she wanted to be called "Mona"—no last name, just Mona. Like Cher.

Chic's wedding was not the same caliber as Bill and Annie's, but you can judge for yourself. Here's a copy of Chic's wedding invitation:

Mr. & Mrs. Glitzle Chickowski
request the honor of your presents*
at the wedding of their
LEGENDARY Son
*** C * H * I * C ***
(who is currently appearing in Macbeth with Brett Summers
at the Brew & Burger TheaterGarden City, N.Y.)
to Mona What's-Her-Name.
To take place on
Saturday evening, December Thirty-first
Nineteen Hundred and Eighty-seven
Aboard the luxury yacht
APPLAUSE XXIII
At ten-thirty p.m. o'clock
Reception immediately following
Hors d'oeuvres available at cut-rate prices
Cash bar
R.S.V.P.
Collect calls not accepted!
*(presents $5 in value per person/$10 per couple)
(Chic's silverware registry: Horn & Hardart; Linens: Holiday
Inn; China: TWA First Class; Glassware: Smuckers)

You'll notice that Chic's invite *did* specify gifts, but with a value of $5 per person, $10 per couple. People found it easy to shop for Chic and Mona, but like all newlyweds, they got plenty of duplicates. Like, they got at least three sets of plastic ketchup and mustard squirt bottles, and three sets of fuzzy toilet seat covers—fortunately, in different colors!

RED, WHITE, AND BILL

Bill was fiercely patriotic, and so was I. Well, I still am, but not today, because I'm writing this on April 15th and I just paid my income taxes!

But the time-honored American symbols have always meant a lot to me. For years, every Fourth of July I've outlined my boat in red, white, and blue chaser lights and flown the American flag from the highest mast. One Fourth of July, I even bought a few dozen flags so anyone at the marina who wanted to could fly one on their boat. Bill loved the idea. You already know how Bill felt about the Statue of Liberty and he was equally proud of the flag.

But of course, that didn't mean that the flag was immune from MAD. For issue #300, the staff decided on a cover that depicted George Bush (who was president at the time) burning a sort of American flag. Bush had made flag-burning an issue in his presidential campaign, so we were playing off that, but since this was MAD, there was of course a twist—the flag bore a picture of Alfred E. Neuman. So the cover posed an interesting question: Would President George Bush burn the flag *because* it had Alfred's picture on it?

In this issue we burn GONE WITH THE WIND
WIZARD OF OZ CASABLANCA DICK TRACY
MAD
January 1991
300th ISSUE

"...Would President George Bush burn the flag because it had Alfred's picture on it?"

Bill was a little unsure about the cover and he called me into his office and asked if I had seen the rough art. I told him I had. He said he was worried that it looked un-American, and that it would be taken as a slam against the flag. I told him I didn't think it was unAmerican and that I saw it as humorous, and thought-provoking. Would George Bush, so righteously American, burn the flag because he couldn't stand Alfred?! Bill said our talk made him feel better and that he'd let the cover go as scheduled.

Hussein Asylum Edition

But the cover never ran. Shortly after it was sent down to the printers, Operation Desert Shield began, with its massive movement of soldiers and equipment to the Middle East. Worried that four months down the line the cover would mean a lot of things we never intended, the art was struck, and a different cover was rushed into the works. MAD cover #300 was dated January, 1991, so it was on sale just before Christmas of 1990. Then we were really thankful it didn't have the "flag" cover, because tensions were building when that issue hit the stands. And a few weeks later, the war began. That was when I discovered that Nick, John, Bill, and I were not only patriotic, we all had ESP. While on my way into the office one morning, for some reason I recalled that "60 Minutes" had received much mail from ex-servicemen. Most had said how much they loved receiving MAD while overseas because reading the satires kept them in touch with what was happening back in the States. So when I got in, I asked Nick and John if we should ask Bill to start sending MAD overseas. Surprise! They had just come from asking Bill! But the bigger surprise was that earlier in the day Bill had ordered an extra 25,000 copies of MAD to be sent to the troops overseas. (Yes—to OUR troops! Maybe we should have forced them on the enemy, but we didn't!) And over the next several months, regular issues of MAD, with a small picture of Alfred E. Neuman in Desert Storm gear added to the cover, were sent to the troops overseas.

"...earlier in the day Bill had ordered an extra 25,000 copies of MAD to be sent to the troops overseas. (Yes—to OUR troops! Maybe we should have forced them on the enemy, but we didn't!)"

READING THE MAIL

Just about to the very end, Bill opened all the subscriber mail, and he sorted and added up the sales figures for the MAD subscriptions.
Obviously this was something Brian Fitterman of Please Promotions didn't know.
Brian was responsible for having MAD jackets made for the staff—at our own expense, of course—and the "Spy vs. Spy" and Alfred E. Neuman pins used for premium giveaways for the two- and three-year subscriptions to MAD.

Now, Brian wanted a subscription of his own, but he felt that if he asked Gaines how to get one, Gaines would feel obligated to "comp" him one. So, Brian just decided to order a subscription through the mail like a regular person. Which he did.

A few weeks later, Brian's check was returned to him with a note from Gaines.

"Dear Mr. Fitterman:

"I am sorry, we don't accept checks from Jews. So we are sending it back. However, we are entering a free three-year subscription for you!"

Brian called me, saying in disbelief, "Dick, how could Gaines, the *publisher* of MAD know I had subscribed! Who do you think gave him my letter?"

"Brian," I said, "Gaines always has—and probably always will—open all the MAD subscription mail himself! So very little gets past him!"

John Caldwell on Bill Gaines

Bill Gaines and I had little in common. He relished fine wine, and I grew up in upstate New York. He delighted in practical jokes, while I worked for a brief time as a cartographer. He had a fondness for dirigibles, and I put ketchup on just about everything. He enjoyed non sequiturs, while I once tried to hitchhike to Finland. But we did share one important link. He enjoyed publishing MAD Magazine, just as much as I, first in my youth, enjoyed reading it, and now as an adult, enjoy being a contributor.

ALL EMPLOYEES MUST WASH HANDS BEFORE LEAVING! VISITORS CAN GO AWAY YECCHY!

The first time I encountered Bill Gaines was in the men's room outside the MAD offices. I was on my way in to meet, for the first time, Nick Meglin and the late John Putnam. (No, I wasn't meeting them in the men's room. The fact is, I have the bladder of a lab rat and I had to relieve myself before going in to show my wares to Nick and John.) As I stood at the urinal Bill walked in and bellied up to the next pissoir. I was dumbfounded. Several of my bodily functions temporarily ceased, including the one that obliged me to ask for the key to that particular salon in the first place. Naturally I knew who he was, but he had no clue to my identity. (This was years before my massive rhinoplasty and species change surgery.) As I recall, it was around noon, so he probably figured me to be someone delivering sandwiches. (No, not to the men's room! You know what I mean.)

As I waited for my temporary power shortage to run its course, I could see Bill was finishing his immediate business. As he zipped up, the thought occurred to me to reach over and flush his urinal, saying something like, "This one's on me, Mr. Gaines." But I poultried out and let the moment pass. It wasn't until perhaps three years later that I actually was introduced to Bill. By then, too much (if you'll pardon the expression) water had gone over the dam for me to bring up our previous non-meeting.

One night at dinner on Bill's last and my first MAD trip, I made Bill laugh. We were aboard the cruise ship *Horizon* enroute to Bermuda, a few hundred miles out and several courses into our meal. I had heard Bill laugh before, but I was never the source of his outbursts. Finally, something I said had triggered a howl of staggering proportions. I'm certain the ship rocked and compasses spun. Nobody enjoyed laughing more than Bill, and at last I could delight in serving up a between-course, palette-cleansing chuckle. Later that evening my wife, Diane, and I had this exchange: "I made Bill laugh tonight." "I know. Wasn't it great?" "Yeah. What was it I said?" "I don't remember." "Neither do I."

I still don't remember.

UNDERSTANDING STATISTICS

Statistics can lie. And so can chapter headings. This chapter has nothing to do with statistics. Remember how I told you Gaines was convinced that the publisher of the MAD paperback books never really read the contracts—and so he put in more and more bizarre terms which they unknowingly agreed to? Well, the publication of this book is on a very tight schedule, and I'm convinced that the editor of this book, Joan Fucillo, isn't reading everything I write!

Therefore, I threw this chapter in as a test. I figured with a chapter heading like "Understanding Statistics," she'll skip right over it. I'll tell you a little bit about Joan. She doesn't even live in New York City!
She lives in Clinton, New York. That's the *sticks!* My guess is that Thunder's Mouth hired her because she probably pays very little rent in Clinton, and they wouldn't have to pay her New York editor prices! At least Joan does have a phone. Well, sort of. You just call the local drugstore and ask the pharmacist to run upstairs and get her!

Okay, the test is over. I've said enough bad things about Joan. If you're reading this chapter, it's obvious she didn't! Otherwise it would be cut out of the book!*

And now, on to our next regularly scheduled chapter.

---

*Editor's Note: Well finally, a mention in your lousy book ... you bet I'm leaving it in!

HONEST AND AN ATHEIST

Bill was a remarkable man, and without a doubt the most honest person I've ever met. In all his dealings he was loyal, brave, true, and at times, truly bizarre. One particular practice of Bill's really got to me: He dunned people who DIDN'T bill him promptly!

Although his appearance could fool you, Bill was a neat-nick, an "orderly" fanatic, who could only go home when every piece of paper he had put on his desk in the morning was dealt with, and his desk was clear for the following day. By the same token he wanted to close out each month's checkbook with EVERYTHING paid, so it wasn't unusual to hear him on the phone, complaining in a sing-song way, "Didn't I buy something from you? Didn't you send it to me? Wouldn't you like to be paid? Then you'd better bill me right away! It's been a month already, and I want to pay for it now!! Send me a bill!"

Okay, so that was strange, but it wasn't until we got to talking about income taxes that I found out how truly honest Bill was. As you know, Bill loved to travel to Europe, especially in search of great food and fine wine, and since MAD is published in a dozen foreign countries, I knew he was doing a lot of business on these trips. I was curious, so I asked Bill how he kept track of what part of each trip was pleasure, and what part was business. Bill said, "It's easy. I go to a foreign publishers' convention or book fair once a year. That's business. That's all I take."

I couldn't believe it! "But Bill, you're having dinners with publishers all over the globe—that's got to be a business expense!"

Bill was adamant. "It's too much trouble to figure out what's business and what's pleasure. I just write off the one trip a year. Period."

Not long after this conversation, I found out that Bill didn't believe in

God, or a hereafter. That got to me, and I literally yelled at him: "You really ARE nuts!! You mean to tell me you're THAT honest because you want to be—you're not even doing it out of fear of going to Hell? Bill, you're a very sick person!!!" After hearing that, what really puzzled me was that while Bill didn't believe in a Superior Being, he *did* believe in the laying on of hands as a healing power.

CONTRACT

I not only believe in the healing power of the laying on of hands, but I even took a couple of courses in the subject. My interest began over twenty years ago, because of my first dog, Wags. Here's the story:

I had been out for several hours with a friend, and the two of us walked into my apartment. Wags, who was about eleven years old but in okay shape for his age, was lying on the floor, stiff and cold. I could not, would not, believe he was gone! I knelt down and held him, telling him that this could not be. He could not leave me! He slowly became softer, and finally he got up and walked around! My friend exited quickly, more or less backing out of the door, with just a little wave good-bye. Later that evening he telephoned, and in a stammering voice said, "Was I hallucinating this afternoon, or was your dog dead—and then alive?"

I said, "I'm still shaking too, but I think that's what happened. We just came back from a walk, and he's fine!" This led me to firmly believe that the powers of the mind are real—and truly powerful!

Now, Bill was diabetic, really overweight, and wasn't getting around very easily. There were days when he wasn't feeling well at all, and he couldn't get any relief from his various medications. So I told him about the laying on of hands, and I asked if he wanted me to try to help him. He said he'd try anything. It worked, and then it became a fairly regular thing. If Bill was having a bad time of it he would call me into his office. I would touch whatever part of his body that "presented" itself to my mind and I would often relay the "thought pictures" I got while working on him.

...Her throbbing breast glistened in the moonlight.

According to Bill, I was successful most of time, and his relief would last from twenty minutes to several days. However, as fit our relationship, I would usually end a successful session with these words:

DICK: Don't forget, Gaines, these same hands that can heal you can kill you in a second!! You must give me everything I ask for—and want! Or I'll wipe you off the face of the earth, just like that!! (snap fingers!!)

Then as I left his office, I would take Annie aside and say in a stage whisper that Bill was sure to hear, "He's too healthy! Increase the sugar in his insulin! We're never going to get his money at this rate!"

WHINE AND CHEESE

Gaines really loved wine. He had a wine cellar in his apartment. And I'm not talking about some little wine chest! This was a walk-in, walk-around, refrigerated wine cellar that happened to be on the 25th floor! You saw it as soon as you entered his home. It was like stepping into a modern apartment to find that someone had built a large log cabin right in the middle of the living room.

I, on the other hand, know nothing about wine, and rarely drink it. But as a matter of fact, Bill often invited me to wine tastings, and we made a great team. Between the two of us, we were able to grade the wines fairly accurately. The formula we used was, the better I liked the taste of a wine, the more Bill knew it was sweet and cheap; a wine I considered vile was excellent and expensive! But I don't think Bill took me along just for my taste—laughter was as important to him as wine.

One of the most sumptuous of the wine and food affairs I went to with Bill was at the Waldorf-Astoria. Chefs from all over the world were flown in, and exotic wines were gathered from the far corners of the globe.

This occurred about fifteen years ago, and it cost $100 a plate, which was quite expensive at the time. When I found this out I told Gaines to ask how much extra silverware would cost—because I REFUSED to eat with my hands!

Since Bill treated me to the dinner, I picked up the tab for the two cups of coffee we had at the Automat on the way up to the Waldorf. Of course, this was a black tie affair, so we were both in tuxedos. That was one of the great things about Bill. How many people would stop at the Automat before going to the Waldorf-Astoria for chow, er, to dine? But that's the great thing about New York, too. You can go into any dining establishment from a dingy coffee shop to the Waldorf in a tux, and not raise an eyebrow. (But now that I think about it, I'm not sure Bill's tux was a tux—I think it was a black suit, white shirt, and bowtie. But, hey, close enough. At least he wasn't wearing Jaffee's T-shirt!)

As you can imagine, there was much pomp and circumstance at this gourmet affair. All the guests were gathered in front of the closed dining room doors. At *exactly* 7 p.m., the doors were flung open, and we saw rows of tables laden with candles, flowers, and at least a dozen wine glasses at each of the massive place settings. I turned to one of the maitre d's and said, "Didn't I tell you NOT to fuss?" During the dinner, I sipped each different wine as it was served, and made my pronouncements to Gaines. Things like: this is an arrogant little wine—this is a humorous wine—this wine is a pain in the ass—this is a presumptuous little wine—this wine thinks it's just a little bit too big for its glass....You know, wine talk!

"...this wine is a pain in the ass—this is a presumptuous little wine—this wine thinks it's just a little bit too big for its glass....You know, wine talk!"

About five hours later, we left. The host stood by the door shaking everyone's hand, and when it was my turn, I said, "Next time you'll have to come to *our* place for chow." As Gaines and I were waiting for the elevator, I could see the empty wine cases piled by one of the dining room exit doors. I said to Bill, "Look, the boxes our nine-course frozen dinners came in!"

Bill really loved that! As a matter of fact he said, "God, Dick, if they ever have an affair like this again, we should have John Putnam make up some fake boxes like that, and we'll leave them next to the elevator. Then we can just watch people's reactions as they see them when they leave!"

ORDERING FOOD, THE GAINES WAY

Bill ordered main courses pretty much the way I liked to order desserts. He'd order two or three entrees for himself, and then he always ordered "one for the table." One for the table was an extra entree that anyone at the table could taste.

"...It was not unusual at a MAD dinner for there to be eight diners and more than twice as many appetizer and entree orders."

Of course, anyone eating out with Bill was also entitled to order "one for the table." If we were at a restaurant where Bill's ordering habits weren't known, it wasn't unusual for the waiter or waitress to say, "How many more will be joining your party?" Hearing that offended Bill, but he would just say, "It's for us. Just bring it!"

Another good part of eating out with Bill was that he almost always picked up the check. I say "almost always" because, if it was just the two of us, I would often pick up the check. Okay, SOMETIMES I would pick up the check! Once in a while? Once in a blue moon? The truth is, I would occasionally pick up the check, and Bill was very grateful when I did. Certainly not because he didn't have the money to pay the tab himself, but I believe that for Bill it really was the thought that counted.

John Ficarra on Bill Gaines

When I hear the name Bill Gaines, several words immediately come to mind—cheap...generous...insane. But the one word that would probably top my list when I think of Bill Gaines would be *food*. Much of Bill Gaines' life was devoted to the pursuit of a great meal (with an appropriate great wine, of course). And when you were with Bill, it was very easy to get caught up in the great food chase.

When I first started working at MAD, I was a dumb, "gastronomically challenged" kid. At my first official MAD dinner, Bill took Nick Meglin, Lenny Brenner, and me to a renowned Italian restaurant in Brooklyn. I promptly ordered shrimp cocktail and a steak—an order for which Bill mercilessly mocked and ridiculed me for many years thereafter. But it wasn't long before Bill had me gorging on world-class delicacies such as caviar, truffles, and more. Like all great armies, the MAD staff traveled on its stomach, led by Bill, our General Patton, who was quite willing to slap any headwaiter who stood in the way of him getting a good meal.

Dining out with Bill was always an adventure. It was with Bill that I first learned the expression "order it for the table." Bill's idea was that if you saw something on the menu that you even remotely thought you might enjoy, immediately order it for the entire table to sample. It mattered not that you had already chosen an appetizer and entree, order it for the table. It was not unusual at a MAD dinner for there to be eight diners and more than twice as many appetizer and entree orders.

I remember once eating with Bill and the staff at New York's famed Gotham Bar and Grill. As always, Bill sat at the head of the table orchestrating the dinner, making sure that everyone had everything they could possibly want and then selecting the perfect wine to complement each dish. After about a dozen appetizers, champagne, several bottles of wine, and a plethora of entrees still to come, the waitress came over to our table. "The chef sent me out," she said. "He wants to know, Who *are* you?"

I always enjoyed the look on the waiter's face when Bill would summon him over and proceed to order the entire menu. And I will never forget a meal the staff once had at Brooklyn's Gage and Tollner where, at Bill's urging, Nick Meglin ordered eight different sweet potato appetizers, just for himself. And that was only the beginning of a four-hour-plus eating orgy! Eventually the waiters brought over a *second table* just for all the plates, platters, and wine bottles.

But Bill was by no means a food snob. In fact, one of his favorite foods was White Castle hamburgers, which he fondly remembered from his youth. One day I went into Bill's office and told him a new White Castle had just opened near my home in Staten Island. Bill's eyes lit up and he immediately proposed a deal to me. If I would host a dinner party at my home and supply him with White Castle hamburgers and fries, he would supply the food for the rest of the staff. That seemed perfectly fair and reasonable enough to me, so I accepted.

Two weeks later the entire editorial staff gathered at my house. Bill happily sat at the end of the table wolfing down the dozen or so hamburgers I bought for him, not giving a second thought to the fact that those dozen burgers had cost him several hundred dollars in world-class caviar, smoked Scottish salmon, foie gras, and prosciutto and Buffalo mozzarella for the rest of the staff.

If you are born under the right stars, live a clean, exemplary life and are really, really lucky, once in your lifetime you will meet someone with the warmth, generosity, and insanity of Bill Gaines.

FOOD FLIGHT

But Bill didn't make the trip to the Ficarras' on Staten Island just to eat White Castle hamburgers. Once or twice a year, along with a few other MAD staffers, he went there for a *real* dinner, and a dinner in Bill's honor at the Ficarras' house was more like a Roman Food Feast. If you don't believe me, just check out the menu each person received as they entered the feast. *Yes, everything on the menu was served!!*

John's wife, Marilyn, engineered the entire meal. She claimed that she actually loved having the MAD guys over to eat because "they ate so much and took home any leftovers"! I, of course, just picked, until we got the good part of the meal—dessert. And I helped Marilyn out, too, by taking the extra desserts home. (By the way, "Uncle Boo" was yet another pet name for William M. Gaines.)

NO PALM OIL WAS USED IN PRINTING THIS CHAPTER

UNCLE BOO'S COMMAND MEAT MADNESS MANIA MAD MEETING

MEAT

-Polish Paté on Rye
-Boar's Head Coney Island Hot Dogs
-Italian Sausage
-Parsley & Cheese Sausage
-Bar-B-Que Chicken
-Chicken Pinwheels (with Ham, Cheese & Herbs)
-Polish Kielbasa
-Steak Sandwiches

SALADS

-Rotini Pasta Salad (with Red & Yellow Peppers)
-Fred's Own Potato Salad

FILLERS

-Corn on the Cob
-French Bread
-Soft Rolls

DESSERTS

-Peach Pie
-Homemade Chocolate Chip Ice Cream
-Fresh Fruit Salad
-Chocolate Mousse

DRINKS

-Coke/Diet Pepsi
-Iced Tea
-Beer (Guiness Stout, Guiness Gold, Heineken, Budweiser)
Your Host: Yankee DoodleMay 27, 1990

ENJOY!!!ENJOY!!!ENJOY!!!ENJOY!!!ENJOY!!!ENJOY!!!ENJOY!!!ENJOYENJOY!!!ENJOY!!!

GETTING MY JUST DESSERTS

Just as much as Bill loved wine, I love desserts. It's my favorite part of a meal. And when I moved away from home and got my own apartment, I increased my consumption of desserts at dinner and reduced the main part of the meal. Then one night, I had a thought: *Hey, I live alone! No one can criticize my eating habits!* So I eliminated the main part of dinner altogether and just ate desserts. I was in seventh heaven!

For an appetizer, I'd have an apple turnover. For the main course, half a blueberry pie. And for dessert, chocolate chip cookies and ice cream. I made the chocolate chip cookies myself, not because they tasted better, but because I liked to eat the raw dough. I ate so much dough that even though the recipe said "yields two dozen cookies," I often ended up with just four or five baked cookies. Since I seemed to be thriving on my all-dessert diet, I decided to stop pretending to bake the cookies—I simply made the dough and ate the whole bowl raw! It tasted great, and what an easy cleanup—no cookie pan to wash! And no hot kitchen. My all-dessert diet lasted almost a week;

then I got really sick!

I barfed, got diarrhea, and had terrible stomach pains. That night changed the way I ate forever. Now I eat a salad or a vegetable, at least once a month!

During my first dinner out with Bill, I told him that I always look at the restaurant's dessert menu first. That way I'd know whether to order a large entree or a small one. Bill told me to get whatever I wanted for the main course, and to leave dessert to him. So after we consumed the main course, the waiter came over and asked if we wanted to see the dessert menu again. But Bill told him not to bother with the menu and just to "bring one of every dessert you have!" He was *serious*. The waiter rolled a dessert cart over to my side and left it there. And I knew that Bill was a guy who really understood what it meant to be a dessert freak!

I never let Bill be that extravagant again, but when we went to dinner, I didn't hold back. If there were three, four, or five things on the dessert menu I wanted to try, I'd order them all!

On the airplane rides to our MAD trips, Bill couldn't actually order dessert (or the food, for that matter), but he would do the next best thing. He'd have all the artists and writers who could live without desserts agree to give them up. Then he would alert the stewardess serving the meal, and tell her that all those desserts should go on my tray. You can imagine the looks I got from the people on the plane who weren't in on the joke, when their trays arrived with one piece of chocolate cake and mine came loaded with at least a dozen!

SPEED READING

Gaines called me into his office.

BILL: I want to take the Evelyn Wood Speed Reading Course.

DICK: Surprise, Bill, you're a grown man. You can take it! You don't need my permission.

BILL: I want you to take it with me. I don't want to go alone.

DICK: You won't be alone, Evelyn Wood will be there.

BILL: Come on, take it with me! I'll pay for both of us.

DICK: Bill, I don't *like* to read, so why would I take the course? So I won't like to read three times faster?

BILL: Come on, take it, we'll have fun. We'll eat out before every class.

DICK: Will there be cake?

BILL: Plenty of cake.

DICK: Oh, okay....

So Bill signed the two of us up. He felt we couldn't go wrong because Evelyn Wood had a money-back guarantee: If we didn't triple our reading speed while increasing our comprehension, we'd get our money back. So off to school we went.

The first few classes were really interesting. We read articles as fast as we could; and then later we learned that those test articles had phrases and words missing. That exercise showed us that the brain could fill in the missing parts of the stuff we'd read. So, if we read extremely fast, our brain would fill in anything we missed.

We started reading faster and faster. The instructors kept telling us that we didn't have to read slowly to get enjoyment from reading, but I was reading so fast, I didn't know what the hell I had read! We read *Moby Dick* in eleven seconds. I told Bill I remembered something about fishing, but that was it.

Yet, the funny thing was that both Bill and I continued doing well on the comprehension tests. Then I discovered something about those tests: If you just used logic, you could probably pass the test without reading anything. Here's a sample question to illustrate the point:

When his master came home from work, Spot the dog:
A. was setting the timer on the VCR.
B. had left a note saying he went shopping.
C. wagged his tail.

Obviously, the answer's "C"...unless, of course, you have an incredibly gifted dog named Spot. So Bill and I decided that from that night on, we would only answer the question if we specifically remembered reading the information in the text. If we specifically remembered reading "Spot wagged his tail when his master came home," we'd answer the question correctly. If not, we'd just leave it blank. Surprise! Our grades started to fall, and neither one of us passed the final exam.

So Bill got his money back. And in fairness to Evelyn Wood, (who by the way, never did show up in person), we did increase our reading speed, but we didn't triple it, and that was the guarantee.

Thus far, this chapter contains 483 words. Find your reading speed on the following chart:

MINUTES TO READ THE CHAPTER		YOUR AVERAGE SPEED
TEN MINUTES	——————→	*You read 48.3 words per minute. Take a speed-reading class!*
FIVE MINUTES	——————→	*You read 96.6 words per minute*
THREE MINUTES	——————→	*You read 161 words per minute*
ONE MINUTE	——————→	*You're lying. Not even Evelyn Wood herself reads that fast!*

Now, test your comprehension by answering the following questions.

1. Dick took the Evelyn Wood Speed-Reading Course with:
A. William M. Gaines.
B. Tonya Harding.
C. Superman.

2. After the class was over, Dick and Bill:
A. got their money back.
B. painted their apartments black.
C. were killed in a plane crash.

3. The object of the speed-reading class was to:
A. learn how to read faster.
B. prepare for a career as a beautician.
C. understand the current tax code.

ANSWERS: Don't you feel stupid turning this book upside down? Like you expected the answers to be anything but "A" all the way! Now, do me a favor, turn the book back right side up, and continue reading. But SLOW DOWN. There's going to be a test!

CLOSE ENCOUNTERS OF THE MAD KIND

MAD fans are legion. For a while there was even a magazine about MAD called *MAD Freaks*, which was published by a bunch of fans. But we met only a very few of our fans in person until 1977. The occasion was MAD's 25th anniversary, and about six of us went on a national tour to celebrate. (As I recall, we stalled going on the tour for a couple of months so we could celebrate MAD's **25.2**-year anniversary—the **.2** part fit better with our image!) It was the first time MAD had done anything along the lines of a publicity campaign.

The six MAD-reps were paired up and sent into the world. I traveled with Al Jaffee to Dallas, Houston, and San Antonio, and we had a wonderful time, especially doing radio shows. On one particular program, I broke Jaffee up when a listener phoned in with the question: "What do you guys wear?" I assume he meant to the office, but I answered, "I'm wearing a formal blue gown, and Jaffee is wearing a beautiful pants suit!" Jaffee cracked up, and from then on, if I couldn't work in that answer, he would make it happen, by saying, "Dick, I bet the listeners would like to know what we wear when we travel"—or something like that.

The reception Al and I, and all the MAD guys, got was incredible. Our business cards were as prized as if they were $50 bills. (When I figured that out,

I tried to charge $50, but unfortunately, that didn't work.) Even years later, I'd run into people who were still carrying my MAD card in their wallets!

Even traveling on my own to conventions or lectures, being the man from MAD has gotten me some incredible treatment. Like the time one winter night when an entire hotel got extra heat because *I* had a chill. Here's the story: I had called the front desk to say that my room was cold, and they sent up the building engineer. He explained that because it was an old hotel, it had no individual room temperature controls, and there was nothing he could do about it. I thanked him for his time, and gave him a copy of a MAD paperback I'd written. He freaked out and insisted on seeing my driver's license, because he could not believe it was really me staying at the hotel! Beaming, he left my room to go to the basement and crank up the boilers. Everyone was plenty warm that night!

MAD fans come in a variety of shapes and sizes. Once at a comic convention, I watched a group of bikers strolling through the aisles. These were big bikers: big arms, big bellies, lots of facial hair, tattoos everywhere—and the men were even tougher! As they made their way to the MAD booth, I couldn't imagine what was in store. They didn't stop to chat, but they all stopped to give Alfred the thumbs-up sign. One even ventured to utter a few words: "Alfred's cool, man!" Alfred sure does have wide appeal.

MAD fans have a wonderful sense of humor. At one San Diego Comic Convention held years ago, we gave away MAD tattoos. The tattoos were a bonus in one of the MAD Collector's Specials, but we had about 10,000 extra sheets printed as giveaways. As I handed them out, I would say things like, "They go on with water, they come off with sulfuric acid!"

I got a lot of snappy answers, like, "Great, I have some sulfuric acid with me!" and "Sulfuric acid? Good, I'll give them to my kids!"

One of my most fun presentations was for the New Jersey Chapter of Mensa. When I booked it, I had no idea that Mensa was an organization of above-average people, many of them certifiable geniuses (they had to pass a test!). After I found that out, I was worried that they would be a tough audience—but they weren't. In fact, they were the best audience I ever had! They laughed at every punchline, often two or three words before the finish. And, they even spent time thinking about my slide show after it was over.

In my MAD lecture, I run this slide:

MAD

This page is in black and white, but the slide wasn't. (Oh come on, you can imagine the colors.) While the slide was on the screen, I would give this description: "The red line is the number of copies printed. The green line is the number sold. The yellow line is mustard—we made this chart while we were eating lunch. And the purple line is the color of the carpeting we've been trying to get for the MAD offices."

About a week after that particular performance, samples of purple carpeting started coming in. I called one of the people who had set up the lecture and asked if she had any idea about what was going on. She said, "Obviously, various members of Mensa are trying to help you get that exact shade of purple carpeting for your offices. They've contacted dozens of rug manufacturers!"

MAD fans have had a tremendous effect on me personally. After Bill died in June of 1992, I thought maybe it was time to move on, because I didn't think I wanted to be at MAD without Bill. But a month later at the San Diego Comic Convention, so many people grasped my hand and pleaded, "Make sure MAD continues to publish," that I decided to stay on for the duration.

MAD AND THE RISE OF THE EDUCATED CONSUMER

One of the cornerstones of MAD's philosophy, and mine as well, is, Don't believe everything you read, or everything you see. In fact, it was my commitment to truth in advertising that launched my MAD career thirty-odd years ago. (What? You've forgotten already?) And over those years, I've written innumerable articles that puncture Madison Avenue's balloon.

(Okay, so maybe the articles are NUMBERABLE—numerable?—but who cares??) I also wrote an original MAD paperback called MADvertising, way back in 1972, when Ralph Nader was still wearing diapers—under a three-piece suit, of course.

Bill claimed that I was actually performing a public service and that I was responsible for alerting consumers to many of the misleading tactics companies used in advertising and packaging, like planned obsolescence, hyping useless features, and touting meaningless statistics. Statistics can be so misleading! For example, did you know that nine out of ten people I interviewed said this book was the funniest book published in 1994! But what would the result be if I asked people who *didn't* work for Thunder's Mouth Press, the book's publisher?

In *MADvertising*, I have a chapter on how manufacturers use deceptive ways to make their products look better. For example, an airline or a car company can make their seats look gigantic by hiring tiny models for their ads.

That might be cheating a bit, but it isn't *that* far from reality. But further along those lines, one of my favorite mail order rip-offs was something called the Early American Style "Country Store Organizer."

The photo in the ad for the "Organizer" showed a small cabinet with a plant and a coffee mug on top, and letters and things in the slots below. The copy said, "adds warmth to any room—helps end messy clutter." In reality, the Country Store Organizer was only 9 inches high and 7 1/2 inches wide—it would only add warmth to A VERY SMALL ROOM! And as far as organizing things goes, you *could* stick envelopes into the slots, but only if you cut them in pieces first! That's because the piece was only 3 1/2 inches deep. A mug and a plant couldn't fit on top—they must have used toys for the picture in the ad. I had a lot of fun demonstrating this one on TV—I'd appear with a huge pair of scissors and cut up envelopes and try to fit them in the slots. I showed the Country Store Organizer on "Live! With Regis & Kathie Lee," the "Phil Donahue Show," and Sally Jessy Raphael's program.

But, you know, people don't think. First of all, no dimensions were listed in the ad—a bad sign. Second, the Country Store Organizer only cost about $9. What do you think you're going to get for $9? Actually, you get a lot less than you'd think!

Researching such products means you buy a lot of them, and I do believe I single-handedly kept a manufacturer of tacky copper-bottomed pots in business with my TV work. The pots looked good in the ad; they even looked good on camera. I would show off the pots, and then I'd say, "But the ad doesn't mention one additional feature—if you want to take your frying pan with you on a trip, it folds up for easy packing!" The metal on the frying pan was SO thin, I actually could—and did—fold it in half on the air. It always got a big laugh, but I've demonstrated it so many times on TV, I've ended up buying at least a dozen sets of those flimsy pans!

My friends at the Better Business Bureau tell me that mail order fraud runs into the billions of dollars, so be wary when you read ads that offer too much for too little. Over the years I've collected hundreds of mail order rip-offs, and I have a warehouse full of prize stuff: $15 luggage sets, which are chintzy nylon shells; $10 genuine diamond rings, which are diamond chips

CONSUMER

...Consumer Reporter Stuart Rado shot this when we were on the Sally Jesse Raphael show. I'm holding one of those bargain "Copper bottom pots.

mounted in tinfoil; $15 "sewing machines," which are much more like small staple guns! You get the picture. If it sounds too good to be true—it probably is!

One of my very favorite satirical pieces for MAD was "Sneaky Tactics to Get You to Open Junk Mail." This article ran way back in October of 1980. Hopefully it was humorous back then, but look it over now, and see just how many of those sneaky tactics have actually been used!! Maybe I wasn't writing a humor piece. Maybe I was actually writing a handbook for junk mailers!

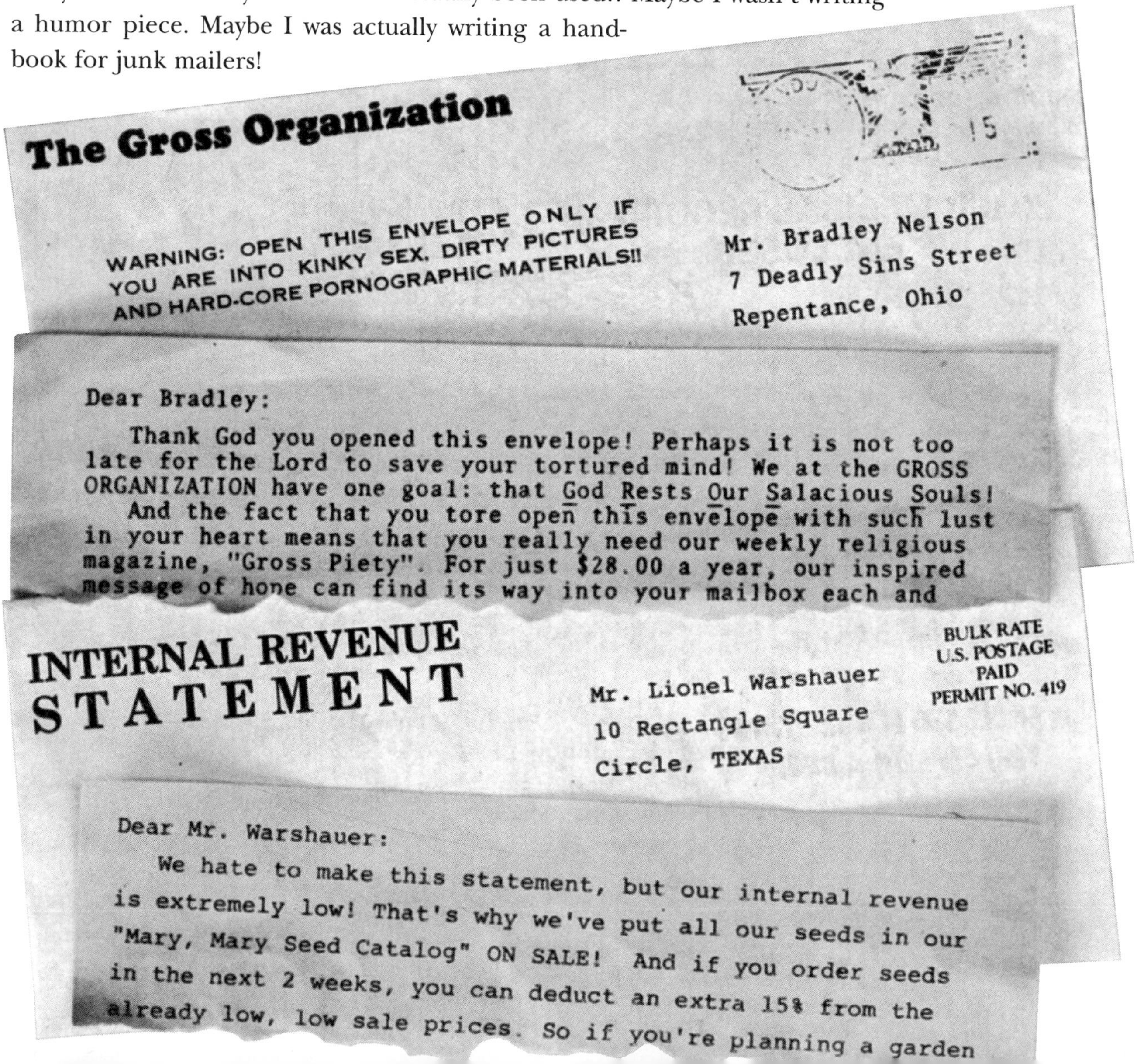
The Gross Organization
WARNING: OPEN THIS ENVELOPE ONLY IF YOU ARE INTO KINKY SEX, DIRTY PICTURES AND HARD-CORE PORNOGRAPHIC MATERIALS!!
Mr. Bradley Nelson
7 Deadly Sins Street
Repentance, Ohio
Dear Bradley:
Thank God you opened this envelope! Perhaps it is not too late for the Lord to save your tortured mind! We at the GROSS ORGANIZATION have one goal: that God Rests Our Salacious Souls!
And the fact that you tore open this envelope with such lust in your heart means that you really need our weekly religious magazine, "Gross Piety". For just $28.00 a year, our inspired message of hope can find its way into your mailbox each and
INTERNAL REVENUE STATEMENT
Mr. Lionel Warshauer
10 Rectangle Square
Circle, TEXAS
BULK RATE
U.S. POSTAGE
PAID
PERMIT NO. 419
Dear Mr. Warshauer:
We hate to make this statement, but our internal revenue is extremely low! That's why we've put all our seeds in our "Mary, Mary Seed Catalog" ON SALE! And if you order seeds in the next 2 weeks, you can deduct an extra 15% from the already low, low sale prices. So if you're planning a garden

Here's more valuable advice for the consumer taken from my paperback book MADVERTISING, illustrated by Bob Clarcke.

"Beware of the asterisk (*) next to the big print in an ad. Advertisers use it to give you "bad news" or "qualifying statements". For instance:

Now Fly to Miami Via
ITA Airlines for Only
$56 ROUND TRIP*
*Fly any Wednesday during Passover that the plane is less than 1/8 full, including the crew, and you must stay in Miami for at least two years, four months, three weeks and five days and return on a windy Thursday in Lent on any flight that is carrying penguins as air freight.

The Bald One
PIANO
GUARANTEED FOR 5 YEARS*
*The five years are: 1944, 1963, 1969, 1973 and 1999. If your piano becomes defective during any one of those five years, return in the original carton, along with a self-addressed prepaid return carton to our factory in Hong Kong. Be sure to include the piano bench and the person or persons who play the piano. Allow two years for return, and keep in mind that a trip to a faraway place like Hong Kong is very bad for a delicate musical instrument like a piano.

CELEBRITY RESPONSES TO MAD BASHING (MOSTLY BARFING) AND MAD RESPONSES TO BEING CELEBRITIES (MOSTLY BOASTING)

It's always fun to get feedback on your work. Once when I was watching "The Tonight Show," I saw Johnny Carson ask Michael J. Fox, "When did you know you MADe it big in show business?" and Michael reply, "When MAD Magazine satirized *Back to the Future,* I knew I had arrived! Having my likeness drawn by Mort Drucker was just awesome!"

Another celebrity loved something Mort and I did for MAD, but this celebrity's attorneys did not. Here's the whole story. I wrote "Star Bores," a take-off on the blockbuster movie *Star Wars.* The MAD version featured Oldie Von Moldie, Chewbacco, and Princess Laidup, and it was a huge success with the readers. Right after that issue hit the stands, George Lucas wrote a letter to me and Mort, who of course had drawn his usual fantastic caricatures, calling us the "George Bernard Shaw and Leonardo da Vinci" of satire. *AND* he said, he wished there were Academy Awards for us! (Hey, I don't have to quote from memory. If I search around I bet I can find the actual document....Now let's see, where did I put that thing? Oh, here is it! In a gold frame with a spotlight on it, right next to my couch.)

Days later, we got a different kind of letter. This one was from Lucas' attorneys demanding the original art as well as a portion of the profits from the issue containing the parody. We decided to use Bill's letter-answering technique and scribbled on the lawyers' letter—"Gee, your boss, George, liked it!" —and attached a copy of Lucas' letter. We never heard from them again!

That reminds me of another incident, when a couple of gentlemen from the FBI came to the office. Seems like we had produced an Alfred E. Neuman dollar that was so well-designed, it worked in those vending machines that took paper currency!! Just like the lawyers, the G-men demanded the original art and plates, but Bill doesn't give original art to ANY-ONE, and that includes the FBI! He did, however, give his word that he would never reproduce that dollar again. I don't know why the Feds accepted Bill's word, but they did. Maybe his innate honesty just comes through, even to strangers.

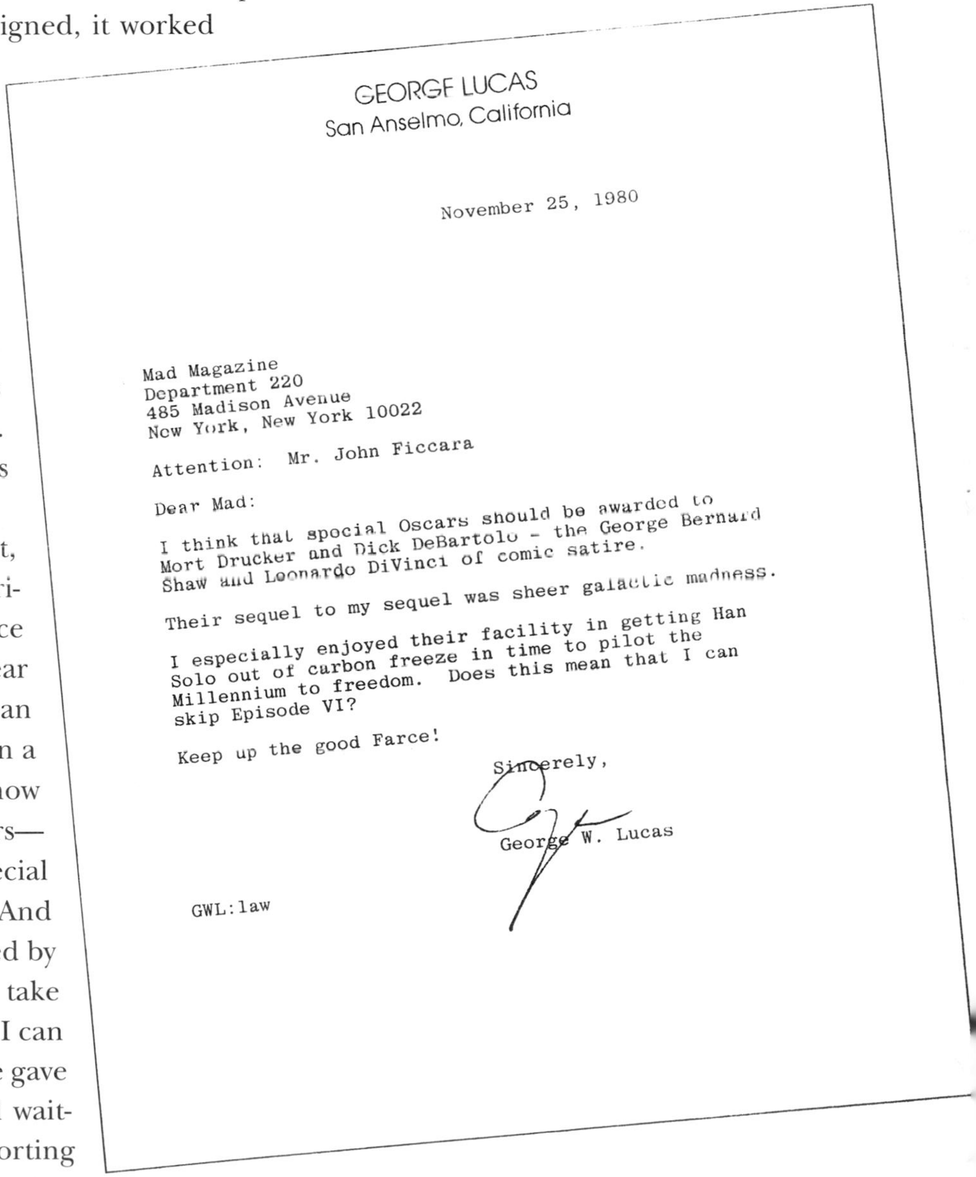

GEORGE LUCAS
San Anselmo, California

November 25, 1980

Mad Magazine
Department 220
485 Madison Avenue
New York, New York 10022

Attention: Mr. John Ficcara

Dear Mad:

I think that special Oscars should be awarded to Mort Drucker and Dick DeBartolo - the George Bernard Shaw and Leonardo DiVinci of comic satire.

Their sequel to my sequel was sheer galactic madness.

I especially enjoyed their facility in getting Han Solo out of carbon freeze in time to pilot the Millennium to freedom. Does this mean that I can skip Episode VI?

Keep up the good Farce!

Sincerely,

George W. Lucas

GWL:law

Aside from lawyers and heat, we get the occasional drop-in celebrity. Carol Burnett came by the office one day to show us that her left ear was *not* seven millimeters longer than her right one, as we had indicated in a parody of her show. (Remember how at the end of every show—for years—Carol tugged on her left ear as a special goodnight to her grandmother.) And another time Robert DeNiro stopped by and asked if he and his son could take the MAD Office Tour. I said, "Only if I can co-star in your next movie!" Well, we gave them their lousy tour, and I'm still waiting for Bob to call me about reporting for work on the set.

Being involved in TV has given me some unique opportunities, like getting to meet celebrities who are interested in buying comedy material, not just taking the MAD Tour. I've written jokes for Phyllis Diller, and I've done a lot of work with Soupy Sales. I got to write two one-hour TV specials Soupy starred in. One was a Saturday morning kids' show, and the other was a basketball special featuring Soupy and the Harlem Globetrotters. Soupy and I also went to Canada to work on a version of *Hellzapoppin*. Talk about *off*-Broadway!

And I've gotten to meet many of the people we've satirized in MAD. For example, a l-o-n-g time ago (1974), when "The Match Game" was taped in New York City, George Segal was a guest on the show and I got to tell him that he was featured in the new issue of MAD, in our version of *The Owl and the Pussycat*—"The Foul and the Prissy Cats." George was so excited he told me to meet him at the beginning of the lunch break, so I could take him to the nearest newsstand. He bought ten copies of the magazine. When June Lockhart was a "Match Game" guest, she was still filming "Lost in Space," and I got to give her a copy of the latest MAD, which featured my spoof of her show. (What great timing!) In "Loused Up in Space," the Robinson family's space capsule lands on a planet where everything is of enormous size—in one panel they come across a giant watermelon which turns out to be a REALLY giant pea! After she read the piece, June said, "You're not only funny, you have ESP! We're shooting a show now where we crash land on a planet where everything is giant-sized!" These days I get to meet a lot of the celebrities MAD is currently satirizing when I'm on "Live! With Regis & Kathie Lee."

"...calling us the George Bernard Shaw and Leonardo da Vinci of satire. AND he said, he wished there were Academy Awards for us!"

I know from these experiences that celebrities like to see themselves in MAD, but I never dreamed that I would find my name in other magazines. That's happened twice. The first time was back in 1971, when *National Lampoon* did a huge, fifteen-page take-off on MAD Magazine, written by the very funny John Boni. Naturally, the spoof featured a movie parody—called "Citizen Gaines." In this take-off on *Citizen Kane*, John Boni came down hard on everybody, but strangely enough, veteran MAD writer Larry Siegel and I came away unscathed. All through the piece Citizen Gaines is trying to find someone at MAD who can define "satire." No one in the office can, but someone does remark, "Siegel and DeBartolo would know, but they're not here."

I later met and became good friends with John Boni. He told me that he liked the satires turned out by both Larry and me, and he didn't think we should be raked over the coals in his piece—hence the flattering line. But just to show you that MAD has no hard feelings about being lampooned, I'll tell you that John has written several satires for us. (Of course we haven't paid him yet...and we never intend to! But we do publish his stuff!)

Since Larry Siegel's name just came up, I want to mention that all MAD writers owe Larry a big thank you. Many years ago, the artists were paid double the writers' rate. None of the writers were upset by that arrangement because the art is critical to MAD, and it's obviously very time-consuming to produce. But Larry came up with an interesting argument for equal pay that none of us had—at least I hadn't—thought of. MAD writers have to come up with the premises for the articles, as well as several examples of what the article would be like. So a writer might generate five premises along with the examples for each one, and sell MAD only one premise. Therefore, the other four premises become work on spec that don't produce any income. The artist, on the other hand, is given the writer's completed work, and there's no working on spec involved. After Larry pointed this inequity out to Gaines, we all started receiving the same pay per page.

But back to seeing my name in print. A couple of years ago, a friend came in with a copy of *People* magazine and said, "Hey, your name was mentioned in one of the movie reviews."

"My name?? Why would my name be in a movie

THE PLAYER

Tim Robbins, Greta Scacchi, Vincent D'Onofrio

Two themes move contrapuntally through this Hollywoodcentric film, which is self-important, sanctimonious and, for director Robert (*Nashville, M*A*S*H*) Altman, surprisingly dull.

One theme tracks a murder investigation into the street-brawl death of a screenwriter. The other theme involves satirizing the film industry's ethics and aesthetics, or lack thereof.

The murder plot is pursued in listless fashion, despite flamboyant overacting by Whoopi Goldberg as a homicide detective and a whimsical performance by country singer Lyle Lovett as another cop. The satire is innocuous, not nearly as penetrating as the stuff Dick De Bartolo turns out in *Mad* movie parodies. Altman's apparent shock at finding venality in Hollywood, in fact, rings false, as if he had gone into a lion house and expressed shock at finding so many carnivores.

Robbins (*Jacob's Ladder*) plays a studio executive who screens story ideas and who is receiving threatening postcards from a disgruntled writer.

review in *People*? I've never written a script!" She handed me the piece and sure enough there was my name, just like she said.

But I'm not the only famous person at MAD. By the early sixties, when I started working for MAD, William M. Gaines was a cult hero; and by the mid-eighties he was certainly famous. But he never thought of himself that way. One time I walked into his office and he was all bent out of shape because he had heard about a new restaurant, and he wanted to go there for dinner. He had called, but they had didn't have any tables available for that night.

DICK: Did you tell them who you are?

BILL: They don't care who I am!

DICK: Gaines, they do! You're famous. Restaurants like to suck up to shallow people, and you're one of them! Give me the Goddamn phone and the number of the restaurant!

BILL: (hands me the paper) It won't do you any good! If they're filled up, they're filled up!

DICK: (on phone) Hi, this is Dick DeBartolo at MAD Magazine. Our publisher, William M. Gaines, set aside this evening to dine at your restaurant. But he forgot one thing. He forgot to call you and tell you he was coming...so he doesn't have a reservation. Is there anything you can do? (putting my hand over phone, I ask Gaines) He wants to know if you want eight or eight-thirty or later.

BILL: Eight o'clock.

DICK: Eight p.m., for two. Yes, William M. Gaines! (I hang up) Hmmm... did you realize this phone number is for McDonald's? I never knew you needed reservations for McDonald's!...Okay Gaines, you're all set!

BILL: If they said they were filled up, how could that be?

DICK: Billy, if Paul Newman and Joanne Woodward walked into that restaurant without a reservation, do you think they would be turned away?

BILL: No.

DICK: Well, Paul and Joanne are in Hollywood making a movie, so you got their table! Just pray to God they don't change their plans, or you and Annie are out on the street!

"...Well, Paul and Joanne are in Hollywood making a movie, so you got their table! Just pray to God they don't change their plans, or you and Annie are out on the street!"

On a couple of occasions when we were flying off on our MAD trips,

I was able to get Bill bumped up to first class. He really appreciated that because, as I've said, he was a BIG MAN. When Bill flew on his own, he always went first class, but when he went with the MAD group, he flew coach like the rest of us.

Anyway, this happened back when Frank Borman was running Eastern Airlines. I got to meet Frank because I was doing a story for *Powerboat* about a high performance boat he'd bought. Anyway, when I met Frank I told him that the whole MAD group would soon be flying to Disney World on his airline. Could he do anything to make Gaines more comfortable? Frank told me to give him a call just before the trip. I did, and we got really lucky, because it turned out that the MAD group's trip to Florida was booked on a fairly empty jumbo jet; so Frank graciously upgraded the entire MAD staff. (I didn't get to go first class, though. I was flying down to Orlando from a different location, so I went coach. Darn!) On the way back I was able to upgrade the two MAD "heavyweights," Gaines and Lenny Brenner.

Of course, I didn't let this courtesy to Gaines go unnoticed. A few days after the trip I went into his office to bargain.

DICK: So, did you enjoy your two first-class trips with coach tickets?

BILL: Yes, thanks to you.

DICK: Oh, a big thank you—so that's it. Had you PAID for your first-class tickets, they would have cost eighteen hundred and sixty-six dollars!

BILL: Really?

DICK: Yes, really, but I'm not expecting you to pay me that kind of money.

BILL: What are you expecting?

DICK: A mocha layer cake.

BILL: That sounds reasonable.

DICK: A mocha layer cake from GREENBERG'S!!! (an expensive Manhattan bakery)

BILL: It's still worth it! Will you be here tomorrow?

DICK: For a Greenberg's mocha layer cake, I'll just sit here until tomorrow!

BILL: If I buy you *two* mocha layer cakes, can you get me first-class upgrades to Europe?

DICK: Sorry, Gaines, I don't do Europe!

Since he was famous and he loved to travel, I got the idea that Gaines would be perfect for one of those American Express commercials. You know, the ones where the-not-*quite*-a-star personality would ask, "Do you know who *I* am?" So I found out the name of the advertising agency American Express was using and wrote them a letter suggesting Gaines. I pitched Gaines in two different ways. They could do it normal, the way the commercials had been written, or they could do it in a satirical way. On his commercial, Billy could ask, "Do you know who I am?" Then he'd pause and say, "Because quite frankly, I can't remember!"

Well, I did get a call back from one of the account executives at the agency. He said they were seriously considering Bill, but while there was strong interest on behalf of the client, the list of people being considered was quite long, and the number they used, quite small. Alas, Gaines never did make it into one.

But, as I've said, Bill didn't consider himself, or MAD for that matter, as having any pull. So when Bill heard about all the activities in the works for Liberty Weekend in 1986, which included the re-lighting of the torch on the Statue of Liberty, he asked me what sort of clout *I* had to get him and Annie press passes for the festivities. I told him I was going to apply for press passes in the name of *Powerboat* magazine, and that he should do the same for MAD.

BILL: Why the hell would they give MAD Magazine anything?

DICK: Because, MAD IS a magazine!! Maybe we'll be inspired to write something as a result of Liberty Weekend.

BILL: You're nuts!

Well, I called the press office and the lady on the phone didn't laugh, scoff, or act strange in any way when I requested the credentials for MAD Magazine. I had them send applications to my attention at *Powerboat,* and to Bill's attention at MAD. I knew that security for the event was going to be incredible—but the application for press passes was four pages long! Our names, we were told, would be checked out with the FBI, the IRS, and probably the Pillsbury Dough Boy. After about a month, Bill and I both got letters from the press office saying that the allotment of passes was severely limited because they had received thousands of applications, and we would hear from them again. After another few weeks, we got the news: *Powerboat* was granted one press pass, and yes—MAD Magazine was granted one press pass!

Bill and I had to show up in person to get our passes. They were laminated in plastic, had all sorts of official signatures and numbers on them, and came with neck chains. We were told they had to be worn all the time at each event we chose to attend. Having two passes worked out well. I lent Bill mine when he and Annie wanted to go, and Bill lent me his when the photographer and I went....And, in case you're wondering, I actually *did* cover the event for *Powerboat* magazine.

Bill told me that since I had arranged the press passes, he would take care of getting us a spectacular place to view the rededication fireworks at the Statue—and did he ever! Bill had a friend who lived on one of the top floors of a high-rise in Battery Park City. She had a corner apartment with a wall of windows facing both the Statue and the Brooklyn Bridge. Of course there were tons of food, and for the special event, Bill brought wine, not just any wine, but wine that was bottled in 1886, the same year the Statue was built. It was an outstanding day and night!

...It's almost the end of the book. We can't think of one damn thing to print here!

Another city wide gala bash that Bill, Annie, and I attended was the 200th Anniversary of the Brooklyn Bridge. That was another night to remember—but we had very different reasons. Annie and Bill remembered it as a night of spectacular fireworks, but I've always remembered it as the worst night of navigation I've ever faced. The East River, which runs under the Brooklyn Bridge, is very narrow, and not only were there thousands of boats there to see the fireworks, the Coast Guard had announced that there would be no anchoring! So all the boats, including tugs, Circle Liners, and luxury yachts had to stay in motion, and try to overcome the rapid river currents—and each other. My little twenty-foot work boat was surrounded by huge yachts, and not far from us there were a couple of tugboats pushing barges full of spectators! I don't know if Bill and Annie had any idea of how many times we were nearly rammed or run over, but every time Gaines said, "This is a night I'll never forget"—referring to the fireworks—I echoed, "Neither will I"—referring to trying to stay alive and afloat!

MAD

Angelo Torres on Bill Gaines

I came to work for MAD in 1966, but I had met Bill Gaines some twelve years earlier when he was the publisher of the most exciting and creative line of comic books ever put together. With editors bordering on the genius, and the finest array of freelance artists ever assembled and given free rein to illustrate some outstanding scripts, EC Publications was clearly the envy of the comic world.

It was 1954 and I was an art student at what is now the School of Visual Arts when I had the great fortune to meet and become friends with Al Williamson, one of EC's finest contributing artists. Before long I found myself working with Al on his science fiction pages, and not too long after that I joined him delivering finished art to the now legendary hotbed of creation that was EC. I met a lot of people that day. I said hello to Al Feldstein and I think I just waved to a very busy Harvey Kurtzman. John Severin was there and his sister Marie, Johnny Craig, and others I can't quite remember. And there was Bill, a rather imposing figure to an art student who could only dream of someday, maybe, working for this man. I was greeted by this tall, clean shaven, crew cut, overweight, raucous individual with the same informality, friendliness, and warmth I would know so well years later working for MAD. I made many visits to 225 Lafayette during this period and eventually drew my very own story for EC, but time was fast running out on the EC books, and when the end came only MAD would survive, to eventually become an American institution and Bill's greatest triumph.

In the intervening years I was a frequent visitor to the MAD offices, now moved uptown. Bill's friendship was unwavering, in spite of the fact that I was working for competing humorous magazines, and eventually I came to work for him again.

A few years back I was asked, "Why are you still working for Gaines?" The answer was easy. "Because I love the guy."

IN THE LIMELIGHT

MAD never spends a penny on advertising. And maybe a penny—max—on publicity. But so many people in the entertainment field grew up with MAD and love MAD that we manage to stay in the limelight. Oh, okay, we stay a little bit to the side of the limelight. But speaking of limelight...well, once we really got into the LIMELIGHT.

One New York disco that has managed to keep going while dozens of others have come and gone is the Limelight. When they first opened many years ago, we received a call from one of their staffers asking if they could throw a party for MAD. Bill talked to me about it, asking if I had ever been there and was a MAD party there a good idea. I told him that the Limelight was a trendy place, and if the party didn't cost him anything, why not? So Bill agreed.

The Limelight took care of mailing the invitations, and we sent over various MAD things so they could decorate the inside of the club. I made trays of slides for them to project—mostly MAD covers interspersed with closeups of MAD staffers making faces. But on the day of the party, Bill called me into his office. He was in a panic.

BILL: Did you know there's an admission charge for people who want to get into Limelight?

DICK: All discos charge admission. But didn't they give you two hundred free passes?

BILL: Yeah, the MAD staff and their friends can get in for free, but what about MAD fans who come? Don't you think they'll expect to get in for free?

DICK: Bill, I don't think so. People who go to discos know there's a charge.

BILL: Well, I never thought about an admission charge. I'm going to see if I can cancel the whole thing!

DICK: Bill, the party is in five hours! The Limelight did a mass mailing. They've decorated the place with giant Spies and MAD logos. I've sent over slides for them to project. We've all invited people. You can't cancel it now!

BILL: Okay, then I'm going to pay the admission charge for all the MAD fans who show up! I don't want them to think MAD is making money out of this!

DICK: Bill, I really don't think they will. And if anyone complains, pay THEIR admission fee, or refund their money if they've already paid, but I really don't think people think it's free!

Well, we narrowly avoided that disaster and then there was another near miss at the private cocktail party Limelight gave us before the big bash. Naturally, as soon as we arrived Bill asked, "Where's the food?"

The Limelight people said, "Food? There's no food at a cocktail party—just cocktails!"

It was a statement close to sacrilege, but Bill controlled himself and said, "Hand me the phone. The MAD staff won't stand for cocktails without food!" He called a nearby restaurant and told them to deliver —on the double.

Anyway, the party took place. And Bill took his free passes and stationed someone at door of the Limelight to give them away to the first 200 people who showed up.

"...Hand me the phone. The MAD staff won't stand for cocktails without food!" He called a nearby restaurant and told them to deliver— on the double."

GIFTS FOR THE MAN WHO HAS EVERYTHING

What sort of a gift could you bring when you went to Bill and Annie's house for dinner? Wine? Restaurants came to Bill for wine — they didn't need wine! Dessert? Hell, I was going for the dessert, because I knew Bill and Annie would have something spectacular. How about something with a picture of a Statue of Liberty on it?

Oh yeah, I was going to bring that to people who owned six of the seven ORIGINAL Bartholdi prototypes for the Statue of Liberty. No, the only thing that would make an impression was to bring something outrageously bad. The fun part was making the outrageously bad thing sound good.

Just to show you what I mean, one time when Dennis Wunderlin and I were invited for dinner, we went shopping at Weber's, one of those odd lot-type stores, for something for Annie and Bill. And we found THE gift: a gold, plastic, unicorn clock with fake plastic flowers inside the face. A butterfly attached to one of the hands wound its way through the flowers, which didn't slow it down any, because this precision piece of equipment gained about twenty minutes every hour. A perfect gift for the couple with everything, we thought. And we were SURE they didn't have one of these! While waiting on line to pay for this gem, the woman standing behind us heard us talking about how to gift wrap it. Shaking her head in disbelief she said, "You're not REALLY giving that as a gift, are you?" When we heard that, we knew we really had selected the perfect present! But finding the right gift was just the start; then the transformation would begin. For this piece, I wrote the history of "Das Clocken die Unicorn," and Dennis designed an elaborate "museum quality" shipping case.

Another time, I gave Bill and Annie one place setting of a silverware set. Okay, so it wasn't silverware, it was flatware! But not just any flatware, it was four *un*-matching pieces. But they were especially unmatched because they were part of the "PASTICHE Collection." The place setting came packed in a special Wunderlin-designed "presentation case," accompanied by a certificate of authenticity.

THE STORY BEHIND THE PASTICHE COLLECTION

We asked our artisans to design a silverware set that was aesthetically pleasing, carefully balanced, and not a piece of crap. The knife, the fork, and the spoons contained in your heirloom PASTICHE collection are the same type of utensils used by President Bush and the First Lady when they eat! You could shop the FINE STORES of the world and never find silverware of this QUALITY!
Each piece of your PASTICHE silverware set is as different as a grain of sand!

CARE OF YOUR FINE SILVERWARE

We suggest you wash each fine piece from time to time. One washing after every two or three meals is the minimum. Fortunately, the intricate designs of PASTICHE hide stuck-on egg yolk, spinach, and lipstick, so you do not have to wash them after every meal, as you do with "ordinary" flatware.

If you wish to polish your silverware, we suggest several coats of Kiwi Clear, and a light buffing with a grinding stone or sandpaper.

ADDING TO YOUR MAGNIFICENT COLLECTION

You can buy additional pieces through us, or steal them from hotels, restaurants, and friends. But remember—never steal two of anything! Two matching pieces will ruin the entire effect of PASTICHE!

WHY ARE THERE ONLY FOUR PIECES IN MY SERVICE FOR TWELVE SET?

Over the years we have discovered new owners of PASTICHE were OVERWHELMED when they encountered dozens of different dazzling patterns at one time. Studies show that four pieces is the most anyone can stand seeing at one time! That is the number we pack in our service for twelve sets. For dinner parties that include more than just yourself, we suggest you pass the utensils around so everyone can eat off them.

It makes for very animated conversation, and occasional health problems.

I'm not sure how Bill and Annie felt about the actual flatware, but they loved "The Story Behind the PASTICHE Collection." One day I saw Annie making photocopies to mail and fax to their friends.

When Bill had to go to the hospital to get a pacemaker, Dennis and I went to visit, and we decided to bring him a "BASKET OF GOOD HEALTH" as a gift. We couldn't find *exactly* what we wanted commercially, so we had to make it ourselves. It contained cigars, maple syrup, rock candy (as I said, Bill was diabetic), and a fine wine—with instructions to "SHAKE WELL BEFORE SERVING." Gaines was greatly cheered.

Actually, I brought Bill wine on a number of occasions. One time I presented him with a really nice bottle—not some musty old wine, this was a wine that proudly stated on its label: "FRESH!" One of Dennis' and my running wine jokes was pretending that the salesman had forgotten to remove the price tag. Dennis would make an oversized price tag with an outrageous amount on it—like an $89 sticker on a two-dollar bottle of wine. I would hand Gaines the bottle, shoving the tag in his face as I remarked, "Oh no, didn't that sales clerk remove the price tag?? I'm so embarrassed!"

Other wines I selected for Bill were more than just wines, too. After Dennis got finished with the label on one bottle of $1.98 red, it said:

A Fine Wine,
A Good Disinfectant,
And a Sturdy Floor Wax!

Even with the variety in his water-cooled wine cellar, my guess is that Gaines had never gotten a wine like that before!

HEALTHCARE BILL (GAINES)

This is going to be a real short chapter because basically, Gaines had no health! Bill was overweight and out of shape from the day I met him, and he stayed that way right up to the end. Sometimes he would try to do something about it, and he'd go on yo-yo diets. He'd eat almost nothing for two months before a European trip, and then he'd eat EVERYTHING on the actual trip!

Bill and Annie even went to Pritikin to lose weight. But Bill had close friends Fedex him packages with cleverly concealed salami and ham, and all the stuff he was there to avoid! He must have known better than to ask me to help him get forbidden foods at Pritikin because, as much as it would have pained me to refuse him, I wouldn't have sent him anything. At least, I **think** I wouldn't have sent him anything!

When I wrote the MAD take-off on that stomach exerciser that was such a big seller—for a while it was constantly on TV—we all sat around wondering who we should get to model for the photo. Someone suggested Gaines, and everyone laughed, so Gaines was it! We just had to find out if he was willing.

Bill was agreeable, but he wanted his two "health addict"

buddies to be in the ad with him: Al Goldstein (yes, THAT Al Goldstein), and Lyle Stuart (yes, THAT Lyle Stuart). They had all gone to school together, and had all gone into publishing together, but they ended up publishing very different kinds of things. Goldstein publishes *Screw* magazine, and Lyle has had several very successful publishing companies, publishing controversial works such as *The* MAD *World of William M. Gaines.*

When we told longtime MAD photographer Irving Schild that all three publishing heavyweights were coming to his studio at one time, he suggested we shoot on the first floor to avoid damaging the upper floors!

Of course we didn't have to pay Gaines a modeling fee, and it turned out that we didn't have to pay Lyle or Al either. They just heard "free food," and they were there! And once they arrived, they stripped down to their underwear, and started eating and posing. It was not a pretty sight!

BONUS #14

The Belly Burner Ad.

Why are we giving away the Bulgin' Belly Burner™ for only $10?
(Because we tried to give it away for $20 and that didn't work!)
Bulgin' Belly Burner™
AS SEEN ON TV*
Don't waste your hard-earned cash on inferior imitations when you can get the inferior original for the same price!
*On Nationwide Consumer Fraud Reports
Intensive back-stretch sends blood rushing to lower abdomen and thighs!
Reverse leg-lifts leave hands free to take important nutritional supplements!
Power sit-ups work your arteries to their bursting point!
To see how desperate overweight people are, our Special Consumer Alert Movement (SCAM) is offering this truly amazing device.
NOT AVAILABLE IN ANY STORE
The amazing Bulgin' Belly Burner will not be sold in any store! It's only offered by mail, where you can't get your hands on one until you have already paid for it!
Use it to flatten your tummy, firm your buttocks, mow your lawn, grate your cheese, slice your eggs—just about anything you can think of!
Forget about expensive gyms, difficult rowing machines and all the ridiculous claims in this ad. Just 10 minutes with the Bulgin' Belly Burner makes you feel as nauseous as if you had worked 40 minutes with heavy weights.
IRON CLAD MONEY-BACK GUARANTEE
Use the Bulgin' Belly Burner just 10 minutes a day for 5 years. If you're not 100% delighted with the new "you," try using it 20 minutes a day for the next 10 years. If you're still not in better shape than our professional models shown above, return the unit for a full refund. (Must be in brand-new condition, in original package, to qualify. Please include a $15 restocking charge.)
ONLY ONE BELLY BURNER PER PERSON!
Only one unit per customer may be purchased. But we won't insult your intelligence by checking to see if you sent in multiple orders, so feel free to do so!
To order, mail this original ad together with $10 for each Bulgin' Belly Burner, plus $19.95 postage and handling and $12.76 insurance, and an additional $7.95 for the translated-from-Japanese instruction sheet. Allow 6 to 8 months for us to ship it and for you to forget that you ordered it.
Bulgin' Belly Burner, Cockamamie Products, Dept. Y-U, Gullibility, TX.

OUR FEW SERIOUS TALKS

I was rarely serious with Bill. And if I was, it didn't last for more than one sentence, but I got really upset when Bill bought a wheelchair.

Bill hated to walk, and with the shape he was in, I'm sure it was difficult. He took a cab if he was going to have to walk more than one block, and I could live with that. At MAD, he at least walked to his office from the elevator, and walked to the men's room. But once he got his wheelchair, he hardly got out of it. He even used it for the trip to the men's room. I tried to convince him that the little bit of walking he used to do was at least some movement for his body, and I asked him to give up the wheelchair, at least in the office. But Bill didn't want to hear it! As a matter of fact, he told me he wished he had thought of getting one earlier.

He was especially pleased at the effect it had when he had to go to the very infrequent meetings about MAD at Time Warner. And, he said, now the meetings were very short because the executives at Time felt he should be gotten out of there as quickly as possible.

Another thing I tried to discuss with him—and which he also didn't want to hear about—was writing down his wishes for MAD should he depart this earth. That conversation ALWAYS went like this:

DICK: Bill, what if you should die?

BILL: So?

DICK: Well, I'm not saying you are going to die. And no matter what you think, Annie and I *are not* putting small undetectable amounts of sugar in your medicine to hasten the process, which doesn't seem to be working, anyway. But why don't you leave a letter expressing your wishes for MAD after you're gone?

BILL: Because no one will care!

DICK: Everybody will care.

BILL: No, they won't.

DICK: Okay, let's suppose they DO care. Wouldn't you like your wishes known?

BILL: No.

DICK: Why not?

BILL: Because I'll be dead!

THE LAST FEW DAYS

What turned out to be my last conversations with Bill were absolutely normal—they ended with a joke. Two days before he left us, I spoke to him at home and said I would gladly come over and sit with him. Bill said, no, and he thanked me. But then I couldn't resist adding, "But of course I'd rather sit with you during BUSINESS HOURS so I can at least get paid for my time." When I called Bill a day later, he told me he was feeling really bad. I reminded him that he had felt really bad in the past and he'd always managed to pull through. He agreed, and said he would indeed get better. But just before I hung up, I had to add, "But Bill, if you don't pull through, can I have that new Toshiba thirty-two inch TV you just bought?" My last memory of Bill is his booming laughter coming over the phone.

On Wednesday morning I went to MAD as usual. As I walked into John Ficarra's office, John said softly, "Billy died this morning." I went back to my office, closed the door, and cried for a very long time.

Anyone I've ever spoken to who has lost a close friend and loved one, even one in bad health, has always had the same reaction: "I knew it could happen, but I didn't believe it when it did happen." That was certainly how I felt with Bill. I thought it would just be a matter of days before I would push open his office door, hurl insults at him, and hear him laugh. Fortunately, I'd heard

A24 THE NEW YORK TIMES, WEDNESDAY, JUNE 10, 1992

MAD

WE'LL CARRY ON WITH THE LAUGHTER, THE IRREVERENCE, THE MISCHIEF AND, OH YEAH, THE MAGAZINE, TOO.

WE'LL MISS YOU, BILL

LOVE,

"THE USUAL GANG OF IDIOTS"

it so much in life, I can easily hear it again when I think about Bill.

Later in the day, I heard the announcement about Bill's death on the radio. The next day it was in all the newspapers. It was even on the front page of *The New York Times*. I was really pleased that Bill's contribution to society was so widely heralded.

Our phones rang constantly for three days after the bad news about Bill was made public. Fans had called first to express their deep sorrow, but then to ask, "Will MAD stay in business?" We decided that MAD would run an ad in *The New York Times*, both to acknowledge Bill's passing and to say that MAD would continue.

The full page ad in *The New York Times* was a staff effort, and I think it fit the moment perfectly.

I read a lot of the mail that came in for weeks after Bill died. All of it was very emotional, but there were a couple of letters that I will never forget. When telling people about them, I still can't get through describing the sentiments without choking up, even two years later. We ran those letters in MAD, but I found them so moving, I've run them again in this memoir. These are from MAD #315, dated December, 1992:

> My deepest condolences on the passing of MAD's wonderfully insane creator. I'm sure his spirit is in Heaven giving God a slight wince. I remember my first foray to MAD's offices at age 13. I just showed up and they let me in. As I peered into Bill's office, he looked up from his work and roared, "Well, either come in or get the @#%! out!" I spent the rest of the day with him. As someone in the profession, I have yet to find a similar welcome anywhere else!
>
> Jonathan Schneider
> New York, NY

I just heard of Mr. Gaines's death and am at a loss for words other than walking around uttering "I'm so sorry, I'm so sorry." I guess there are no snappy answers when dealing with the loss of someone of such great foresight and imagination. Thank you, Mr. Gaines, for making me laugh and encouraging me to think about the world I live in.

Anna Maria Pingarron
Los Angeles, C

Today I heard the news. My heart sank, I got a lump in my throat and the tears seemed to flow instantly. A man I'd never met before had passed away and I cried as if I'd lost my best friend. In a way, I guess I had. William Gaines was responsible for 99 percent of all my laughter in this world. He and his band of idiots invaded my life in 1980 and I've never been the same. I look forward to seeing Alfred every month in some new act of mischievous behavior. Thank you, Bill, for making me smile.

Jared Brent Johnson
Goodlettsville, TN

The night before Bill's memorial service, I visited his daughters Wendy and Cathy, and his wife, Annie. They reminded me that Bill loved to be kidded, and said *PLEASE* do not be maudlin at the ceremony. Although it took guts and a great deal of composure, at that service I made my final comments about Bill. They began:

"This has been a very sad week for me. Wednesday, Billy left us.... Thursday, I found out I wasn't in the will. After more than thirty years of ass kissing, you would think I would at least have gotten a stinking bottle of wine...."

A CONVERSATION WITH BILL FROM THE BEYOND

I'll never forget a clever ploy pulled off by one of the tabloids some years ago. The tabloids are a great source of material for satire—although much of the time it's difficult to write funnier stories than they do! Anyway, this particular paper had an astrologer who wrote a weekly horoscope column. Then one day, she died. I didn't know if she'd predicted her own death or not, but I did wonder if the paper would get a new astrologer or abandon horoscopes altogether. Well, it took the tabloid hardly any time to come up with an answer.

Two weeks after the astrologer's death, the paper's headline read:
"JEANNE DIXON'S FORECAST—SHE PREDICTS YOUR FUTURE—FROM BEYOND THE GRAVE."

Hey, if she can do it, maybe Gaines will talk to us from the great beyond. Annie has tried using psychics to help her contact Bill, but has had no success, so I figured I'd give it a shot on my own. I didn't consult a psychic or hold a seance, I just tried to think of the best place to go from where I could contact Bill. And like a bolt of lightning from the beyond, it hit me...*Nathan's!* So with paper and pen—and a few bucks for frankfurters, I headed out to

Nathan's. And what luck—Bill was there!! This is the way the conversation went...and I DEFY you to prove otherwise!

DICK: Billy, are you all right?

BILL: For a dead person, I'm great.

DICK: So there is a Heaven?

BILL: There's something, I mean, I'm answering you, aren't I?

DICK: Can I buy you some frankfurters?

BILL: No, thanks. I get all I want—and they're free, and I have no stomach, so I don't worry about gaining weight.

DICK: Free frankfurters is what Heaven is all about?

BILL: It's whatever you want it to be. It can be full of dogs for you, for me it's full of free franks, and free wine.

DICK: I'm writing a book about MAD and me—and a lot of it is about you.

BILL: I'm flattered. Tell people I said they should buy your book or they'll die prematurely, and not come to this place.

DICK: Why is that?

BILL: Because I'm trying to help you sell your crappy little book.

DICK: It's a hardcover book and it's not so little.

BILL: I'm impressed. Okay, so I'm trying to help you sell your crappy big, hardcover book.

DICK: Have you run into anybody else there you knew from earth?

BILL: Yeah, John Putnam.

DICK: Why don't you and John get together and try to perform some miracle, so Annie and I will know you're really communicating with us?

BILL: Like what?

DICK: Why don't you make the Statue of Liberty disappear?

BILL: Too ambitious. It took me over a year just to find out how to get to Nathan's.

DICK: Do you think about the changes at MAD since you left?

BILL: No, it's too painful to think about MAD at all. I just think about Annie, and you.

DICK: Really?

BILL: No, I really mostly think about Annie, I included you because I know this conversation is going into the book!

DICK: How did you know that?

BILL: I'm dead, not stupid.

DICK: I'm writing this during the 1993 Christmas season to come out before the 1994 Christmas season. Do you think you can get the new bosses at DC Comics to give me a Christmas bonus?

BILL: I think it's easier to make the Statue of Liberty disappear! Actually, by the time this book comes out, they should figure out that you're an asset to MAD, and do something special for you, like give you an extra box of paper clips.

DICK: If you were still in charge, what would you give me for Christmas?

BILL: TWO boxes of paper clips!

DICK: Do you ever visit the MAD offices?

BILL: Yes, late at night, I sit in my chair in my office. Or at least I have the feeling I'm doing that. I wish it were more like those old *Topper* movies, and that I could move things around and scare the shit out of people I don't like, but so far, that stuff is only in the movies.

DICK: Do you use the bathroom at the MAD office and pee on the floor?

BILL: I don't pee at all. Another advantage of being dead.

DICK: Do you recommend death?

BILL: When you're finished with life, it's a nice alternative.

DICK: If I want to talk to you again, can I contact you at the MAD office?

BILL: Sure, but the frankfurters are better here! You can also contact me on your boat. I got a lot of pleasure out of your boats, and it's easy for me to feel at home there, even now.

DICK: Do you have any messages for anyone else at MAD?

BILL: No, only Annie. I miss her. I can't say anything to anyone else or all the people I *don't* mention will be angry!

DICK: Do you have any other thoughts?

BILL: Yeah, be sure to take the price of the food you ate here as a deduction on your income taxes. By talking to me about your book, this was a business lunch!

God, even from beyond the grave, Bill has a good business sense, even though he never would've taken that deduction himself!

EPILOGUE

Shortly after Bill Gaines died, William Sarnoff, chairman of Warner Books, came to the MAD offices with an announcement: MAD would no longer be a part of Time magazine.

No, that's not a joke, Gaines did report to the head honchos at Time. Which was ironic because when MAD first started, Time had dismissed the new comic with six little words: "MAD—a short lived satirical pulp." Years later MAD was a profitable part of Time, and at age 42 MAD was still going strong. In the part of my MAD slide show where I talk about our association with Time, I mention their earlier attitude and add: "To get even, every Friday night, each MAD staff member steals six Time magazine legal pads from the supply closet. Sooner or later, they'll feel the pinch!"

Anyway, the other part of Bill Sarnoff's announcement was that we were going to be made part of DC Comics. (I guess the powers that be at Time Warner felt we were a better match—many of the writers and artists at DC aren't corporate fashion plates, either.) And since that time, our new bosses have been the people at the head of

DC Comics—Jenette Kahn and Paul Levitz. It was quite a while before they put their names on the MAD masthead because, as Paul put it, "We're not part of 'the usual gang of idiots'—and we'll have to earn that right before our names go on." That, in my mind, was real considerate of them.

Then there's Joe Orlando, the person in charge of special projects at DC, who now joins us at the MAD offices two days a week. Real MAD freaks will recognize Joe's name immediately, because for many years he was a prolific MAD artist! So he's a welcome and familiar addition to the MAD family; I'm glad we never bothered cleaning out his old desk.

My future at MAD? Well, naturally it's up to the dynamic, brilliant, and congenial team of Jenette and Paul, whose foresight and impeccable good judgment will allow them to continue to recognize genius—whoever that longtime contributer with the big mustache might be!

YOUR QUESTIONS ANSWERED BEFORE YOU EVEN ASK THEM

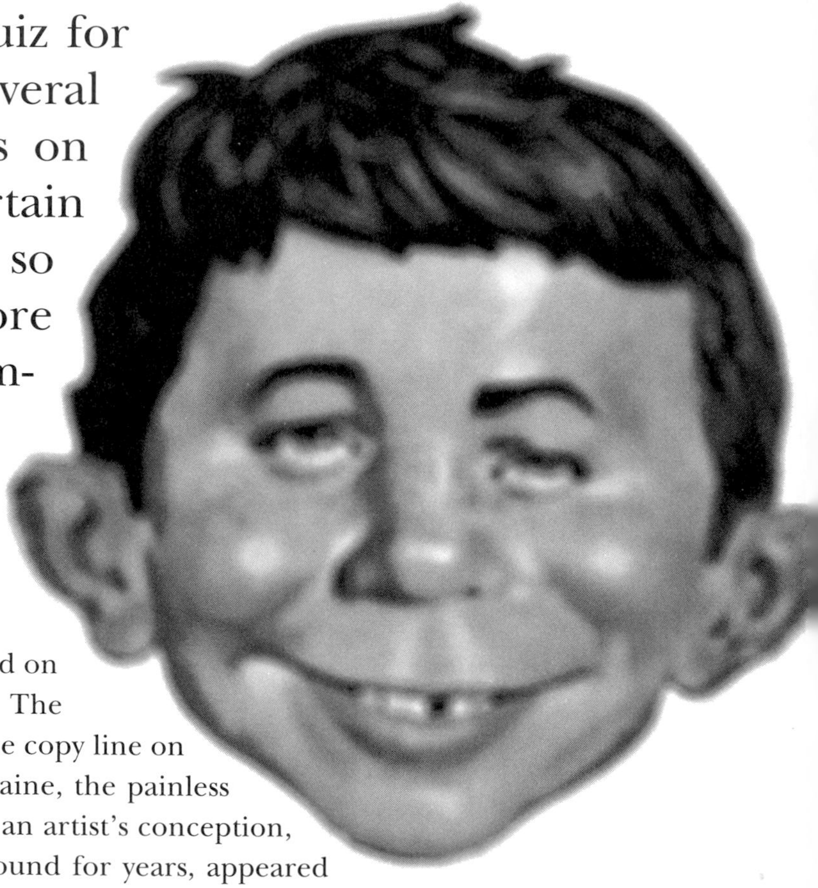

Now it's time for the quiz, a quiz for me, because after making several hundred personal appearances on behalf of MAD, I know that certain questions *never* fail to come up, so I will give you the answers before you even ask. The all-time number one asked question is (John, a drumroll please), Where did Alfred E. Neuman come from?

A kid who looked very much like Alfred was pictured on an ad for a painless dentist back in the late 1890s. The goofy kid with the missing tooth was smiling, and the copy line on the poster read, "What me worry? I go to Dr. Romaine, the painless dentist!" No one knows for sure if it was a real kid, an artist's conception, or a combination of both. But the face floated around for years, appeared in various places, and finally ended up in MAD. For the first few issues of MAD, the gap-toothed kid had different names, but after a while, the name Alfred E. Neuman stuck.

Does MAD accept outside submissions?

This was true 33 years ago for me, and it's still true today. If you think you have a funny article, or even just an idea for a article, MAD does read outside submissions. To get started, send a self-addressed, stamped envelope to MAD Magazine, 485 MADison Avenue, New York City, N.Y., 10022, and ask for either the writer's or the artist's guidelines. If you're real talented, ask for both!

I would also like to note here that I do not read submissions to MAD. The reason is simple. I don't want to be put in the position of having someone say I panned their idea, so I could sell MAD my idea! So there are no brownie points for addressing submissions to me (even if you did buy my book). It only delays the process.

Are early MADs worth money?

The answer is yes, but how much they're worth depends on how much the person you're selling them to wants them. *The Comic Buyers Guide* (available at large comic book shops) lists prices for individual copies. As you can imagine, the most sought-after issue is issue #1 of MAD the comic. At the last comic book convention I was at, in the fall of 1993, the asking price for that issue was $1,400! Prices on the other original MAD comic books drop off considerably. I've seen issues #4, #5, and #6 for sale in the $30 to $80 range, depending on the condition. (And it is inevitable that many of you are now looking up at the ceiling and shouting, *"I had the whole MAD collection, and my mother threw it out!"*)

And that, dear reader, is really that! (Except for some more Bonuses!)

"...The goofy kid with the missing tooth was smiling, and the copy line on the poster read, "What me worry? I go to Dr. Romaine, the painless dentist!"

BONUS #15

Now that you've read the entire book, you might like to customize it so it's more to your liking. So here's a page of extra punctuation! Cut out the commas, periods, dashes, etc. and insert them where you like. Notice that they match the rest of the type exactly!!!

. . . .

. . . .

— —

, ,

“ “

” ”

? ?

? ?

! !

! !

( ) ( )

BONUS #16

Use this page to write YOUR OWN foreword! Yes, you can tell friends you wrote a foreword that appears in a hard-cover BEST-SELLER! *(Please God!)*

BONUS #17

At one of the publisher's conventions, we gave away free ALFRED E. NEUMAN memo pads.

Note how much space we gave Alfred and how much space we gave people for their memos!

ALFRED'S
MAD®
MEMO
PAD!!!
MEMO:
BONUS•BONUS•BONUS•BONUS•BONUS•BONUS

BONUS • BONUS • BONUS • BONUS • BONUS • BONUS

BONUS #18

Now—as promised on the back cover, here are William M. Gaines' Investment and Money-Saving Tips.

Selling property you don't own results in the greatest amount of profit. Insist on cash!!

Setting aside a bit of money each month is better than assuming that the camera crew from Publisher's Clearing House will get to you before your retirement age!

Always use the same bank teller. When you've become good friends, ask if you can open a joint account with someone who has much more money than you do.

When four people eat out at a restaurant, it is cheaper for everyone if you divide the check by six.

If four people eat out a restaurant, it is even cheaper if YOU take the check, and divide it by three. Collect one third of the total from the others. Be sure they don't see the check, or your arithmetic!

BONUS #19

As promised on the back cover, here are your Plumbing Tips, compliments of William M. Gaines.

SYMPTOM	*CAUSE*	*SOLUTION*
Toilet runs constantly	*Float valve stuck*	*Call plumber*
Sink drips	*Worn washer*	*Call plumber*
No hot water	*Hot water heater broken*	*Call plumber*
Toilet overflows	*Unspeakble stuff jammed in pipe*	*Call plumber buy air freshener*
Sewage main breaks while you're away	*Old age*	*Move!*

BONUS #20

As promised on the back cover, here are some Food Tips from William M. Gaines.

PICNIC FRANKFURTERS

Buy FOUR packs of frankfurters and FIVE packs of rolls.

Since there are ten frankfurters in a pack, and only eight rolls in a pack, this is the only way the number will come out even! You will have forty frankfurters and forty rolls.

Save the rolls to feed the birds, and eat the forty frankfurters.

Serves 6.

ALSO, FROM BILL'S PERSONAL COLLECTION:

Stuffed Turkey Dinner with All the Trimmings

Call Annie and say, "Sweetheart, make a stuffed turkey dinner with all the trimmings for six! Okay, dear?"

Serves six.

ALTERNATE RECIPE:

Call Annie and tell her to call caterer and order stuffed turkey dinner with all the trimmings for six

BONUS #21

As promised on the back cover, here are your William M. Gaines Exercise Tips.

Buy a good pair of high-top sneakers. High-top sneakers have many more eyelets than regular sneakers, and bending over to tie them is an excellent exercise. After tying them, rest for the remainder of the day.

Try to use a pay phone at least once a day. Walking around trying to find one that works is excellent exercise.

Hang around with people who are in worse shape than you are. You will look good by comparison. If you are in dreadful shape, trying to find people who are in worse shape than you is an excellent exercise.

At the job, once an hour or so, get up, stretch, and go outside for a few breaths of fresh air. This could be dangerous if you're an airline pilot, submarine commander.

Many fitness experts recommend getting your heart rate into the "target zone." This can be done with vigorous exercise, or by calling your boss's home at 3 a.m. and hanging up.

BONUS #22

And finally, here are a few of William M. Gaines' most effective Dieting Tips.

Use a low-cal topping on banana splits.

Keep in mind that if you become too fat, Richard Simmons may really come to your house with a camera crew, like he does on his infomercials!

Buy new clothes five sizes too big. You'll feel like you lost a lot of weight already, and that will inspire you to lose more!

Don't go on yo-yo diets. You could choke on the string.

Check your doctor before you start any diet. An overweight doctor will be more sympathetic.

Scan the daily newspaper for one of those stories that tells you how the government is spending your hard-earned tax dollars. You will be FED UP in no time!

THANK YOU, DEAR READER;

For buying (hopefully at a good discount) and for reading this book. You may now clip out, frame, and proudly display the OFFICIAL "GOOD DAYS AND MAD" READER CERTIFICATE

Cut and frame
ONLY AFTER BUYING this book!

(However, you don't have to READ the book to earn this certificate!)

CERTIFICATE

from GOOD DAYS AND MAD

"E PLURIBUS NEUMAN"

Be it known to all ye who bother to read the small print on stupid certificates like this...

That ____________________ has survived reading this book, with their sense of humor intact!

Signed: Chic Glitz __________

Chic Glitz
Dean of Jokes

"DE GUSTIBUS NON DISPUTANDUM EST!"

P.S: To get a beautiful frame for this Certificate send $49.99 cash to the Author

ACKNOWLE

A book doesn't happen by itself—I know. For two months I kept looking in my word processor directory, and no book about William M. Gaines and my life at MAD seemed to be conceiving itself! So there are people to be thanked for their help in making this work possible.

At the top of the list is the literary agent Jim Hornfischer, who sought me out and insisted that I could write a book, I would write a book, and I would make a lot of money. I thank him for the first two, and hold him personally responsible for the third.

There was immeasurable help from Annie Gaines, who lent me irreplaceable photos, let me roam through her and Bill's personal MAD files, and filled in missing pieces about Bill's life I did not know, or had forgotten. She even let me see Bill's Last Will and Testament, to prove I wasn't in it! She could not, however, explain the torn-out page that started "To my nearest and dearest friend, Dic—"

DGMENTS

Thanks to Nick Meglin and John Ficarra, co-editors of MAD, who helped me locate MAD art and photos, reminded me of Bill stories I had overlooked, and provided forewords for this book.

And many thanks to the writers and artists at MAD who took the time to contribute their unique talents to this book (with almost no badgering), namely: Al Jaffee, Sergio Aragonés, Mort Drucker, Jack Davis,Duck Edwing, Lenny Brenner, Angelo Torres, Paul Coker, Dave Berg, Charlie Kadau, Joe Raiola, Andrew Schwartzberg, Bob Clarke, Rick Tulka, John Caldwell, Paul Peter Porges, Arnie Kogen, Frank Jacobs, George Woodbridge and Harry North .

To Irving Schild for his photos of Gaines, and to Steve Friedman for his one rotten photo of Regis Philbin, Kathie Lee, and me—for which I went through hell. Also to Michael Gelman, I mean, Mr. Gelman, executive producer of "Live! With Regis & Kathie Lee," for his foreword, and for backing down on his demand that he be listed as "co-author," because he DID write a foreword for the book!

To Joan Fucillo, who edited this book without resorting to drugs or moving to New York. When I first spoke to Joan she told me one of her jobs "was to make sure my book was grammatically correct throughout." My heart sank! Then she added, "or grammatically incorrect throughout, depending on how you work." I was relieved! We respected each other's work and ideas throughout the book.

To Eric Baker, who took my vision and made it into an incredible book—unfortunately, not this book, but he did do a great job on this one, too.

To all the folks at Thunder's Mouth Press—especially Neil Ortenberg, Joseph Mills, and Rebecca Corris, a special thank you. You were excited about this book from the outset and, even more important, stayed excited throughout the project. (I was amazed to learn from Neil that, unlike MAD, where the publisher takes the writer on vacation, at Thunder's Mouth the author is required to take the publisher on vacation.)

To my wife and kids who never nagged or tried to

pull me away from the computer, I say, “Just who the hell are you people? I don’t have a wife and kids!”

And thanks to my dog, TJ, who never once ate, or wet on, any of the completed manuscript pages!

I also want to thank you, dear reader, for taking the time to read (and enjoy??) this book. Although I intended it as a tribute to William M. Gaines, I would gladly swap it to have Bill back—but this is the best I could do, under the circumstances.

APPENDIX

Mr. DeBartolo's appendix was removed
in 1952 at Kings County Hospital,
Brooklyn, New York.

Book and jacket design by Eric Baker Design Associates, Inc. NYC
Back jacket photo by Dennis Wunderlin.